PowerPoint 2016 Level 1
Student Edition

30 Bird Media
510 Clinton Square
Rochester NY 14604
www.30Bird.com

PowerPoint 2016 Level 1

Student Edition

CEO, 30 Bird Media: Adam A. Wilcox

Series designed by: Clifford J. Coryea, Donald P. Tremblay, and Adam A Wilcox

Managing Editor: Donald P. Tremblay

Instructional Design Lead: Clifford J. Coryea

Instructional Designer: Robert S. Kulik

Keytester: Kurt J. Specht

COPYRIGHT © 2016 30 Bird Media LLC. All rights reserved

No part of this work may be reproduced or used in any other form without the prior written consent of the publisher.

Visit www.30bird.com for more information.

Trademarks

Some of the product names and company names used in this book have been used for identification purposes only and may be trademarks or registered trademarks of their respective manufacturers and sellers.

Disclaimer

We reserve the right to revise this publication without notice.

PPNT2016-L1-R10-SCB

Table of Contents

Introduction 1
   Course setup 2

Chapter 1: Fundamentals 3
   Module A: Exploring the PowerPoint environment 4

Chapter 2: Creating a presentation 17
   Module A: Creating a presentation 18
   Module B: Creating and modifying slide content 24

Chapter 3: Formatting 47
   Module A: Working with slide masters and layouts 48
   Module B: Formatting slides and text 73

Chapter 4: Working with shapes and images 95
   Module A: Creating and formatting shapes 96
   Module B: Working with images 116

Chapter 5: Working with charts and tables 129
   Module A: Working with charts 130
   Module B: Working with tables 146

Chapter 6: Customization 159
   Module A: Slide transitions 160
   Module B: Additional text options 165
   Module C: Printing 174

Alphabetical Index 187

Introduction

Welcome to *PowerPoint 2016 Level 1*. This course provides the basic concepts and skills that you need to start being productive with Microsoft PowerPoint 2016: How to create, navigate, format, and customize PowerPoint presentations. This course and the Level 2 course map to the objectives of the Microsoft Office exams for PowerPoint 2016. Objective coverage is marked throughout the course, and you can download an objective map for the series from http://www.30bird.com.

You will benefit most from this course if you want to accomplish basic workplace tasks in PowerPoint 2016, or if you want to have a solid foundation for continuing on to master PowerPoint. If you intend to take a Microsoft Office exam for PowerPoint, this course is a good place to start your preparation, but you will also need to complete the Level 2 course to be fully prepared for either exam.

The course assumes you know how to use a computer, and that you're familiar with Microsoft Windows. It does not assume that you've used a different version of PowerPoint or any other presentation program before.

After you complete this course, you will know:

- How to open and interact with PowerPoint and how to save and close presentations
- How to modify the structure of a presentation, and arrange and format its various elements
- How to work with shapes and images
- How to import and create charts and tables
- How to create custom slide presentations, and create WordArt from text
- About printing options

This is the first course in a series. After you complete it, consider going on to the next one:

- *PowerPoint 2016: Level 2*

Course setup

To complete this course, each student and instructor needs to have a computer running PowerPoint 2013. Setup instructions and activities are written assuming Windows 10; however, with slight modification the course works using Windows XP Service Pack 3, Windows Vista Service Pack 1, or Windows 8 or 8.1.

Hardware requirements for Windows 10 course setup include:

- 1 GHz or faster processor (32- or 64-bit) or SoC
- 1 GB (32-bit) or 2 GB (64-bit) RAM
- 25 GB total hard drive space (50 GB or more recommended)
- DirectX 9 (or later) video card or integrated graphics, with a minimum of 128 MB of graphics memory
- Monitor with 1280x800 or higher resolution
- Wi-Fi or Ethernet adapter

Software requirements include:

- Windows 10 (or alternative as above)
- Microsoft PowerPoint 2016 or any Microsoft Office 2016 edition that includes PowerPoint
- The PowerPoint 2016 Level 1 data files and PowerPoint slides, available at http://www.30bird.com

Network requirements include:

- An Internet connection in order to complete the sharing exercise and the exercise on downloading and using a template (which can be skipped or demonstrated by the instructor)

Because the exercises in this course include viewing and changing some PowerPoint defaults, beginning with a fresh installation of the software is recommended. But this is certainly not necessary. Just be aware that if you are not using a fresh installation, some exercises might work slightly differently and some screens might look slightly different.

1. Install Windows 10, including all recommended updates and service packs. Use a different computer and user name for each student.
2. Install Microsoft PowerPoint 2016, using all defaults during installation.
3. Copy the PowerPoint 2016 Level 1 data files to the Documents folder.

Chapter 1: Fundamentals

You will learn how to:

- Use the PowerPoint interface to interact with the program and its presentations

Module A: Exploring the PowerPoint environment

When you start PowerPoint, at the top of the screen you'll see a set of tools called *the ribbon*. You click the commands and buttons on the ribbon to get work done.

You will learn:

- How to start PowerPoint
- To identify basic features of a presentation
- How to exit PowerPoint

Starting PowerPoint and opening a presentation

In Windows 10, you can start PowerPoint by clicking either its tile in the Start menu or its icon on the Task bar. When you start PowerPoint, you're first greeted with the Open Presentation window. From here, you can open either an existing presentation or a blank one.

1. Click **Start** to open the Start menu.
2. There are a couple of ways to start PowerPoint from here:
   - Find and click the PowerPoint 2016 tile.
   - Click **All Apps** > **PowerPoint 2016**.
     You can also set up icons on the desktop—or anywhere else you like—for starting PowerPoint.

     The Open Presentation window is displayed.

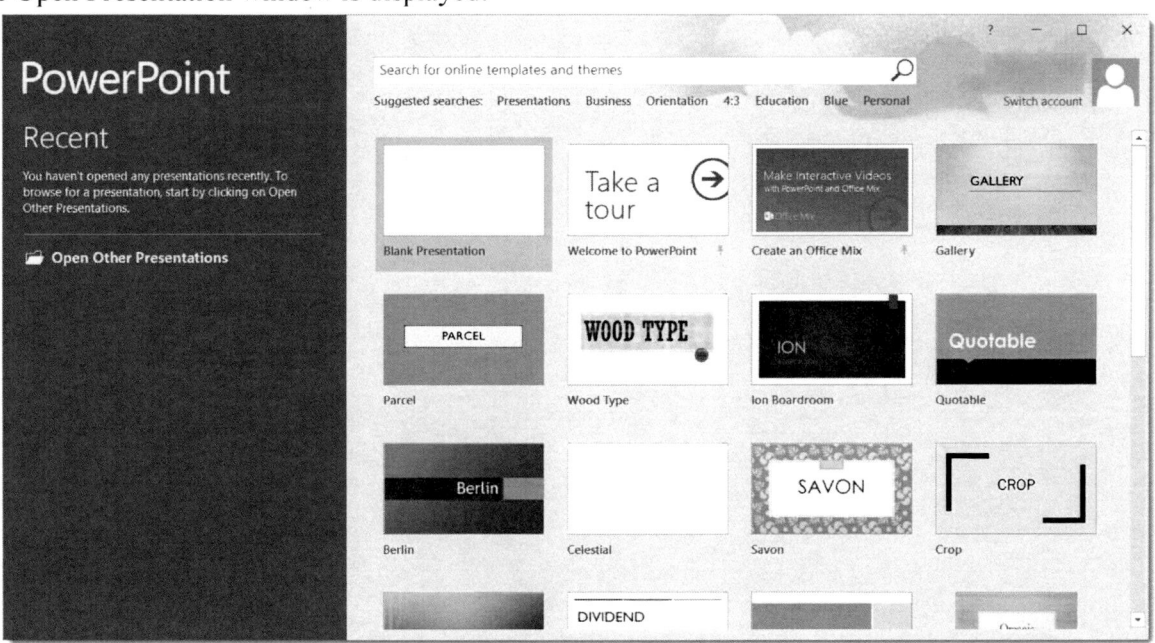

3. Click **Open Other Presentations**.
    In the left pane of the window.

The Open options are displayed.

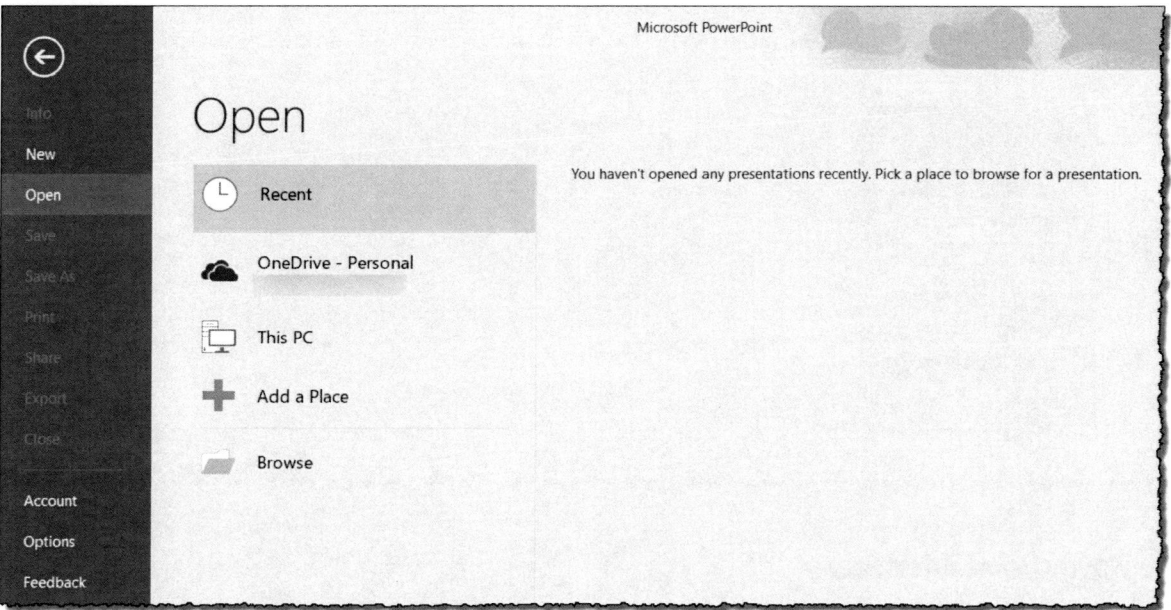

4. Click **Browse**.

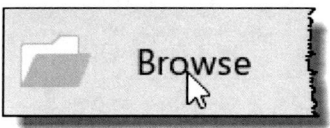

The Open window is displayed.

5. Navigate to the folder containing the presentation you want to open, click the presentation, then click **Open**.
   Or double-click the file name to open the file automatically.

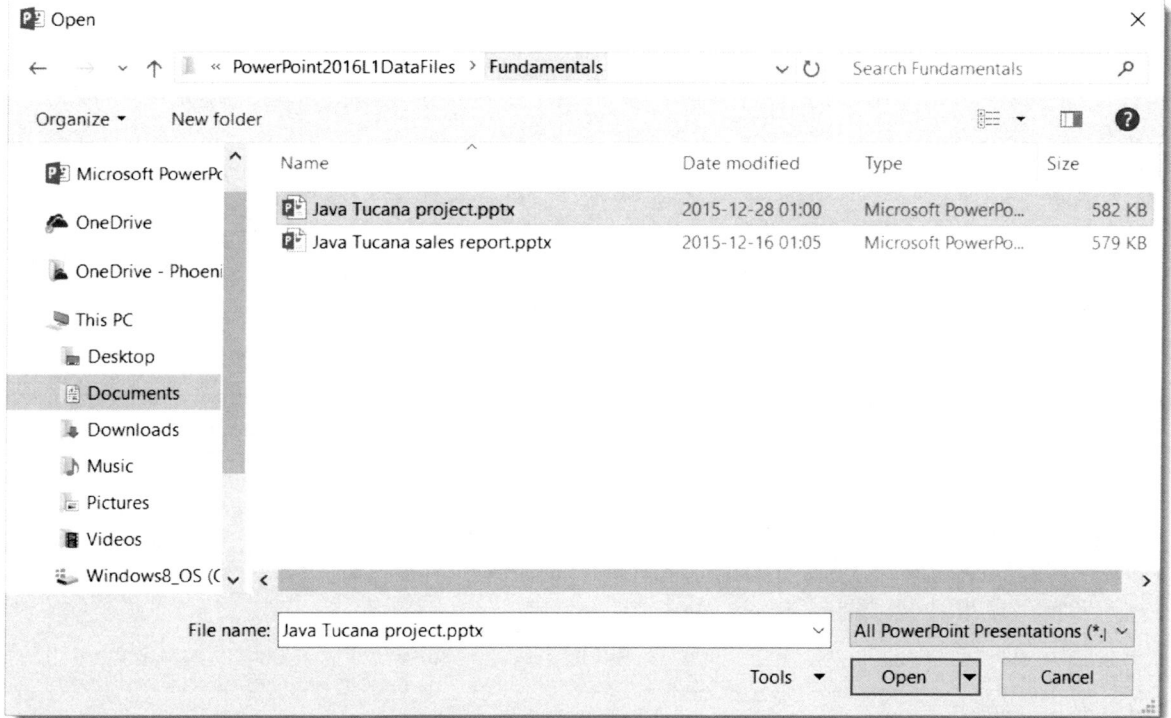

The file opens in the PowerPoint window.

Note: The first time you open a presentation file, the PowerPoint window opens maximized to fill your screen. You can toggle between this maximized-window view and a smaller window by clicking the Maximize/Restore Down icon, respectively, in the upper-right corner of the window.

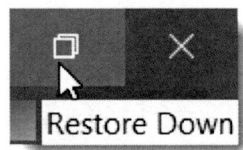

The PowerPoint interface

If you've never used PowerPoint, the interface might be intimidating. But if you break it into pieces, it's fairly straightforward.

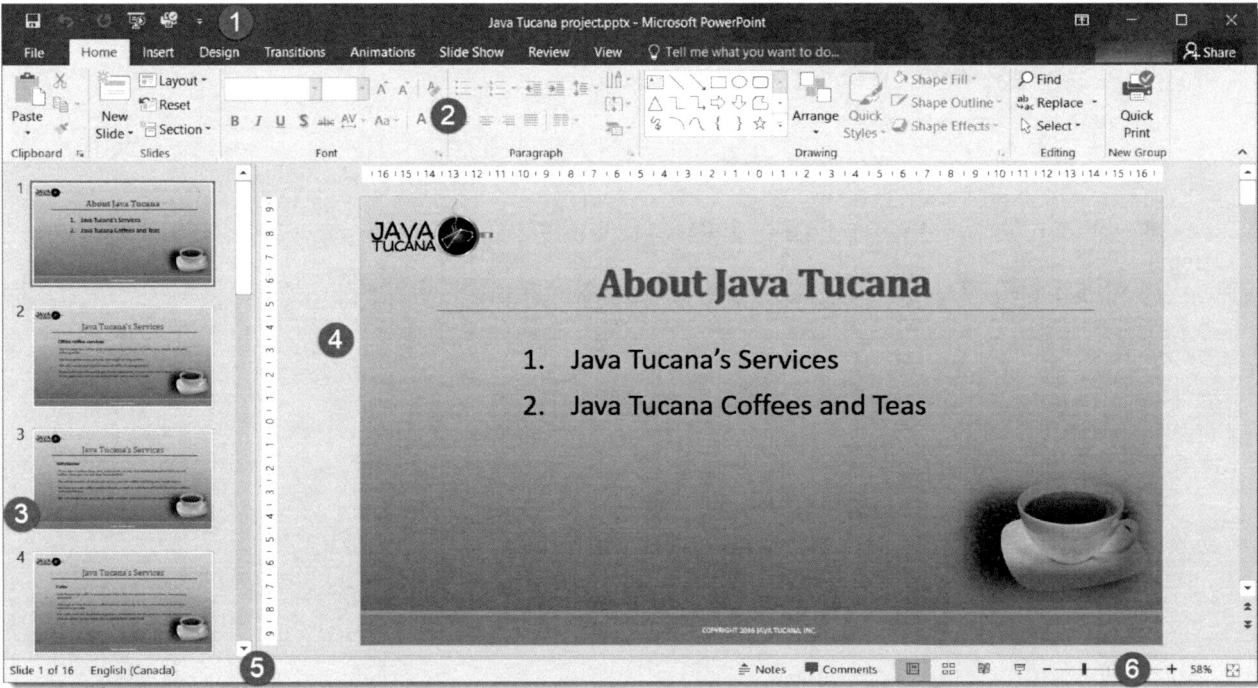

① The *Quick Access toolbar* contains only the most common PowerPoint commands, but you can customize it any way you like. To the right of the toolbar, in the horizontal center, the file name is displayed.

② The *ribbon* contains groups of buttons, lists, menus, and commands that give you access to the most relevant actions you might want to take. They are *context-sensitive*, meaning that they change depending on where you are and what you're doing. The ribbon is organized into *tabs* (File, Home, and so on), and then within tabs by *groups* (Clipboard, Slides, Font, and so on). Get more information about any tool by pointing to it to display a *tooltip* with information about the tool.

③ The *slides pane* displays thumbnail versions of all the slides in a presentation sequentially, from top to bottom. However, its contents can vary, depending on the current view. This pane is also commonly referred to as the *thumbnail pane*.

(4) The *current slide pane*, or *main pane*, displays the slide selected in the Slides pane. This is where you edit the slide selected in the slides pane.

(5) The *status bar* displays information such as the number of the currently selected slide, the number of slides in the presentation, the current language and view, and other features.

(6) The *zoom bar* provides a quick way for you to zoom in on or out from the current slide.

You work on a particular slide by first selecting it in the Slides pane, then manipulating it as you wish in the main part of the window.

Exploring views

In PowerPoint, there are a number of different views. A *view* is a particular organization of elements in the PowerPoint environment. Each view is suited to particular kinds of tasks. Also, there's more than one way to open each view. On the View tab, in the Presentation Views group, are the view buttons. Simply click the corresponding button to change to that view. A few of these views are also represented on the status bar.

   MOS PowerPoint Exam Objective(s): 1.5.2

- *Normal view*: The view you'll likely spend most of your time in while working on PowerPoint presentations. You can also click [icon] on the status bar.

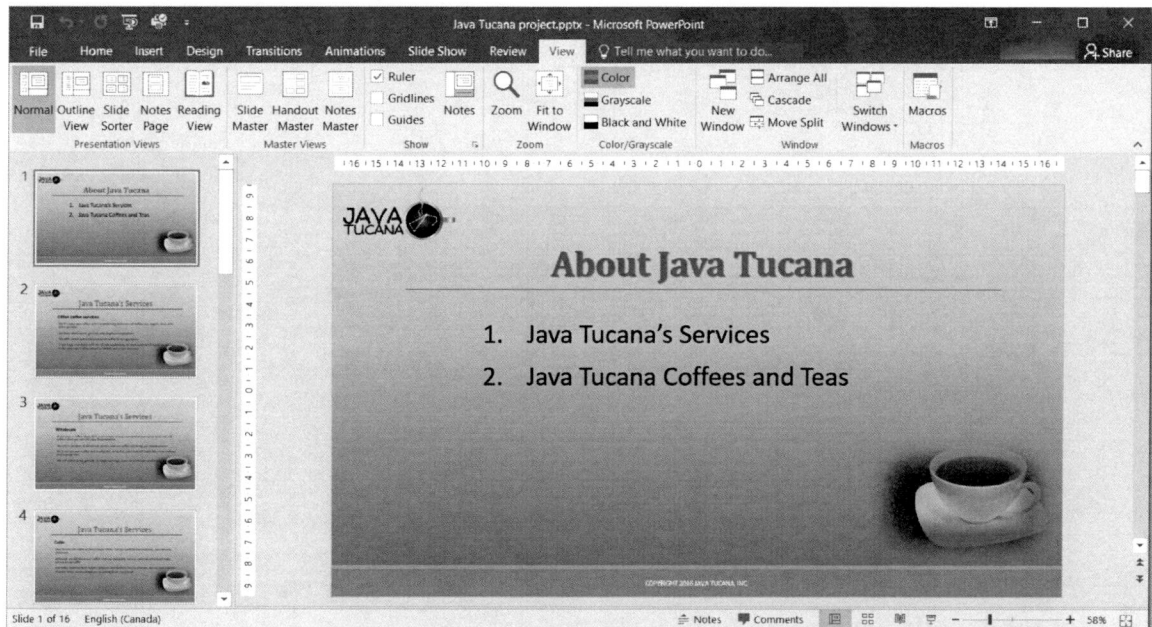

- *Outline view*: Useful for creating an outline of your presentation or exploring storyboard ideas.

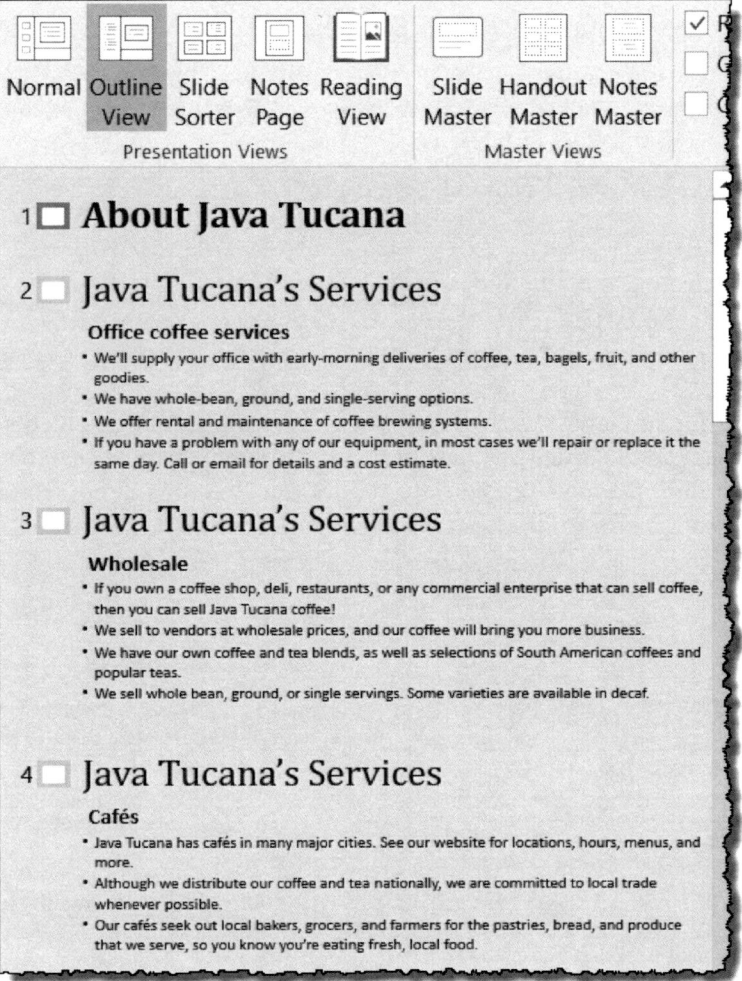

- *Slide Sorter view*: Particularly suited to organizing the slides in your presentation. You can move slides simply by clicking and dragging them to new positions, much as if they were a deck of cards.

    You can also click ▦ on the status bar.

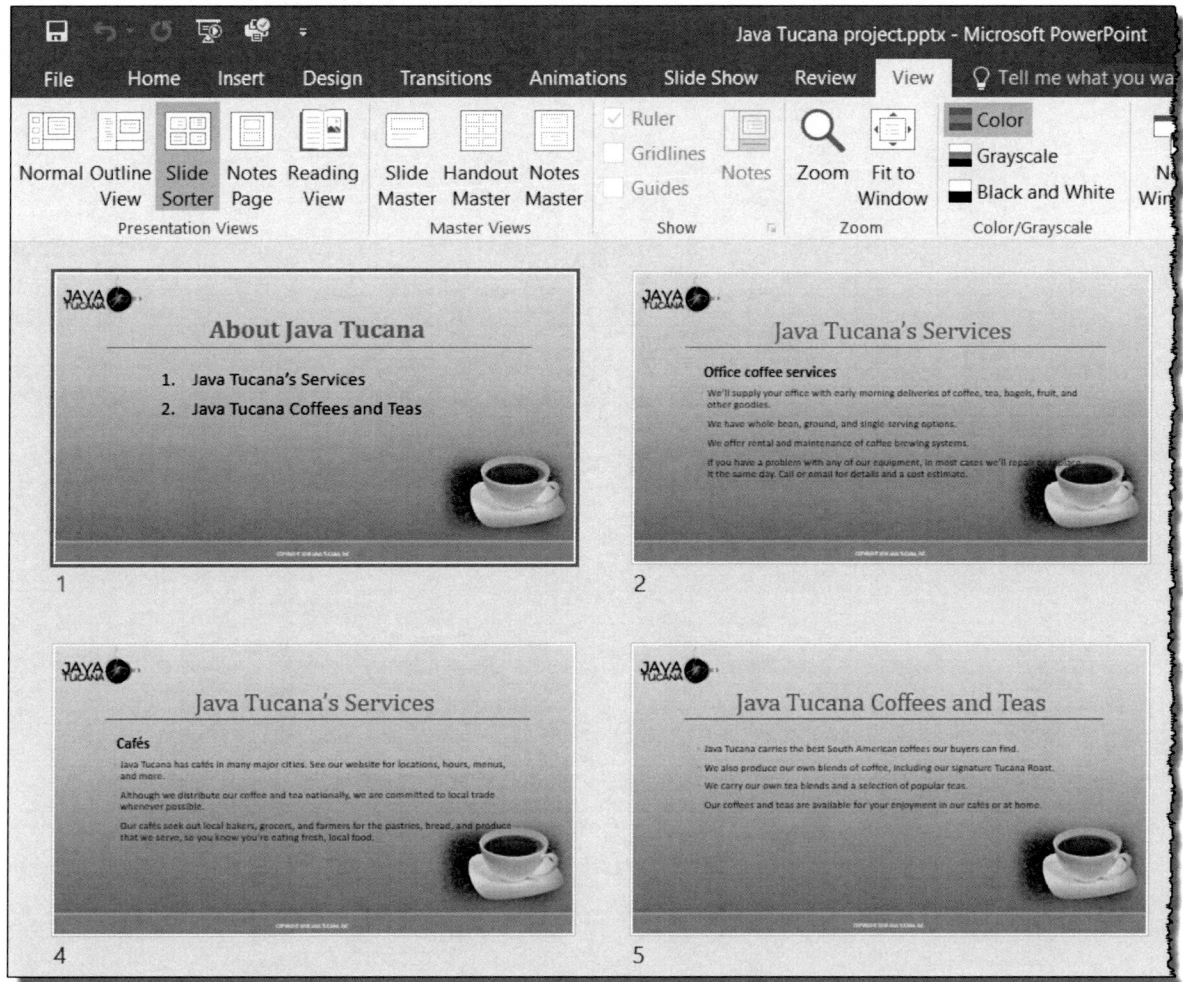

- *Notes Page view*: Opens a page associated with each slide, that allows you to enter and display notes for that slide. Notes pages can be printed for your own use and/or for your audience, and they can be displayed on screen or hidden from view. Accessing Notes view from the ribbon produces a larger notes page under the slide. Clicking ≜ Notes on the status bar displays a smaller Notes area.

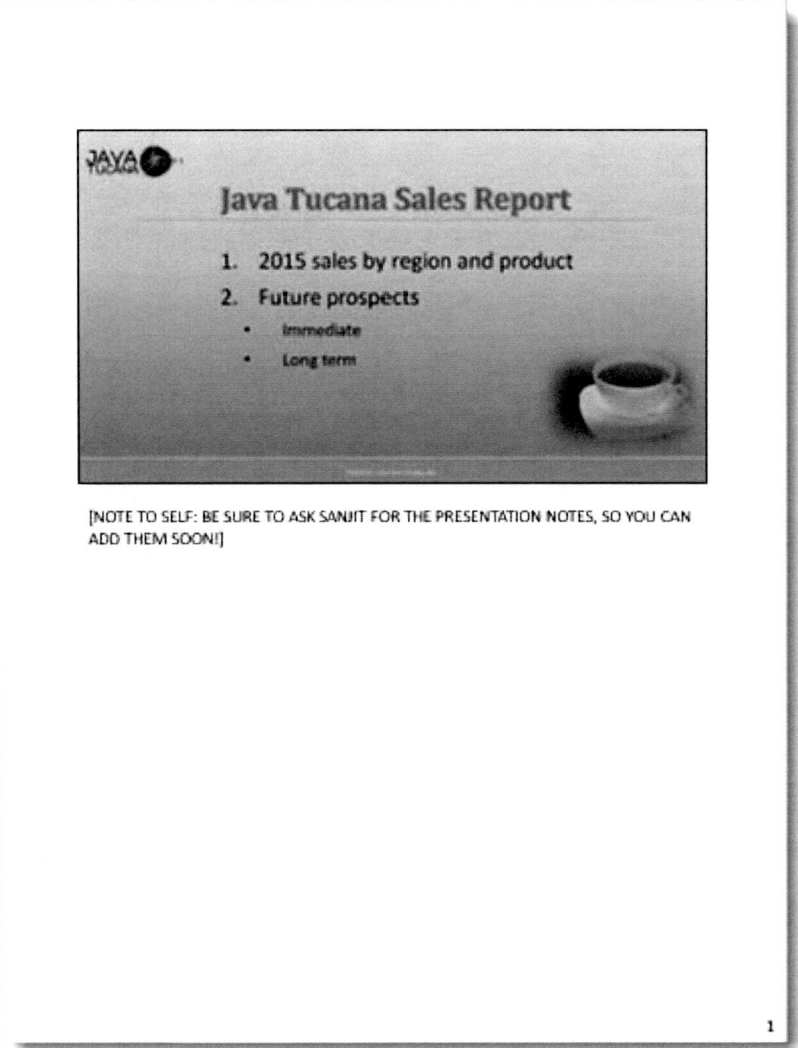

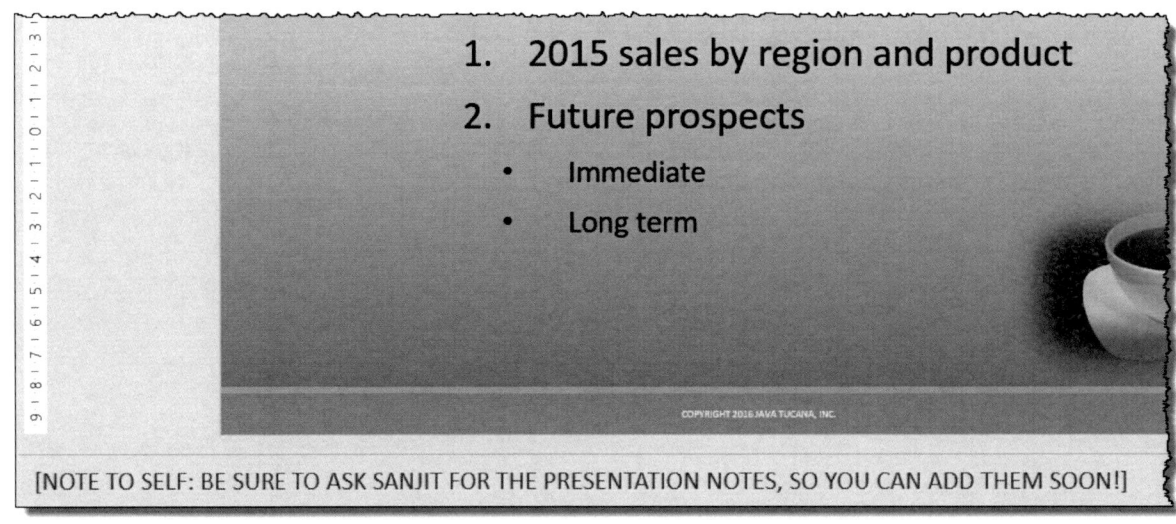

- *Slide Show view*: What you use to play your presentation for an audience. Each slide displays in full screen, and any controls, transitions, effects, and so on that you've added to it will show up here. Obviously, this isn't the view to use when you want to make changes to your presentation. To get to Slide Show view, click 🖳 on the status bar.

- *Reading view*: You'll probably spend the least amount of time in this view. It's similar to Slide Show view, except that you'd use it to play the presentation for yourself, rather than for an audience. You can also get to Reading view by clicking on the status bar. In Reading view, controls for navigation and switching to other views are displayed in the status bar.

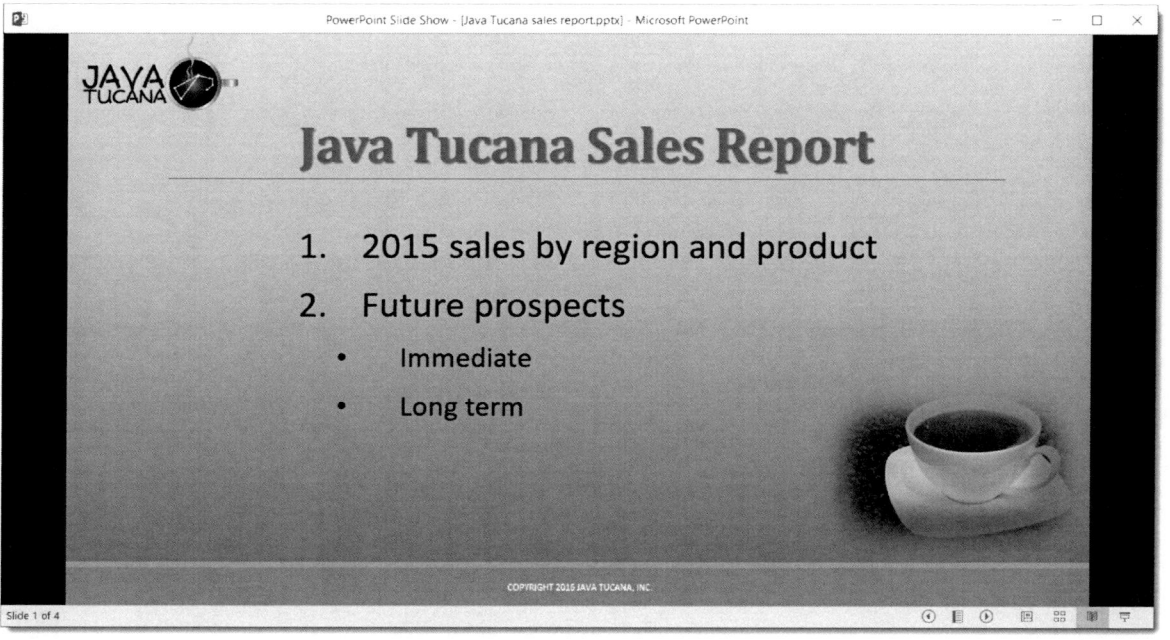

Getting help

To get help in PowerPoint 2016, use the Tell Me box.

1. Click **Tell me what you want to do**.
   To the right of the View tab's name.

   The insertion point is in the Tell Me box.
2. Begin typing the topic you'd like information for.
3. In the list of context options, click the one that most closely matches your topic.
4. If the options listed aren't what you're looking for, you can always click **Get Help**.

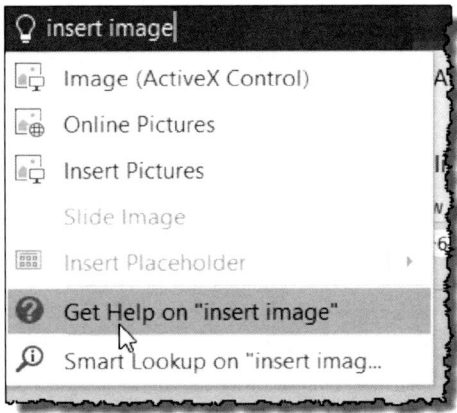

The PowerPoint 2016 Help window opens with additional information that hopefully matches your topic.

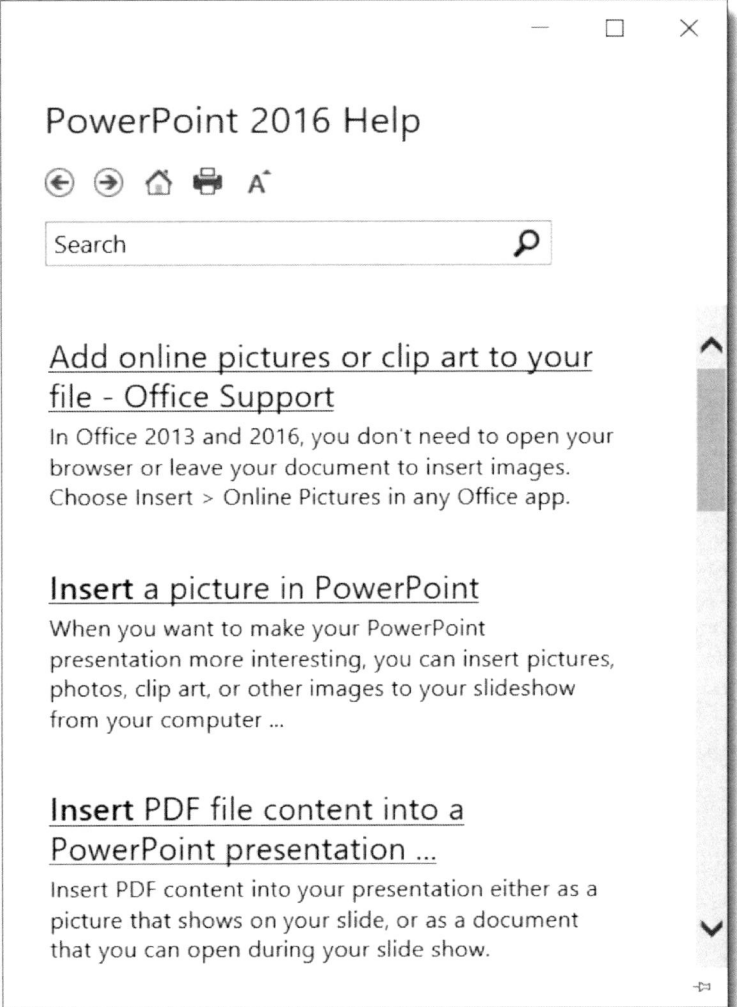

5. Scroll to view the displayed, linked topics, then click to select the desired topic.
   You can also type additional search text in the Search box, then press **Enter** for even more information.

6. When you're finished with your search, close the help window.

Exercise: Checking out PowerPoint

Before you start, be sure that your computer is on and Windows is running. You'll start PowerPoint and take a look around its interface.

Do This	How & Why
1. Follow your instructor's directions to start PowerPoint.	If necessary. The method you use depends on your version of Windows and how it is set up. In Windows 10, you can simply click the PowerPoint icon on the taskbar at the bottom of the screen, or click **Start** and then click the PowerPoint 2016 tile.
2. Navigate to the folder containing the data files for this course, and open `Java Tucana project.pptx`.	If you've just started PowerPoint, click **Open Other Presentations**, and click **Browse**. In the Open window, navigate to the `Fundamentals` data folder, and double-click **Java Tucana project.pptx**.
3. Observe the PowerPoint window.	Most of the window consists of the Slides pane and the current slide.
4. Observe the Slides pane.	All the visible slides of the presentation are displayed.
5. Observe the current slide in the main pane.	The first slide in the presentation is selected and its contents are displayed.
6. Click on another slide.	In the Slides pane. You can also use the Up Arrow and Down Arrow keys to move sequentially through the slides.
7. Observe the status bar.	The number of the selected slide is displayed as you select each one, as well as the total number of slides in the presentation.
8. Use your mouse pointer to grab the zoom bar slider and drag it left and right.	Press and hold as you drag. As you drag the slider left, the slide is reduced in size; as you drag right, it's enlarged. Its current size is represented as a percentage at the right edge of the zoom bar.
9. Observe the ribbon.	This is the large area of buttons, lists, menus, and palettes at the top of the window. It's organized into tabs (File, Home, Insert, and so on), and within in a tab, into groups.
10. Observe the Home tab.	When you open a presentation, the Home tab is selected by default. It contains the most common commands, organized into groups (Clipboard, Slides, Font, Paragraph, and so on). The commands in the Font and Paragraph groups are currently grayed out.
11. Select slide 1 in the presentation.	Click it in the Slides pane. You might need to use the pane's scroll bar to scroll quickly to the top of the presentation.

PowerPoint 2016 Level 1

Do This	How & Why
12. Click on any text in either bulleted item in the list.	In the main pane.
13. Observe the ribbon.	

The commands in the Font and Paragraph groups are now available because you've selected slide text.

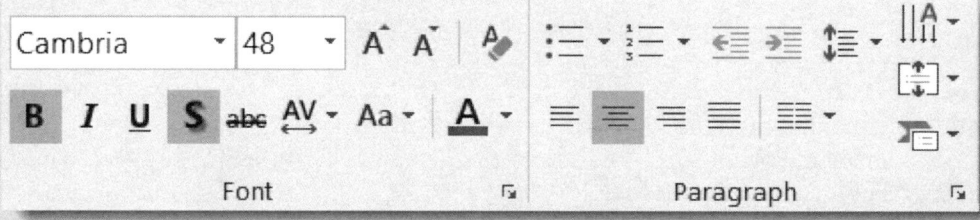

14. Point to the **Bold** button.	To display a tooltip, explaining what the tool does. 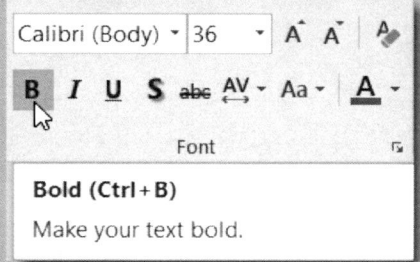
15. Observe the Quick Access toolbar.	This is the small toolbar at the top left.  It has just a few of the most useful commands. You can customize it however you like.
16. Display the presentation in different views.	Use the Presentation Views group buttons on the View tab, as well as the icons on the status bar. To exit Slide Show view at any time, you can press the **Esc** key. 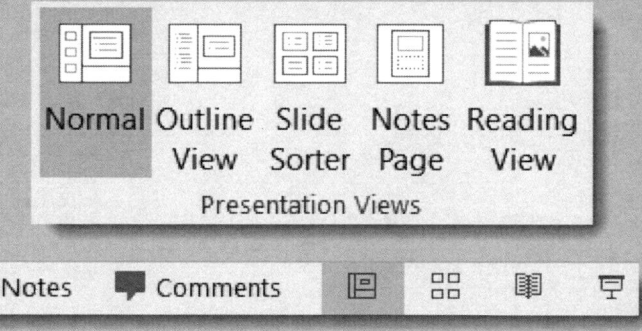

Do This	How & Why
17. Exit PowerPoint without saving the presentation.	Click the **Close** button. 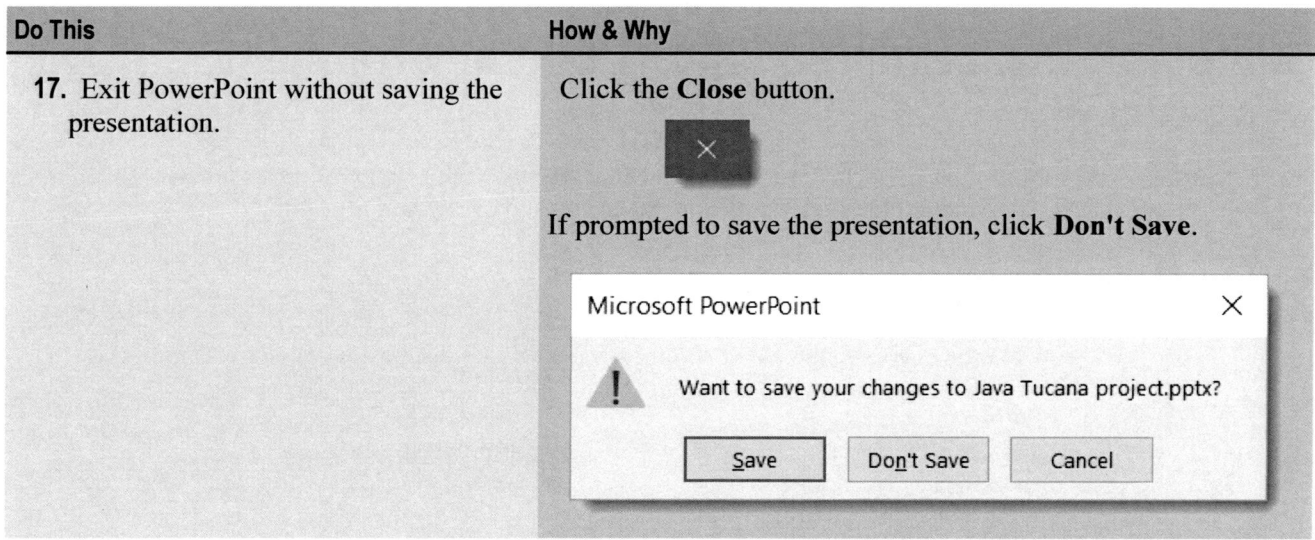 If prompted to save the presentation, click **Don't Save**.

Assessment: Exploring the PowerPoint environment

1. Which of the following are ways to interact with PowerPoint? Choose all that apply.

   - Click buttons on the ribbon.
   - Use the Control Panel.
   - Use the Start menu.
   - Click buttons on the ribbon.
   - Click buttons on the Quick Access toolbar.

2. True or false? You edit a slide in the Slides pane.

   - False
   - True

3. You've opened a PowerPoint presentation and selected a slide in the Slides pane. In the Home tab's Paragraph group, the commands are grayed out and therefore unavailable. Why?

   - You need to wait until PowerPoint warms up.
   - Slides can be edited only in the Slides pane.
   - Ribbon commands become available only after all slide elements are created.
   - Ribbon commands become available when you click on a slide element to which they are applicable.

Summary: Exploring the PowerPoint environment

You should now know how to:

- Start PowerPoint, use the PowerPoint interface to interact with the program and its presentations, navigate among the elements of the PowerPoint window, and close the program

Synthesis: Fundamentals

In this chapter synthesis exercise, you'll start PowerPoint, open a slide presentation, and navigate in the window. Then you'll close the presentation without saving it.

1. Start PowerPoint, and open the `Java Tucana project` presentation.
    From the `Fundamentals` data folder.
2. Scroll through the entire slide presentation and view each slide individually.
3. Zoom in on and out from a selected slide.
4. Do what's necessary to enable the Font group's commands, so that they're no longer grayed out.
5. Open `Java Tucana sales report`.
6. Scroll through and view each slide in the presentation.
7. Select the individual elements of each slide, and observe the effects of doing so on the ribbon.
8. Explore the presentation in different views.
9. Close PowerPoint without saving any changes you might have made to either presentation.

Chapter 2: Creating a presentation

You will learn how to:

- Create a presentation
- Create and modify slide content

Module A: Creating a presentation

In PowerPoint, there is more than one way to create a new presentation, depending on whether you want to do so completely from scratch, or by using an existing structure. Either way, PowerPoint provides you with powerful and helpful tools for creating a presentation.

You will learn how to:

- Create a blank presentation
- Create a presentation from a template

Types of new presentations

PowerPoint provides you with powerful options for creating a presentation. You can create a blank presentation with a completely empty "canvas" for your full creative expression, or you can start with a PowerPoint template. In addition, if you have a particular style of template in mind for your presentation, you can search for one that meets your needs.

Backstage view

As in all Microsoft Office applications, PowerPoint's *Backstage view* is a central location from which you can create, open, and manage your presentations, among other things. You access Backstage view by clicking the File tab on the ribbon.

- When you first click the File tab, the *Info* pane is displayed, containing information about the current presentation.
- The *New* pane contains options for creating a new presentation, including many templates. When you wish to create a blank presentation and PowerPoint's already open, in the New pane, click **Blank Presentation**.

Creating a blank presentation

There are two ways to create a blank presentation in PowerPoint: when opening PowerPoint, and via Backstage view.

 MOS PowerPoint Exam Objective(s): 1.1.1

1. Close PowerPoint.
   If necessary. You'll see how to create a blank presentation when opening PowerPoint.
2. Open PowerPoint.
   Click the PowerPoint 2016 tile; or in the Start menu, find and click **PowerPoint 2016**. PowerPoint's opening window provides you with options for creating a presentation.
3. Click **Blank Presentation**.

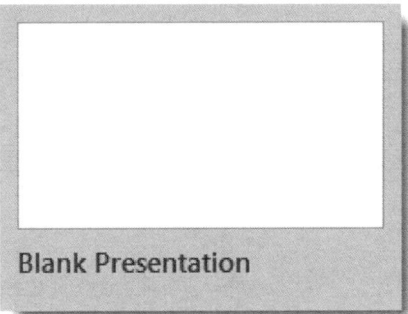

The PowerPoint window opens with a new, blank presentation.

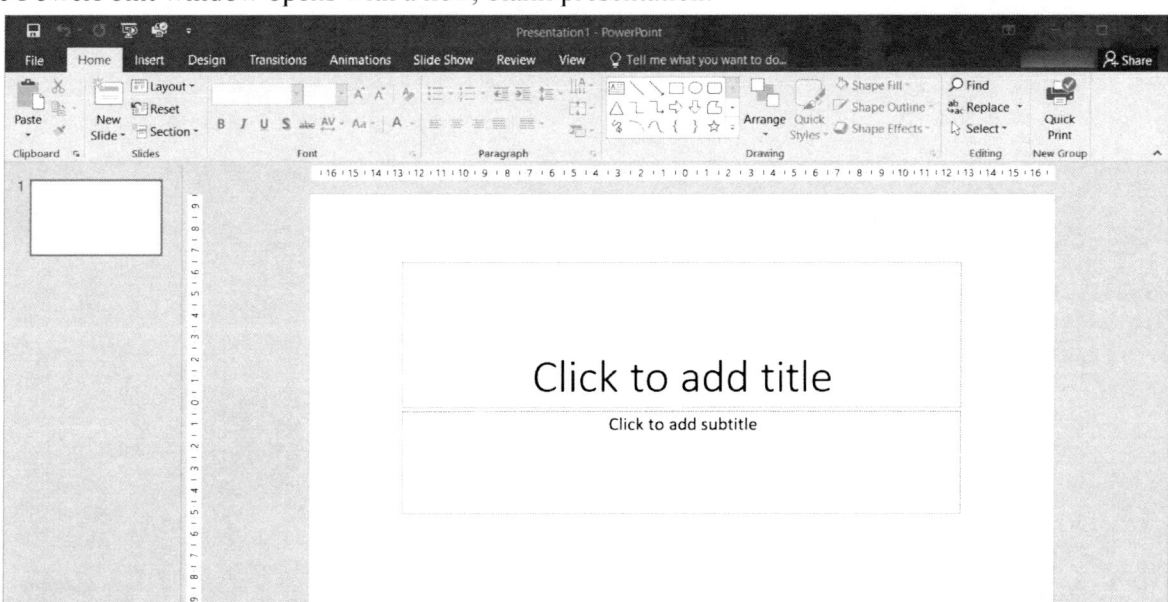

4. Observe the blank presentation.
   It contains only one slide.

5. Display Backstage view.
   On the ribbon, click the **File** tab.

6. Click **New**.
   In the left pane.

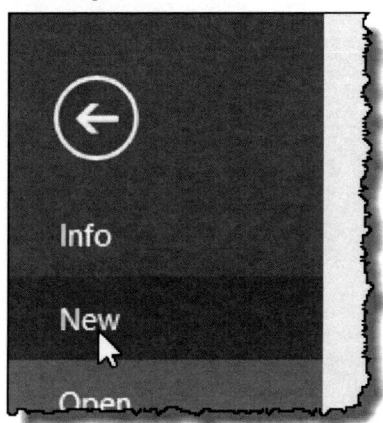

The New pane opens.

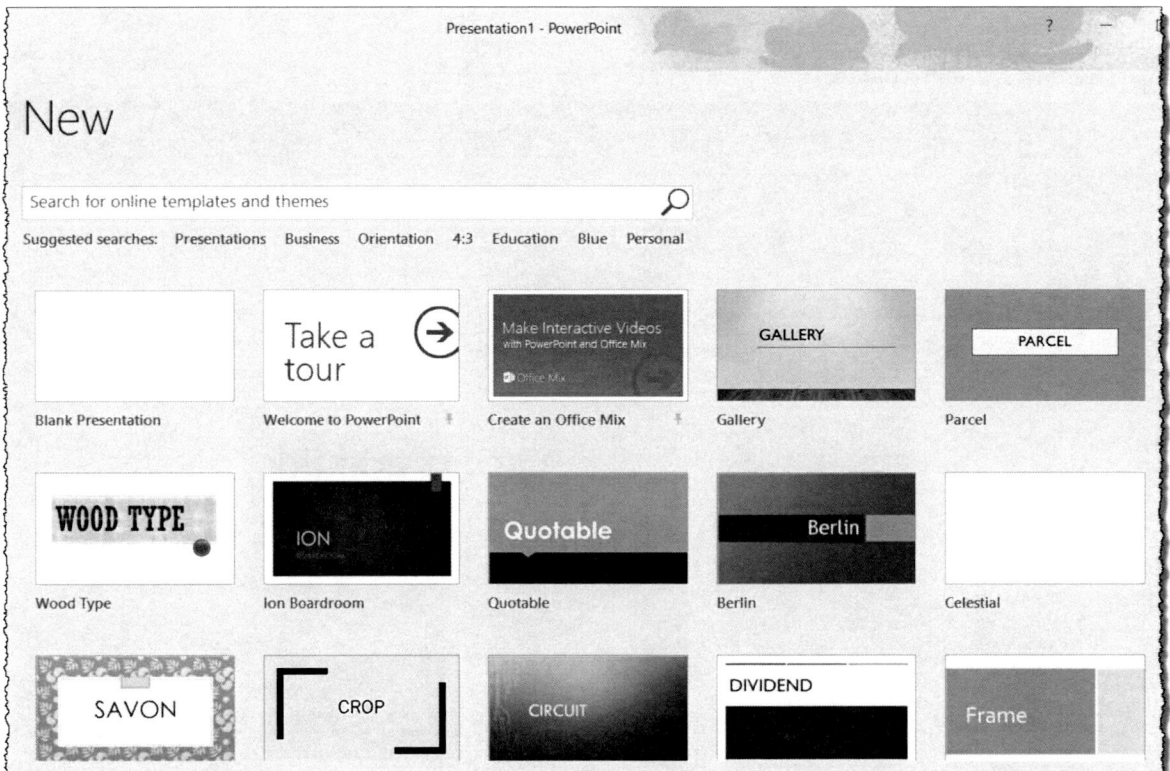

7. Click **Blank Presentation**.

    A second window opens with a new, blank presentation.

8. Observe the window titles.

    The presentations are given temporary names ("Presentation1" and "Presentation2"). Once you save the presentations, their new names replace the temporary ones.

    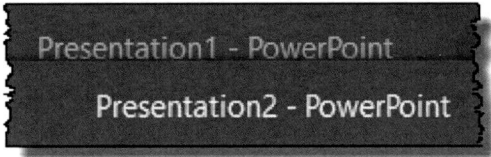

9. Close the Presentation2 window.

    Click its button.

    Only the Presentation1 window remains open.

Creating a presentation from a template

PowerPoint provides you with a number of template designs you can use to create your own presentations.

MOS PowerPoint Exam Objective(s): 1.1.2

1. In Backstage view, click **New**.

    The New pane opens.

2. Scroll to view all the available template options.

    You can also use the Search box to narrow your template options, or search online for even more templates.

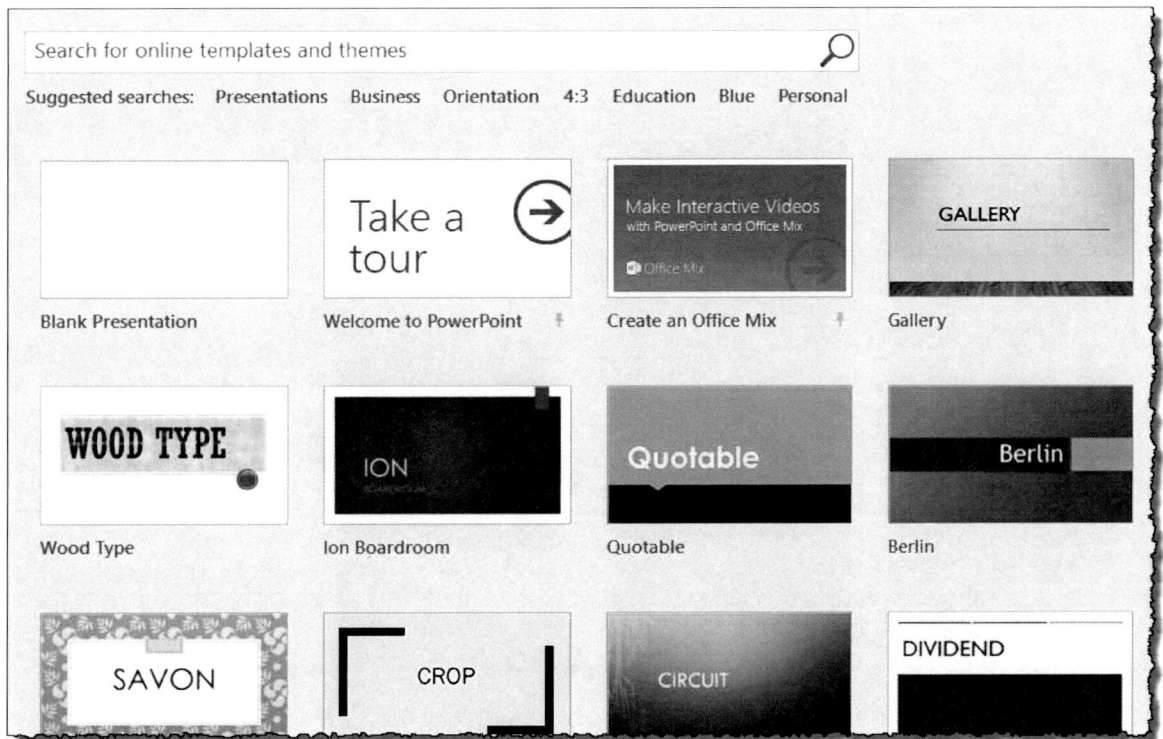

3. Click on a template design to select it.

   A window opens, displaying a magnified preview of how a slide will look with the selected design. Two sets of scroll arrows allow you to flip through more designs using the preview: Use the arrows on either side of the preview window to preview other designs. Use the More Images arrows to display other types of slides using the current design.

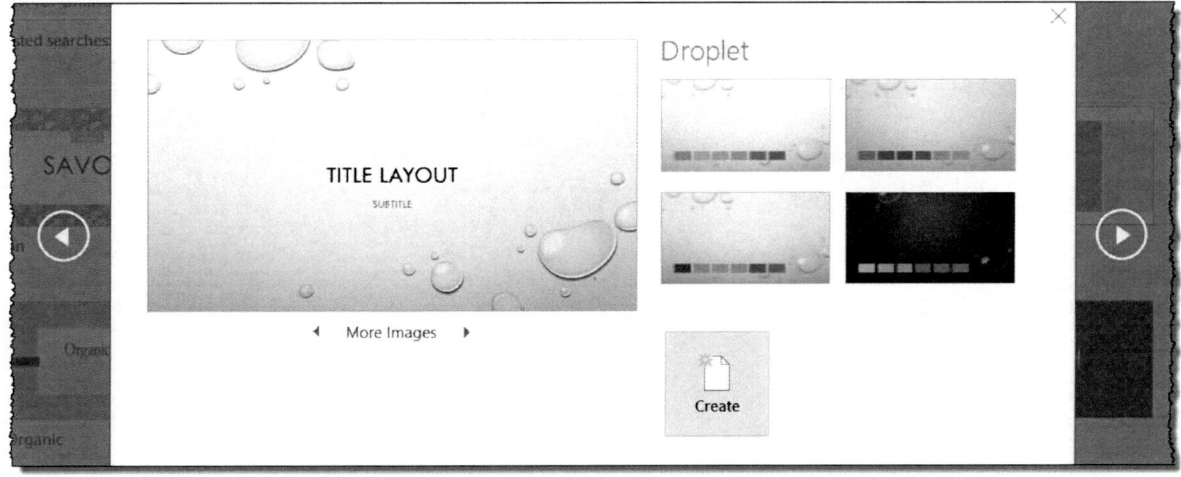

4. Use any of the scroll arrows to preview other designs and/or other types of slides.
5. Once you've selected a design you like, click **Create**.

   The presentation opens in a new PowerPoint window, temporarily titled "Presentation3." PowerPoint numbers presentations consecutively, starting at "1" each time you start the program. It continues to "remember" the sequence even after you save (and thus rename) any of them.

6. Observe the new presentation.

   The design appears on the selected slide, and the presentation contains only one slide. In the main pane, rulers are displayed along the top and left side of the current slide.

Exercise: Creating presentations

Before you begin, PowerPoint is running on your computer. You'll create two new presentations: one blank, one template-based.

Do This	How & Why
1. Click **File**, then click **New**.	To display the options for creating a new presentation in Backstage view's New pane.
2. Click **Blank Presentation**.	A new, blank presentation appears on the screen.
3. Open Backstage view again, and view the available template options.	Click **File > New**. Scroll to view the available templates. You can use the Search box to search for a specific design type. If you have an Internet connection, you can also search online for additional templates.
4. Select a design.	Click on a template. The design opens in a preview window.
5. Use the scroll arrows on either side of the window.	To preview additional designs.
6. Use the More Images scroll arrows.	To preview other types of slides in the current design.
7. Once you've selected a design, click the **Create** button.	In the preview window. The template-based presentation opens in a new window.
8. Close the new, template-based presentation without saving it.	Click ☒ in the upper-right corner of its window.
9. Save the blank presentation as My Cafe Presentation. a) Click **File**, then click **Save As**.	

22   PowerPoint 2016 Level 1

Do This	How & Why
b) Click **Browse**, then navigate to the `Creating a presentation` data folder.	Your instructor can help you find it. [Browse]
c) In the File name box, type `My Cafe Presentation`.	
d) Click **Save**.	
e) Keep My Cafe Presentation open, but close any other open presentation windows without saving.	

Assessment: Creating a presentation

1. True or false? To open, create, or save a PowerPoint presentation, you use Backdoor view.

   - True
   - False

2. What is the command sequence for creating a blank presentation in PowerPoint?

   - Backdoor, New, Blank Presentation
   - File, New, Blank Presentation
   - Open, New, Blank Presentation

3. True or false? When previewing presentation template designs, you can use the More Images arrows to display each sample slide in a different template.

   - True
   - False

Module B: Creating and modifying slide content

PowerPoint makes it easy for you to add text or other design elements to slides. In addition, you can add as many slides as you like to your presentation.

You will learn how to:

- Insert text on a slide
- Add, delete, and hide slides in a presentation
- Insert a hyperlink
- Insert shapes and images

Slides and their elements

A slide is essentially a blank canvas on which you can place text, shapes, or images in order to convey information relevant to your presentation. A presentation can contain any number of slides, but rather than merely deciding on a number, it's best to have a good idea of the salient points, topics, subtopics, and so on that will make the presentation as clear and meaningful as possible. You can always add (or remove) slides later, as needed.

By default, slides contain *placeholders*: special areas designated for holding *objects* such as text, shapes, images, and graphs. Most slides come with one placeholder for the slide's title, and another for a subtitle or body text. However, you can add more placeholders to any slide, as needed. Likewise, you can delete any placeholder.

When deciding on the contents of each slide, it's good to keep in mind a few general guidelines.

- Try to convey or illustrate a single idea, whenever possible. Cluttering a slide with too many different ideas—or simply too much information—can obscure what you're trying to show.
- For any text that isn't a heading, use bullet lists whenever possible, to keep each item concise and memorable. Try to avoid placing a whole paragraph (or more) of text on a slide. If you feel that all the information in the paragraph should be there, simply rewrite the information in the form of a bullet list.
- Graphical elements (shapes, images, and so on) can add esthetic value to a presentation when used prudently, as when illustrating a point. However, try to avoid too many illustrations or, worse yet, pointless ones. For example, a slide intended to show company sales figures might not benefit from a picture of a duck.

Inserting text on a slide

You enter text on a slide by clicking a text placeholder, then typing. Once you click in a text placeholder, it becomes a *text box*, a container for text. When typing text, you can use all the usual word processing tools, such as the Backspace and Delete keys, arrow keys, and so on. You can also select the text and format it as you wish.

  MOS PowerPoint Exam Objective(s): 2.1.1

You can change the size of a text box by dragging its handles, which appear at its corners and sides.

1. Click to select the slide on which you wish to enter text.
   In the Slides pane.

The slide's placeholders are displayed in the main pane: one for a title, the other for a subtitle or body text.

2. Click in the title placeholder.

   The placeholder becomes a text box with handles, an insertion point appears centered in it (replacing the "click to add title" message), and the mouse pointer changes to an *I-beam*, which signals that you can enter text.

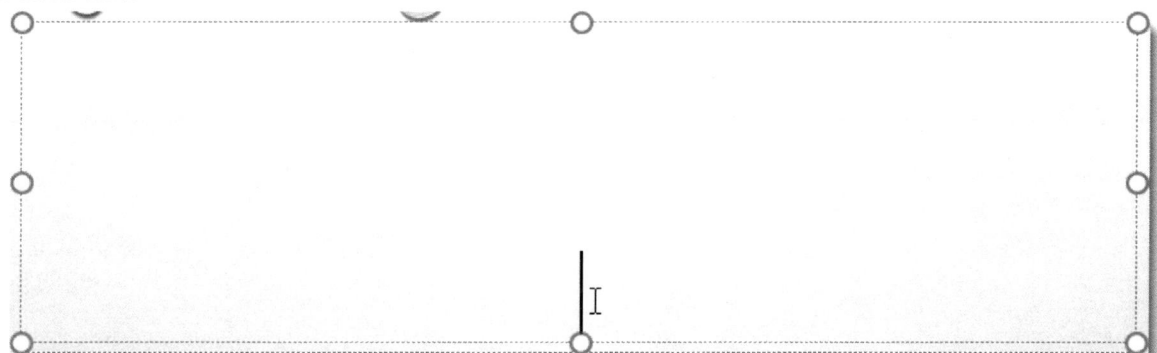

3. Type the title text in the box.
4. Drag the text box handles to change its size.

   - Dragging any corner handle allows you to reduce or enlarge the box's length and width at the same time. As you hover over a corner handle, the mouse pointer becomes a diagonal double-headed arrow. As you drag the handle, the mouse pointer becomes crosshairs.

   - Dragging the left or right side handle reduces or enlarges the box's width. Dragging the top or bottom handle reduces or enlarges the box's height. As you hover over any side handle, the mouse pointer becomes a horizontal or vertical double-headed arrow. As you drag the handle, the mouse pointer becomes crosshairs.

- To maintain the text box's dimensional symmetry, press and hold the **Ctrl** key as you drag a handle. This keeps the box centered in its original position on the slide.
  - **Ctrl**+drag a corner handle to change the size of left-right and/or top-bottom sides.
  - **Ctrl**+drag a left/right handle to change the width of the box equally from both sides.
  - **Ctrl**+drag a top/bottom handle to change the height of the box equally from the top and bottom.

5. Press the **Esc** key, or click anywhere in the slide outside the selected text box.

   The text box, its handles, and the title placeholder itself are no longer visible. Only the new title text is visible.

Adding, deleting, and hiding slides in a presentation

Every new PowerPoint presentation comes with only one slide. But there are many ways to add slides to a presentation. Deleting slides is quite simple. However, you can also simply hide one or more slides, so that they're not deleted, but they don't display in the presentation.

 MOS PowerPoint Exam Objective(s): 1.2.2, 1.2.3, 1.2.4

1. Add a new slide to the presentation by using one of the following techniques.
   - On the Home tab, in the Slides group, click the upper part of the **New Slide** button.

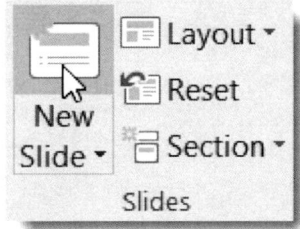

   - Right-click in the Slides pane, and from the context menu, select **New Slide**.

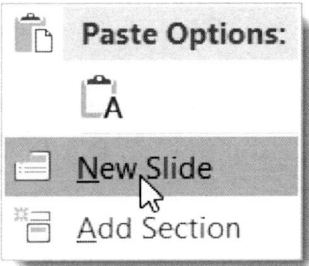

- Press **Ctrl+M**.

   A second, new slide is added in the slides pane. Like the first slide, it contains placeholders only for a title and for a subtitle or other content.

2. This time, click the lower part of the New Slide button.
   On the Home tab, in the Slides group.

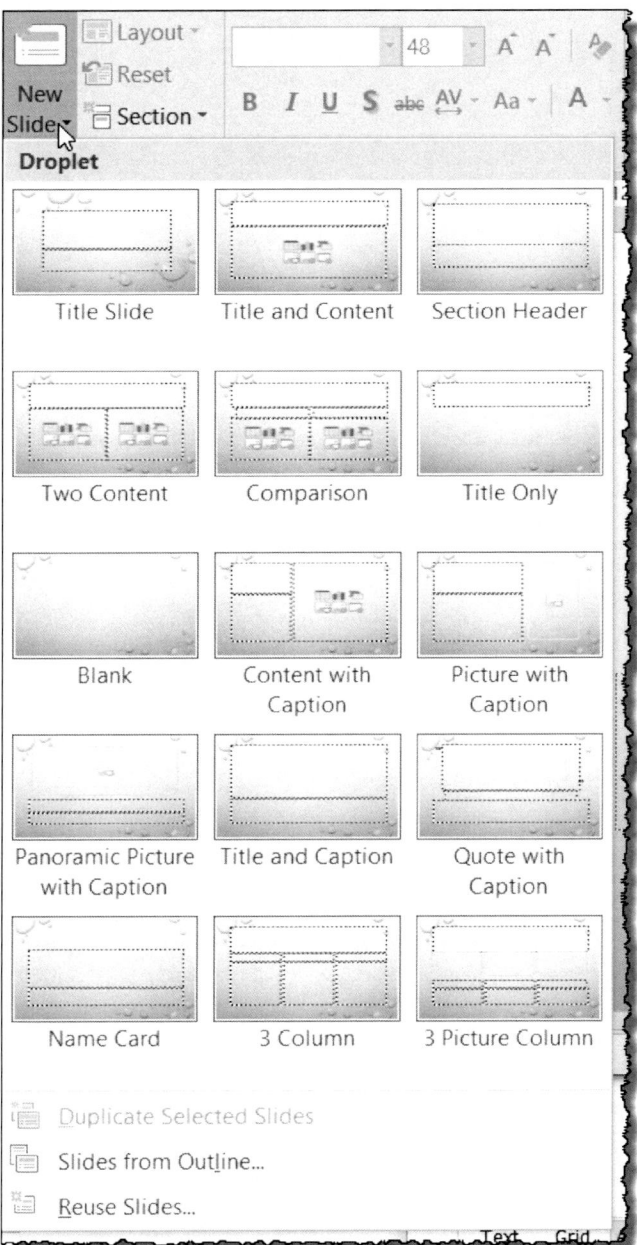

The Office Theme gallery opens, displaying various options for prearranged slide content. Additional menu choices are displayed below the gallery.

- *Duplicate Selected Slides*: Automatically duplicates the format and contents of any selected slide.
- *Slides from Outline*: Opens the Insert Outline window, from which you can navigate to a Word or other text document in outline form. On inserting that document, its outline is automatically rendered as PowerPoint slides.
- *Reuse Slides*: Opens the Reuse Slides pane, which assists you in reusing/salvaging slides from another PowerPoint presentation or other source.

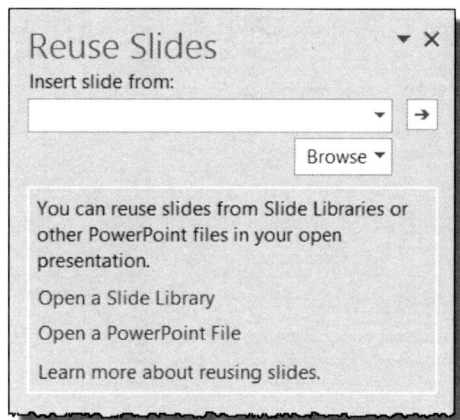

3. Click on a gallery option.

    To add the new slide to the presentation.

4. Right-click the slide you wish to delete.

    It's easiest to do this on slide thumbnails in Normal view or Slide Sorter view. Press and hold **Ctrl** to select multiple slides. Then right-click anywhere in the selection.

    A context menu opens.

5. Click **Delete Slide**.

6. Right-click the slide you wish to hide from display in the presentation.
   Or multiple selected slides.
7. Click **Hide Slide**.

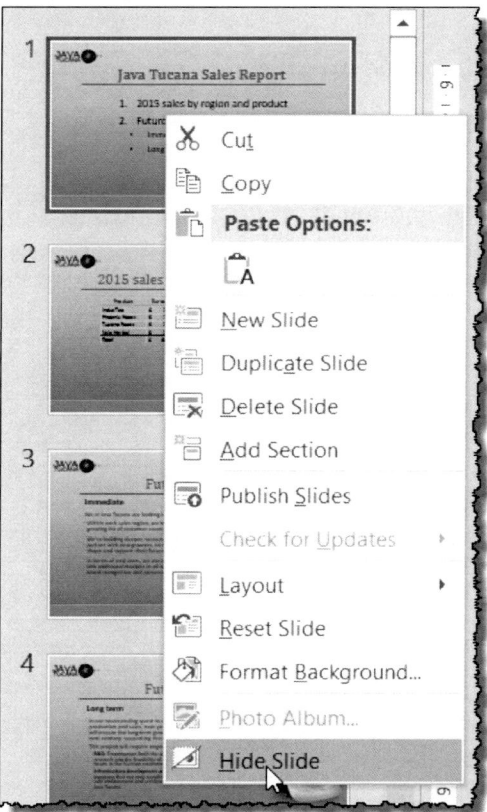

Navigating a presentation

Once your presentation contains more than one slide, there are several handy ways to navigate it.

1. Navigate a multi-slide presentation using one of these methods.
   - In the Slides pane, click the desired slide. Use the Slides pane scroll bar to quickly move through longer presentations.
   - In the lower right of the main pane, click a double-headed arrow to move sequentially through the slides in the direction of the arrow.

    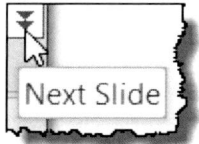

   - In the main pane, use the scroll bar to drag to the desired slide in the presentation. As you drag the scroll box, a tooltip indicates the number and title of the current slide.

- On the keyboard, use the **PgUp** and **PgDn** keys to navigate through the presentation one slide at a time.

Inserting a hyperlink on a slide

 MOS PowerPoint Exam Objective(s): 2.1.6

A *hyperlink* is specially formatted text or a graphic object that's linked to other data in another location. In PowerPoint, you can insert a hyperlink on a slide to link to, for example, another slide (in the same presentation or in another one), another Microsoft Office document, or even a website.

 Note: It's important to remember that hyperlinks become clickable only in Slide Show view.

1. Select the source object—the text or other object—you wish to link to a destination.

2. Format the text as a hyperlink.
   - On the ribbon's Insert tab, in the Links group, click **Hyperlink**.

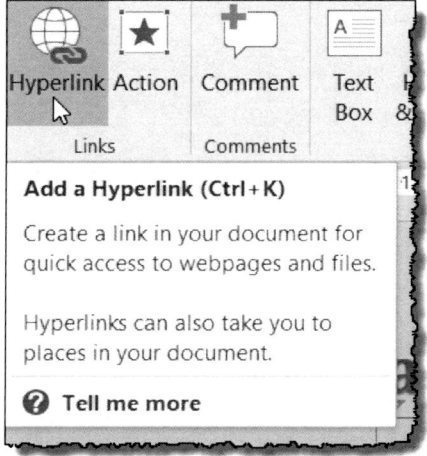

- Press **Ctrl+K**.

  The Insert Hyperlink window opens.

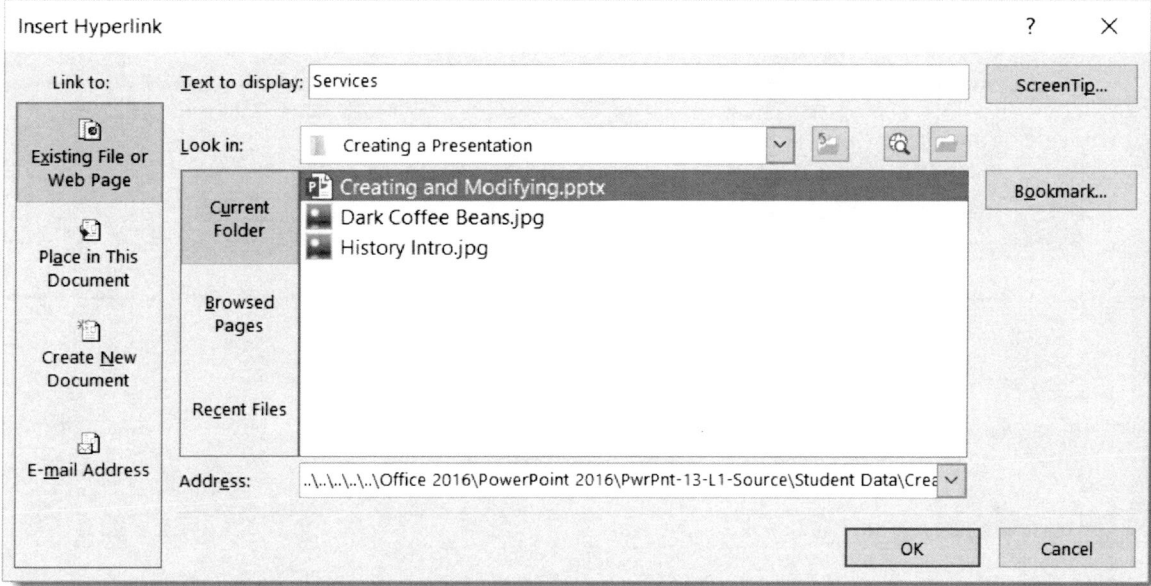

3. Select the destination to which you wish to link the source.

   Use the buttons under "Link to" and "Look in" as necessary. For example, to link to another slide in the current presentation, under "Link to," click **Place in This Document**. The Insert Hyperlink window then lists the slides in the presentation. Select the name of the destination slide in the window, and click **OK**.

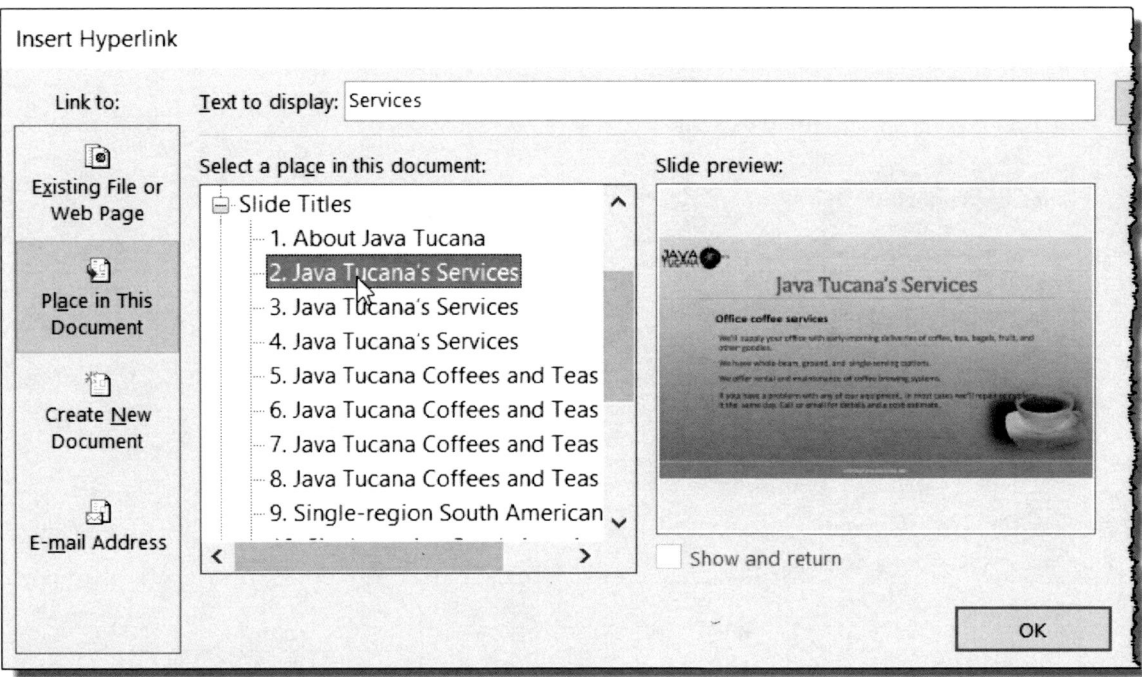

The selected source is now a hyperlink.

1. **Java Tucana's** Services

Inserting shapes

PowerPoint provides a gallery of shapes that you can insert onto your slides. Shapes are accessible from the Insert tab.

 MOS PowerPoint Exam Objective(s): 2.2.4

1. Select the slide onto which you'd like to insert a shape.
2. Insert a shape from the Home tab or the Insert tab.
    - On the ribbon's Home tab, in the Drawing group, click the Shapes gallery's **More** button.

    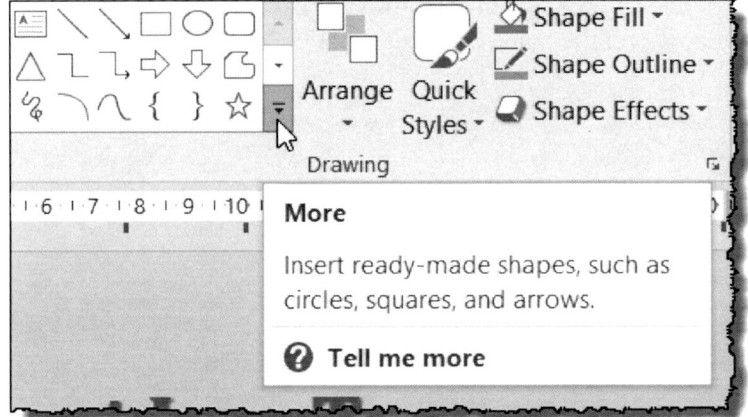

    - On the Insert tab, in the Illustrations group, click **Shapes**.

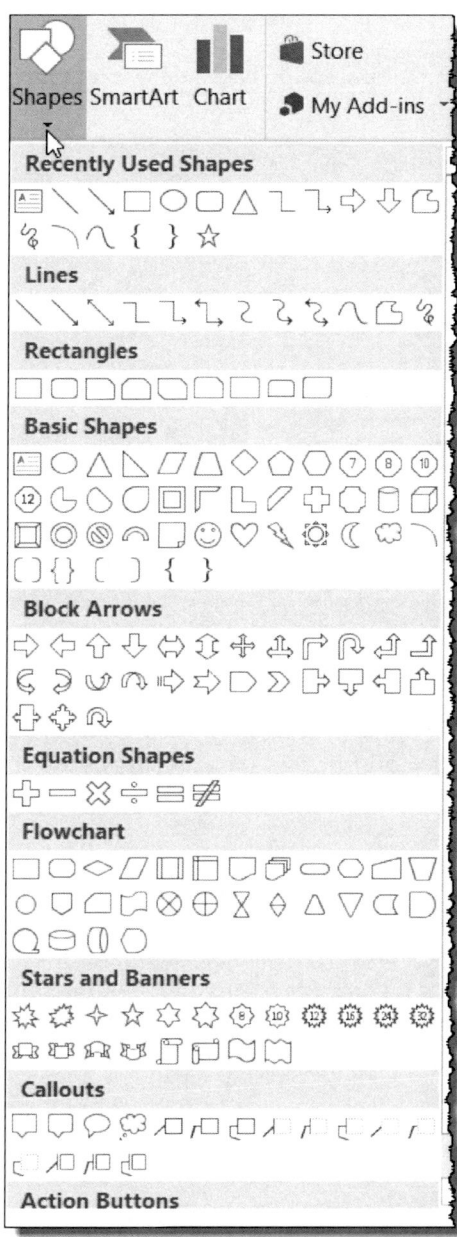

To display the Shapes gallery.

3. Click to select the shape you want to insert.
4. Click on the slide where you'd like to place the shape.

   The shape appears on the slide, and the box enclosing it indicates that it is selected. At the sides and corners of the box are selection handles, which you can use to change its dimensions.

5. Hover over the shape with your mouse pointer.

   The mouse pointer becomes a four-headed arrow, indicating that the shape can be moved in any direction.

   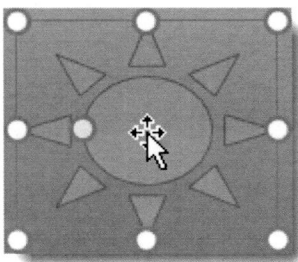

6. With the four-headed arrow displayed, click and drag the shape to place it in the desired location on the slide, then release the mouse button.
7. Press **Esc** or click in a blank area of the slide.

   To deselect the shape.

Types of images

You want your slide presentations to have visual appeal and convey meaning. One way to accomplish this goal is to include images on your slides, where it's appropriate and useful to do so. Fortunately, PowerPoint allows you to insert many kinds of images, or pictures, in a variety of file formats. PowerPoint categorizes image files into two types: bitmap images and vector graphics.

- A *bitmap image* is a file that contains an image made up of *pixels*. The image can be a photograph, a scanned drawing or form, and so on. The number of pixels per unit area (for example, per square centimeter) determine the image's resolution: the greater the number of pixels, the higher the resolution. PowerPoint supports more than a dozen different picture file formats, including .bmp, .jpg, .gif, and .png. However, whenever possible, it's a good idea to use the .jpg format, as its considerable file compression allows you to conserve valuable storage space and can keep your presentations "lean and mean."

- A *vector graphic* is a drawing that contains highly detailed information that describes every point in it in mathematical terms. Thus, the resulting image is highly detailed. In fact, a vector graphic can be enlarged to any degree and maintain all of its resolution. So it shouldn't be surprising that vector graphics are heavily used in the design world. PowerPoint supports all the common vector-graphic file formats, including .cdr, .drw, .eps, and .emf.

In PowerPoint, you can insert an image from a file on your computer or other storage device. However, from the ribbon, you can also download online images.

Inserting an image from a file

The procedure for inserting an image onto a slide is the same for both bitmap images and vector graphics.

1. Select the destination slide for the image.
2. Click **Pictures**.

   On the Insert tab, in the Images group.

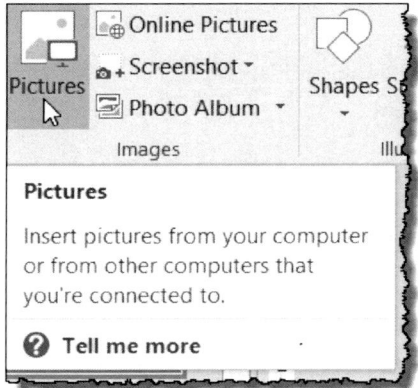

The Insert Picture window opens.

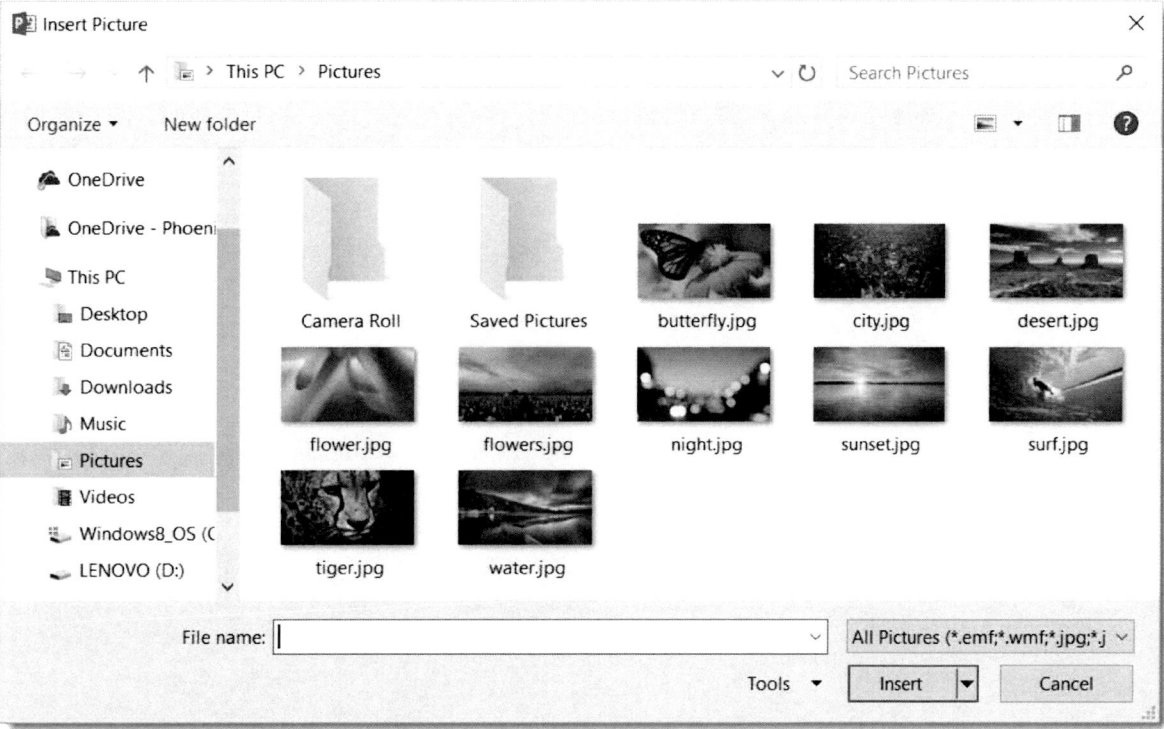

3. Navigate to the location of the image file you wish to insert.
4. Select the image file, and click **Insert**.

    The image file is inserted onto the current slide.
5. Drag the image to position it in the exact location desired.

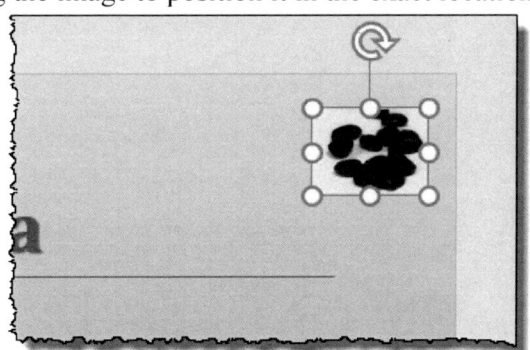

Inserting online images

You can download images from online sources and insert them onto your slides.

1. Select the slide onto which you wish to insert your downloaded image.
2. Click **Online Pictures**.
   On the ribbon's Insert tab, in the Images group.

   The Insert Pictures window opens. Its available options will differ, depending on your current online connection and services.

   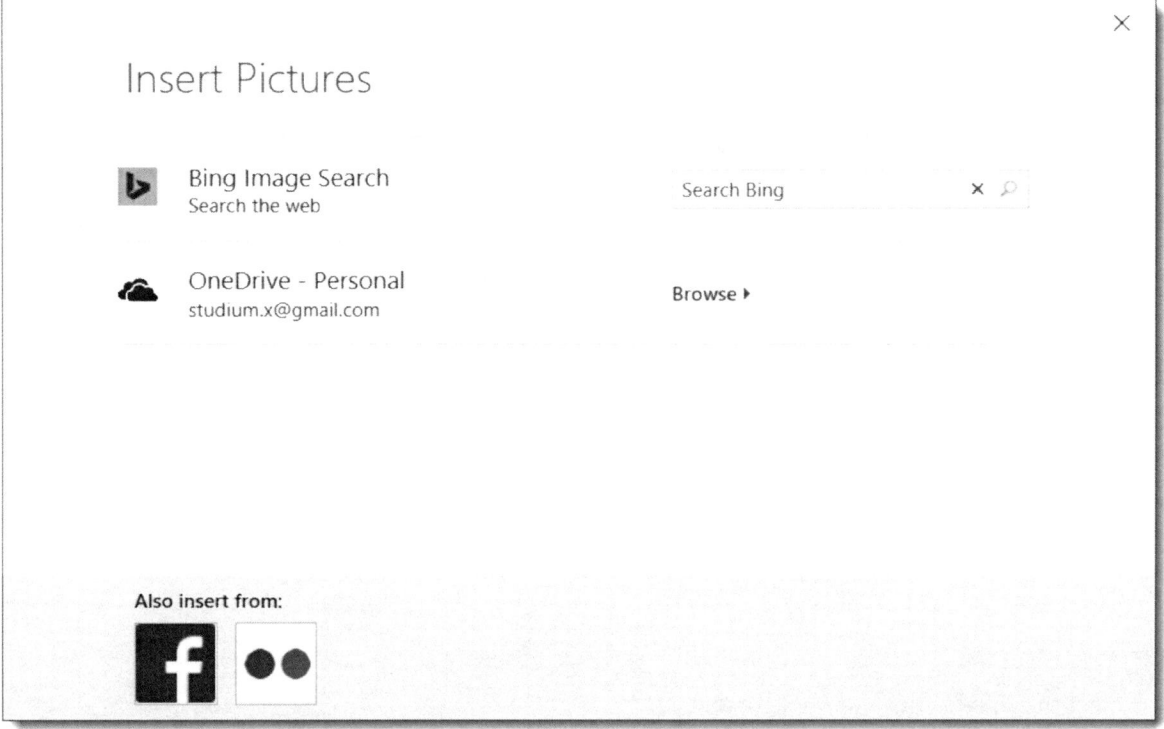

3. Choose a connection to obtain an image.
   - Select an available source, such as OneDrive, and click **Browse**. Then navigate to the desired location and download the image.

- Click in the search box (for example, using Bing Image Search), type a keyword or search string, and press **Enter**. Select an image, and click **Insert**.

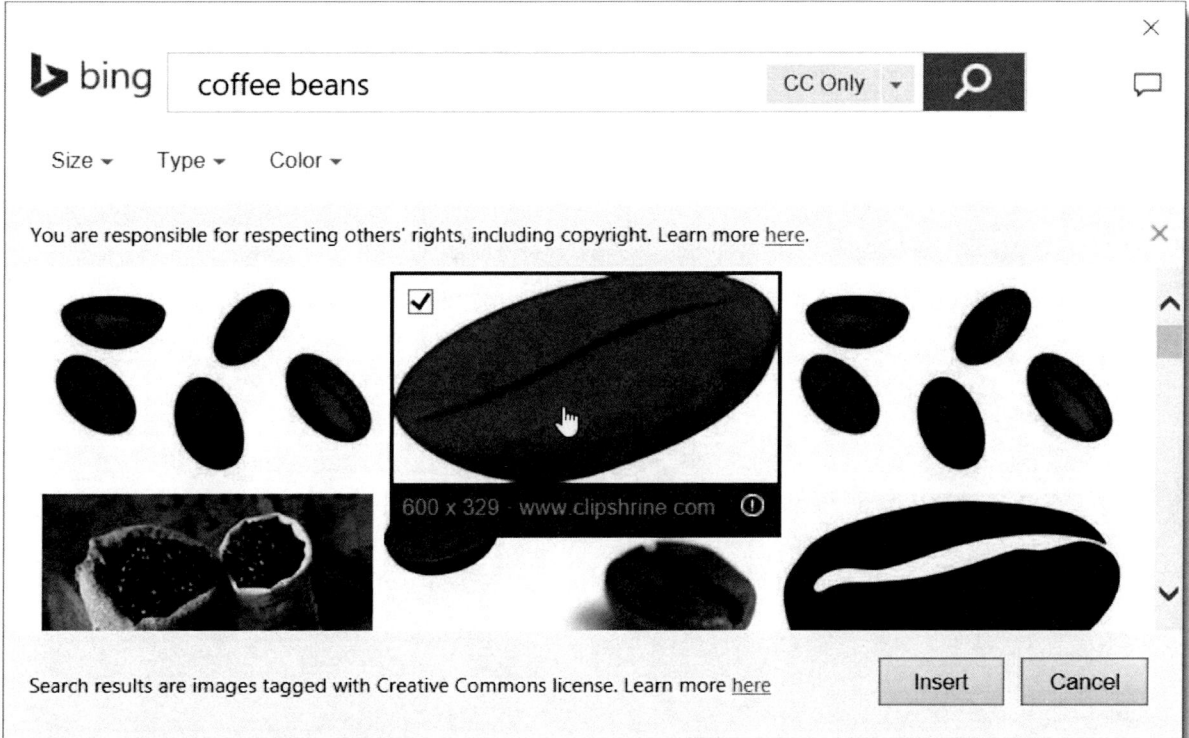

The image appears on the selected slide.

4. Drag the image to position it exactly where you want it to appear.

Exercise: Creating and modifying slide content

You'll add slides to a presentation, and you'll add text and graphics.

Do This	How & Why
1. Open `Creating and Modifying.pptx` and save it as `My Creating and Modifying.pptx`.	It's in the `Creating a presentation` data folder.
2. Scroll through the presentation.	Use either the Slides pane or the main pane. The presentation contains different types of slides ordered and grouped to cover topics and subtopics.
3. View slide 5.	Currently the first slide in the Java Tucana Coffees and Teas section of the presentation. It would be helpful to have a slide that provides a brief overview of this section.
4. View slide 4.	The last slide of the Java Tucana's Services section. You'll insert a slide after this one to begin the next section.

Do This	How & Why

5. Click **New Slide**.

On the Home tab, in the Slides group.

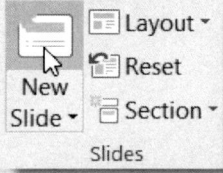

A new, blank slide 5 is inserted and selected.

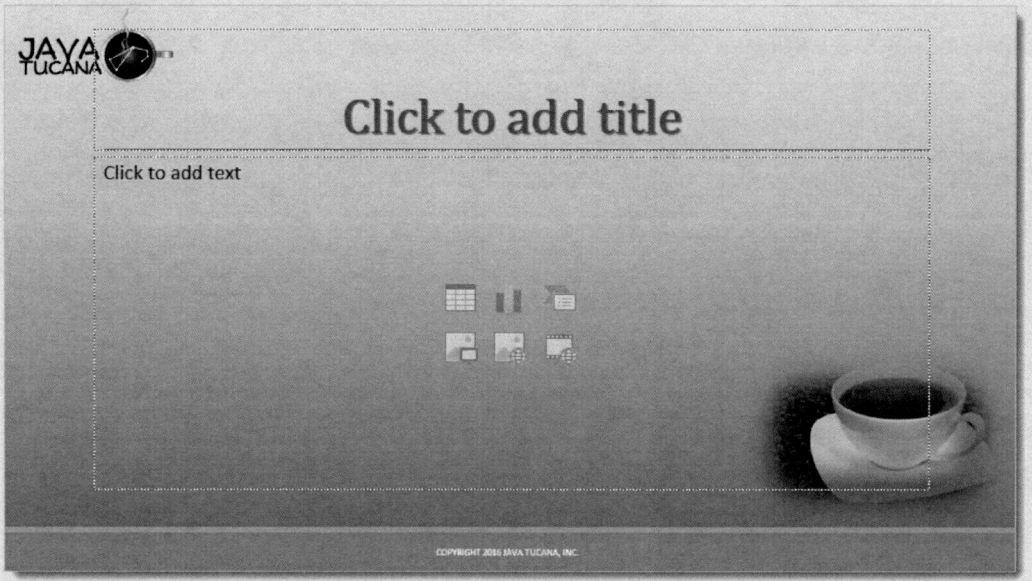

6. Click in the upper text box.

Where it reads "Click to add title." The placeholder text is replaced with an insertion point, and the cursor becomes an I-beam.

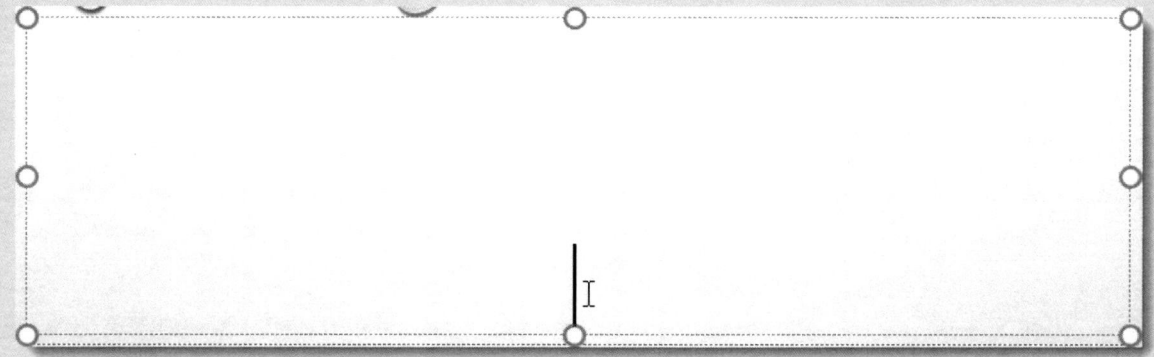

7. Type `Java Tucana Coffees and Teas`.

The heading's font, size, and color is preformatted to match the other slides.

8. Now click in the lower text box.

Which reads "Click to add text." The insertion point appears, aligned at the left edge of the box.

Do This	How & Why
9. Click the arrow to the right of the Bullets button.	On the Home tab, in the Paragraph group. A gallery of bullet styles opens.
10. Select the Filled Round Bullets style.	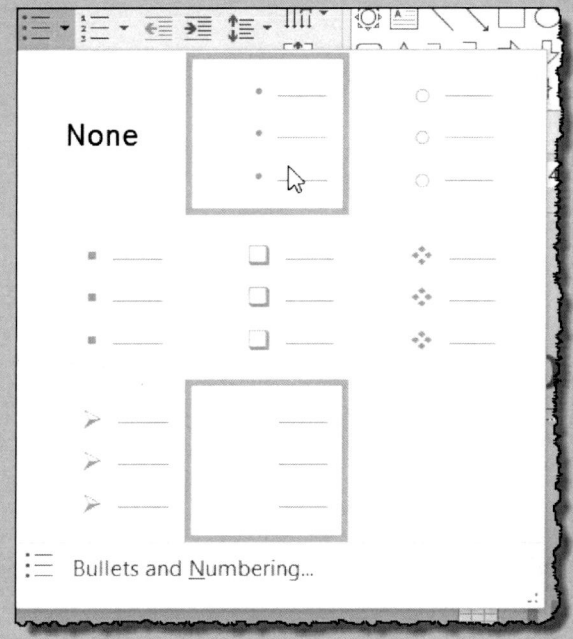 A bullet of the selected style appears at the insertion point.
11. Type `Java Tucana carries the best South American coffees our buyers can find.` Then press **Enter**.	The statement appears as a bullet item. Pressing Enter inserted a second bullet on a new line.
12. Create a second bullet item that reads `We also produce our own blends of coffee, including our signature Tucana Roast.` Then press **Enter**.	
13. Create another bullet that reads `We carry our own tea blends and a selection of popular teas.` Then press **Enter**.	
14. Create a final bullet item that reads `Our coffees and teas are available for your enjoyment in our cafés or at home.`	If you want to include the accented "é" in "cafés," on the Insert tab, in the Symbols group, click **Symbol**. There's no need to press Enter, as this is the final item in the list. 

Do This	How & Why
15. Deselect the text box, and observe the bullet slide title and list you've created. Click in another part of the slide.	

16. On slide 1, format "Services" as a hyperlink to slide 2.	
a) Select slide 1.	
b) Select **Services**, then click **Hyperlink**.	On the Insert tab, in the Links group. 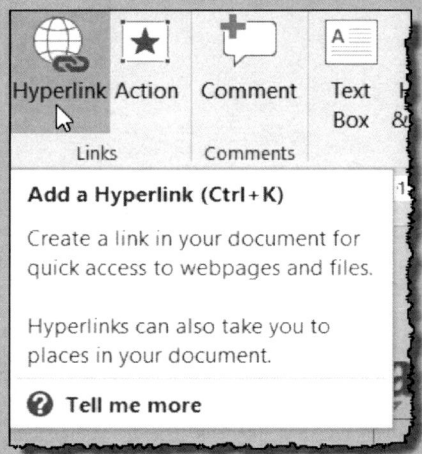
c) Click **Place in This Document**.	In the Insert Hyperlink window, under "Link to."

Do This	How & Why

    d) Click **2. Java Tucana's Services**.

From the list of slide titles under "Select a place in this document."

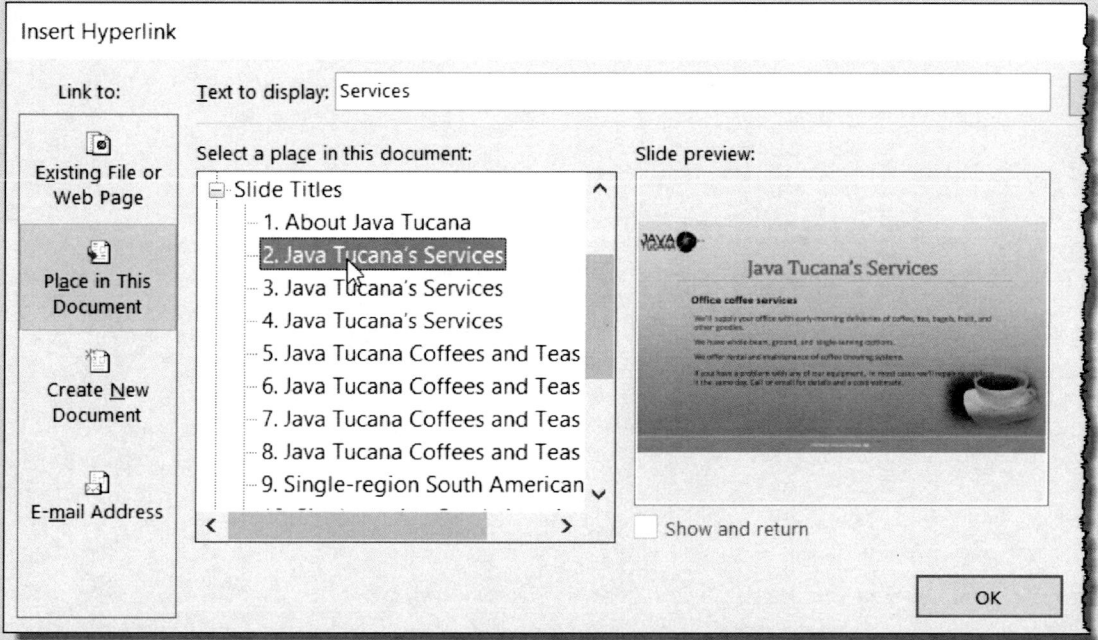

e) Click **OK**.	The Services hyperlink appears on the slide.

17. Also on slide 1, format Coffees and Teas as a hyperlink to slide 5.

Use the same procedure as in the previous step. This time, under "Select a place in this document," select **5. Java Tucana Coffees and Teas**. The two new hyperlinks now appear on the slide.

18. Display slide 9.	The first slide titled "Single-region South American coffees." You'll add a shape to this slide as a visual accent.
19. Click **Shapes**.	On the Insert tab, in the Illustrations group.

Do This	How & Why
20. Click the **Sun** shape.	Under Basic Shapes.
21. Click anywhere under the bullet list.	To insert the shape.
22. Drag the shape where you think it should be placed on the slide.	As you hover over the shape, as long as the mouse pointer is a four-headed arrow, you can drag the shape anywhere on the slide. Also, guide lines, or rules, appear in different places on the slide, which tell you when an object is centered, aligned with another object, and so on.
23. Resize the shape as you see fit.	Use the shape's handles.
24. Elsewhere on the same slide, insert the picture file **Dark Coffee Beans.jpg**.	
a) On the Insert tab, in the Images group, click **Pictures**.	
b) Navigate to the `Creating a presentation data` folder.	
c) Select **Dark Coffee Beans.jpg**, and click **Insert**.	The image appears on the slide.

Do This	How & Why
25. Drag the image to an appropriate location on the slide, and resize it as you see fit. 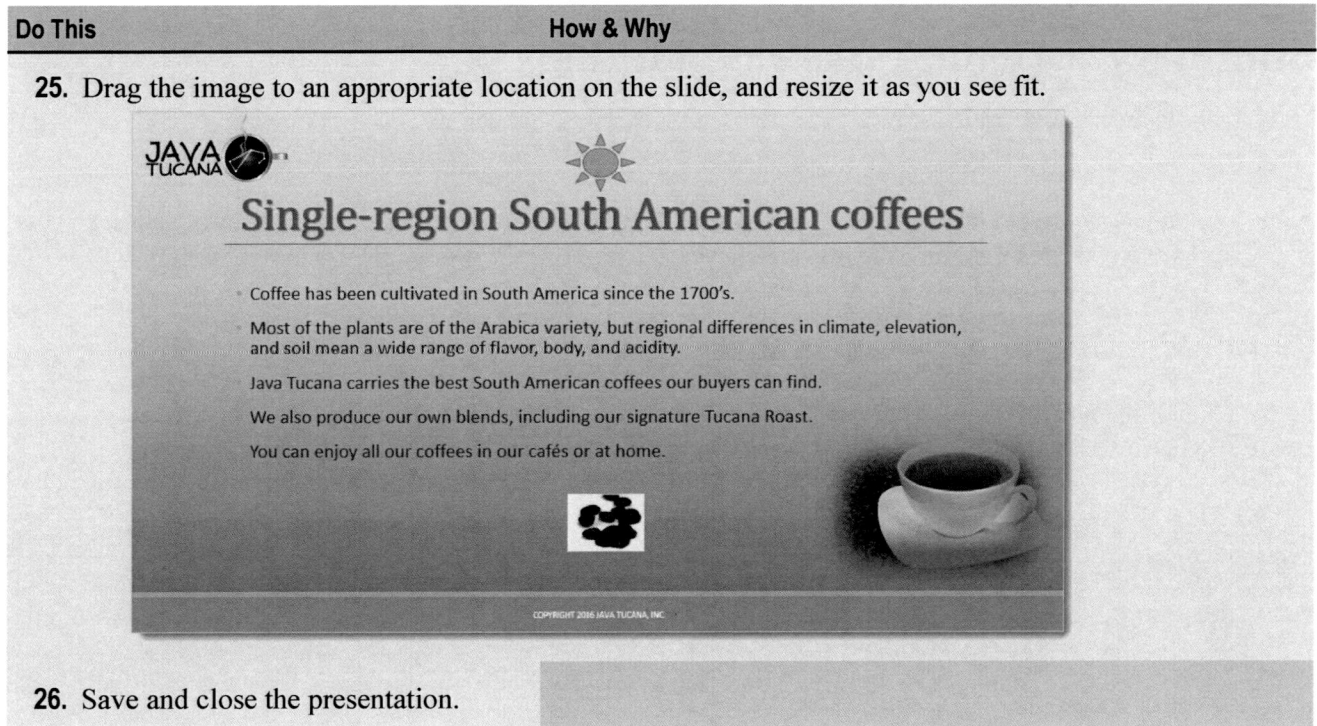	
26. Save and close the presentation.	

Assessment: Creating and modifying slide content

1. When you use the New Slide command, the new slide does which of the following?

    - It replaces the selected slide.
    - It's inserted immediately following the current slide.
    - It's inserted immediately preceding the current slide.
    - It's inserted as the last slide in the presentation.

2. True or false? You can insert text simply by clicking anywhere on a slide and typing.

    - True
    - False

3. True or false? A hyperlinked slide object can link to a destination on the World Wide Web, to another file, or to another location in the same presentation.

    - True
    - False

4. Which of the following statements is true for any images inserted on a slide?

    - Before you insert the image, you must specify its final destination and size.
    - Before you insert the image, you must specify its final destination, but you can resize the image at any point after you've inserted it.
    - Before you insert the image, you must first select a destination slide, but you can move the image and/or resize it afterwards.
    - Before you insert the image, you must first select a destination slide and specify the image's exact size, but you can move it freely afterwards.

Summary: Creating a presentation

You should now know how to:

- Create a blank presentation, and create a presentation from a template
- Create and modify slide content by navigating the presentation, adding slides, formatting slide objects as hyperlinks, and inserting shapes and images

Synthesis: Creating a presentation

In this chapter synthesis, you'll create a new presentation, add text to a slide, add slides to the presentation, create a hyperlink that links to another slide, and insert a shape and an image.

1. Create a new presentation—either a blank one, or one from a template.
2. On slide 1, enter the text as shown.

   History of Coffee
   - Introduction
   - Origins
   - Geography

3. Add a second slide to the presentation, and enter the text as shown.

   History of Coffee: Introduction
   - 10th century (or earlier) origins
   - Believed to have originated in Ethiopia
   - Earliest documented drinking of coffee in 15th century, in Yemen
   - Spread throughout Africa and the Middle East by the 16th century
   - Shortly after, coffee use spread throughout Europe

4. Add a third slide, and enter the text as shown.

   History of Coffee: Origins
   - Etymology
   - First use

5. Add a fourth slide, and enter the text as shown.

History of Coffee: Europe

- Austria
- England
- France
- Germany
- Netherlands

6. Add a fifth slide, and enter the text as shown.

History of Coffee: Americas

- Caribbean
- Central America
- South America
- North America

7. Add a sixth slide, and enter the text as shown.

History of Coffee: Asia

- India
- Japan
- South Korea
- Indonesia

8. Insert a new slide 4 in the presentation, and enter the text as shown.

History of Coffee: Geography

- Europe
- Americas
- Asia

9. On slide 1, format each bullet item as a hyperlink.

   a) Link "Introduction" to slide 2.

   b) Link "Origins" to slide 3.

   c) Link "Geography" to slide 4.

History of Coffee

- Introduction
- Origins
- Geography

10. On slide 2, insert the **History Intro.jpg** picture (from the `Creating a Presentation` data folder).

11. Size and position the image as you would like it to appear on the slide.

12. Insert, size, and position an image from an online source on the slide of your choice.
13. On the slide(s) of your choice, insert some graphic shapes to add visual interest.
14. Size and position the shapes as you see fit.
15. Save the presentation as `My Coffee History.pptx`.

Chapter 3: Formatting

You will learn how to:

- Control the overall look of a presentation with slide masters and layouts
- Format individual slides and their text

Module A: Working with slide masters and layouts

In PowerPoint, you can format individual slides to make them all conform to a theme or look. However, a much simpler and quicker way to make your slides conform to a theme or style is by using slide masters and layouts.

You will learn how to:

- Modify the slide master
- Use the slide master to change a layout

About slide masters

When you want to format or tweak all the slides of your presentation at once, the easiest way to do so is via the slide master, which every presentation created in PowerPoint contains by default. The *slide master* is a single slide that governs the way all its subordinate slides look. Any colors, graphics, and text elements you add to the slide master are automatically applied to all the slides in the presentation that are governed by it. The slide master can also contain one or more layouts. A *layout* governs the arrangement of slide elements, such as text and graphics.

Note: Prior to PowerPoint 2013, presentations contained a Title Master, which governed the format of all title slides. In PowerPoint 2013 and 2016, a Title Slide layout element can be included in the slide master itself. Any title slides will follow the format of the title layout.

The Slide Master tab

When you display Slide Master view, the Slide Master tab is also displayed on the ribbon. The Slide Master tab contains all the important tools for working with and modifying a slide master and its layouts.

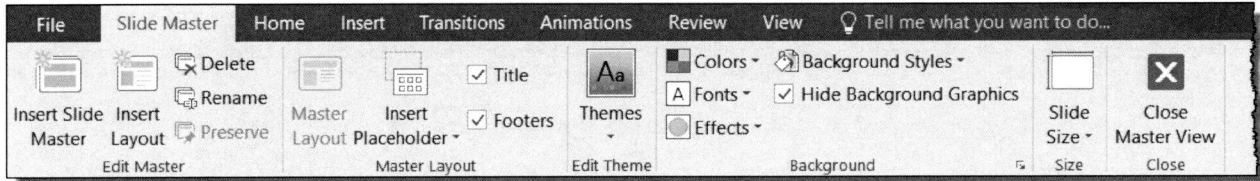

- The *Edit Master* group contains tools for editing the slide master, including adding layouts.
- The *Master Layout* group allows you to edit a layout by adding or removing slide elements.
- The *Edit Theme* group contains only the Themes tool, which allows you to apply a theme to a master or layout.
- The *Background* group allows you to further enhance the appearance of the slides by applying a background style, as well as by modifying slide colors and fonts or adding special effects.
- The *Size* group contains only the Slide Size tool, which allows you to change the slides' aspect ratio to Standard or Widescreen (the default), or change its size to a custom value.
- The *Close* group contains only the Close Master View button.

Modifying the slide master

In Normal view, a presentation's slide master isn't visible. So, before you can work with it, you need to display it.

MOS PowerPoint Exam Objective(s): 1.3.2

1. Click **Slide Master**.

On the ribbon's View tab, in the Master Views group.

Slide Master view is displayed. The Title Slide layout is selected by default. It contains placeholders for a master title and subtitle, as well as three additional placeholders along the bottom of the slide: the Date area, the Footer area, and the Number area.

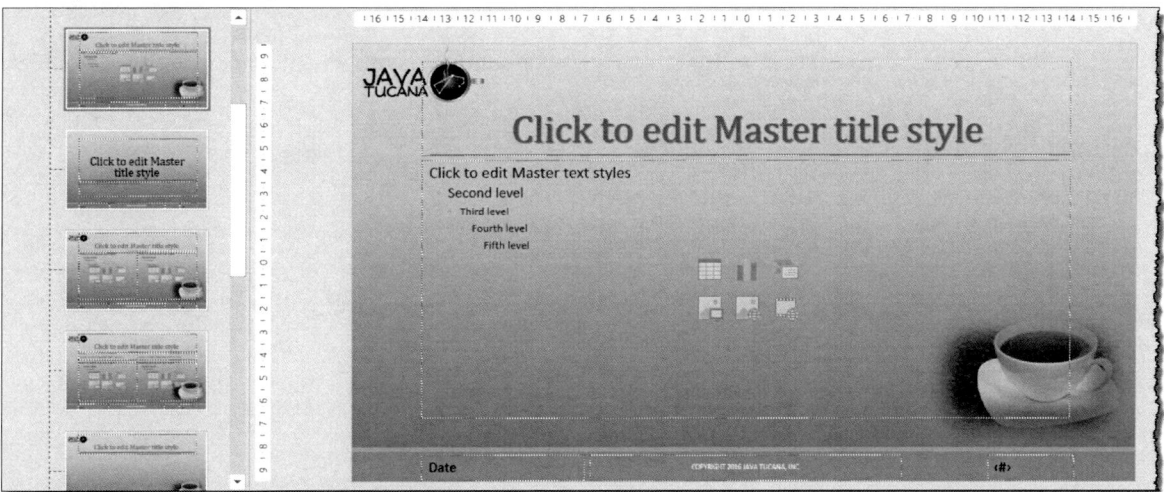

The Slide Master tab is displayed in the ribbon. In Slide Master view, by default, the Slides pane contains a single slide master, called the Office Theme Slide Master. Subordinate to it are individual slide "layouts."

2. Select the slide master.

Scroll up in the Slides pane, or press the up arrow. To modify the slide master, you must select the master itself, not one of its layouts.

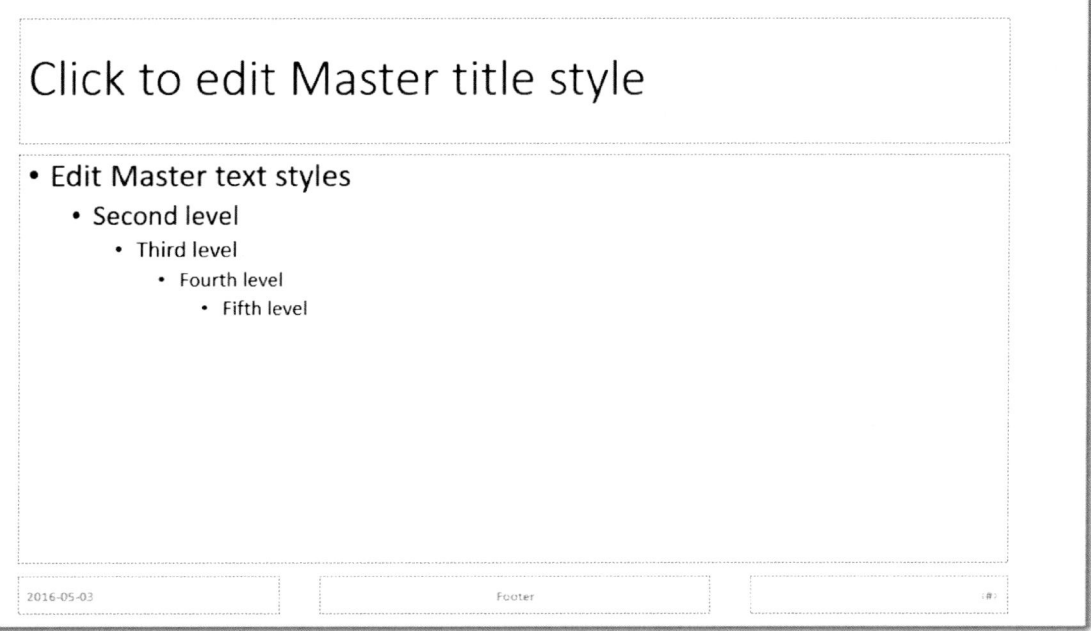

3. Make any desired formatting changes.
    Click in the appropriate placeholder/area to make your changes.
4. Insert any recurring elements.
    For example, you can insert a text box on your slide master by clicking Text Box on the Insert tab, then typing the text and formatting it. You can likewise insert images, sound clips, and video files. Just keep in mind that everything added to the slide master will recur on every slide in the presentation.
5. Change the size and/or position of elements.
    Click an element to select it, then drag to place it wherever you wish on the master slide. Use the element's handles to resize it.
6. Delete any elements you don't want to appear on every slide.
    Click an element to select it, then press **Delete**.

     Note: To delete a text box, first click to select it; next, click on its border; and then press **Delete**.

7. Return to Normal view.
    - On the Slide Master tab, click **Close Master View**.

    - In the status bar, click the **Normal** icon.

    If you wish to override a slide master element on a particular slide, select the slide (in Normal view), select the element or create a new one, and alter it as necessary. Any changes you make affect only the current slide.

Applying a theme to a presentation

You can enhance your presentation using themes that are applied globally to all slides. To do so, your presentation must be in Slide Master view. Use the same method to modify the theme.

 MOS PowerPoint Exam Objective(s): 1.3.1

1. Display your presentation in Slide Master view.
    On the Slide Master tab, click **Slide Master**.
2. Click **Themes**.
    On the Slide Master tab. There's no need to select the slide master in the Slides pane. A theme is applied globally to a master slide and its layouts, thus all are automatically affected.

    A gallery of themes and options opens. *Browse for Themes* allows you to search online for additional themes. *Save Current Theme* allows you to save a selected theme to the location of your choice.

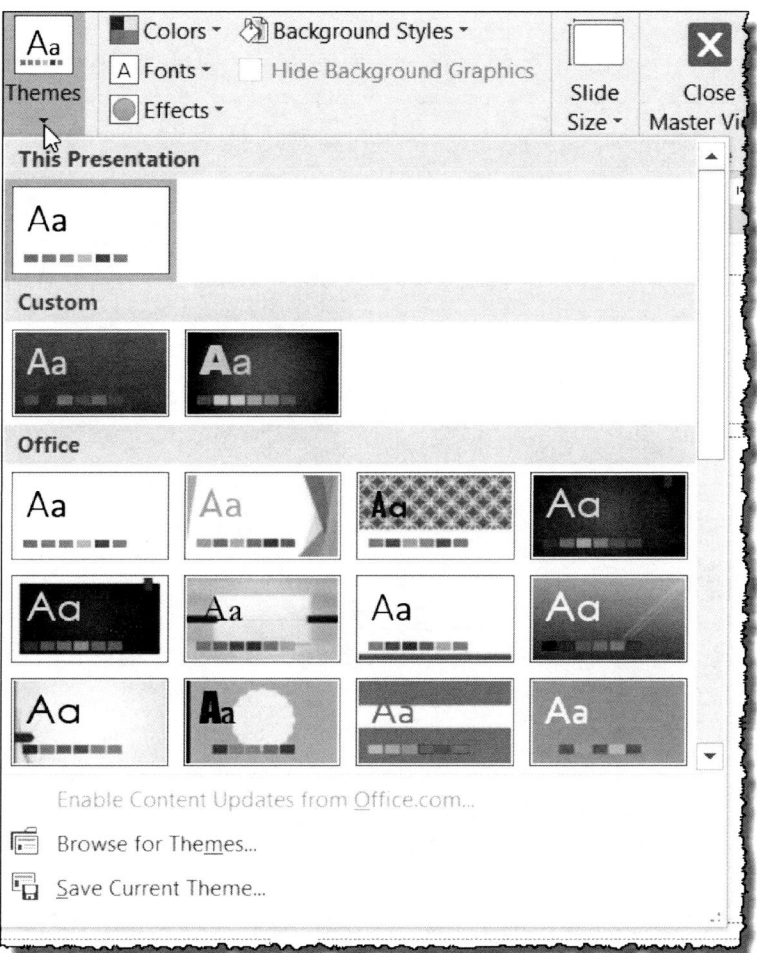

3. Select a presentation theme.

The selected theme is applied to the slide master and its layouts.

Exercise: Working with slide masters

Do This	How & Why
1. Open **JT Slide Master.pptx** and save it as **My JT Slide Master.pptx**.	From the `Formatting` data folder.
2. Scroll through the presentation's slides, and observe some of its features.	It consists of 16 slides, all of which use the same layout, colors, and graphics, including a recurring copyright footer element. Slide 1 also contains three hyperlinks.
3. Switch to Slide Master view.	
a) Click **View**.	To display the View tab.
b) Click **Slide Master**.	In the Master Views group. 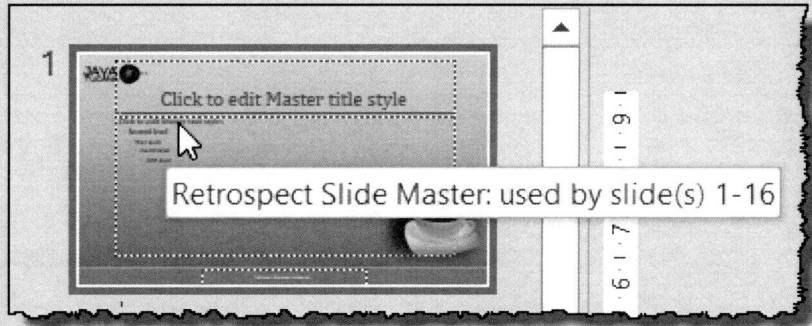 The presentation opens in Slide Master view, and the Slide Master tab is displayed.

4. Hover over the slide master.

In the Slides pane. A tooltip informs you that the master has a theme named Retrospect applied to it, which is used by slides 1–16.

Do This	How & Why

5. Hover over the slide layout directly below the slide master, and observe the tooltip.

In the Slides pane. The tooltip informs you that this layout governs the title slide. Note that the Title Slide layout isn't currently being used by any of the presentation's slides.

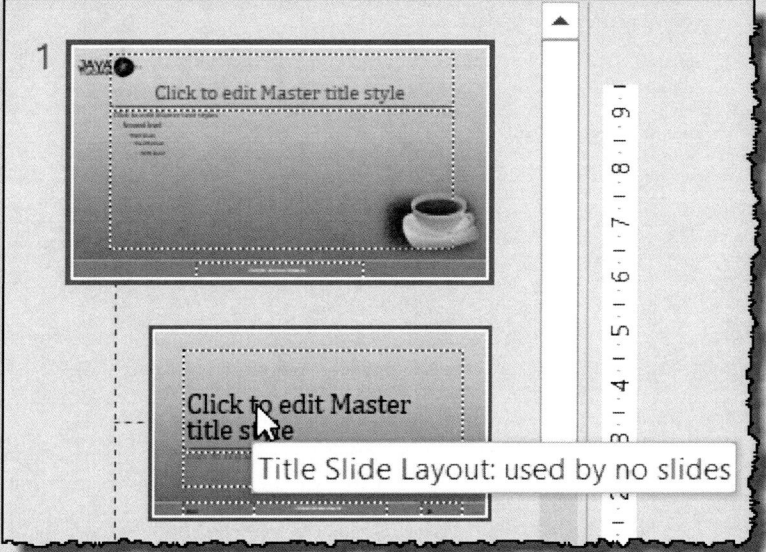

6. If necessary, select the **Title Slide** layout.

This slide doesn't contain any graphics. Because it's used to govern the layout of only the title slide, the only features of the slide master that it retains are the theme and the copyright footer.

| 7. Select the **Slide Master** and observe its elements. | In the Slides pane. It contains text boxes used for editing the master title and master text styles, as well as the logo and coffee-cup graphics. |

Do This	How & Why
8. Click the Java Tucana logo.	To select it. Once it's selected, you can move or resize it however you wish.
9. Move and/or resize the logo on the slide master.	
10. Likewise, select the coffee-cup graphic, then move and/or resize it.	
11. Apply a new theme to the presentation.	
a) Click **Themes**.	In the Edit Themes group. The Themes gallery and options are displayed.
b) Hover over the themes in the gallery.	Scroll to view them all. As you hover over each of the themes, the slide master changes to reflect it.
c) Select a theme.	Click it in the gallery.
12. Observe the new theme in Slide Master view.	The slide master and all layouts are updated to reflect the new theme.
13. Use the **Colors**, **Fonts**, and **Effects** buttons to further enhance your theme.	In the Background group.

Do This	How & Why
14. Return to Normal view.	On the Slide Master tab, click **Close Master View**, or click the **Normal** icon in the status bar.

15. Observe the presentation, scrolling through its slides.

All the slides have been updated to reflect the new theme and modified graphics.

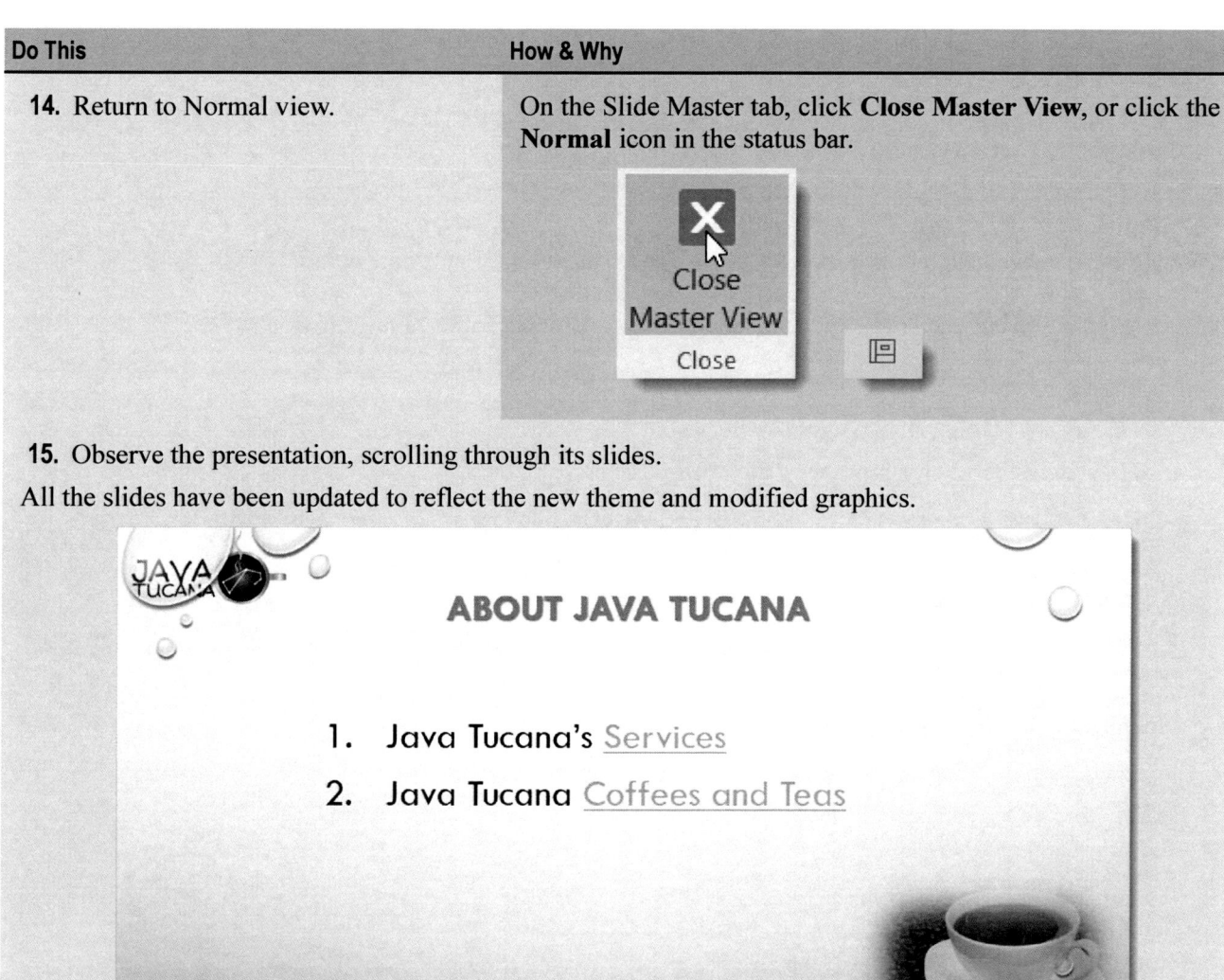

16. Save and close the presentation.

Headers and footers

 MOS PowerPoint Exam Objective(s): 2.3.1

Headers and footers provide a convenient way to place important recurring information in presentations. In PowerPoint, a *header* is recurring information displayed at the top of a handout or notes page. A *footer* is recurring information displayed at the bottom of a slide, handout, or notes page.

PowerPoint slide masters include three placeholders for displaying special information:

- The *Footer area*, for displaying special text that recurs on slides
- The *Date area*, for displaying the date and time
- The *Number area*, for displaying the slide number

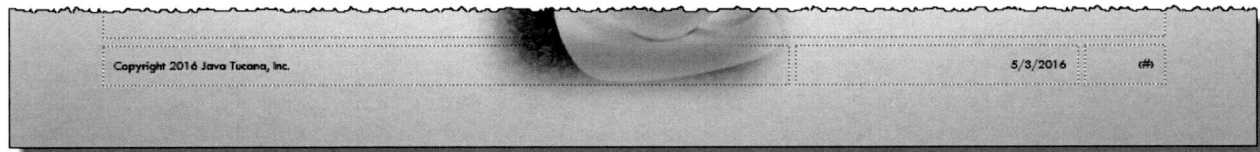

Handout and Notes masters also contain these placeholders, plus one more: the *Header area* displays at the top of handouts and notes pages.

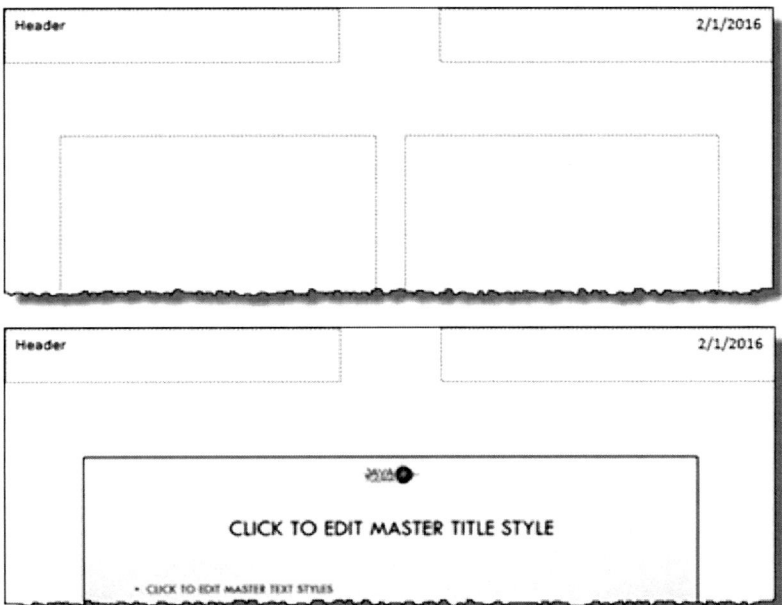

 Note: The Footer, Date, and Number areas appear at the bottom of slides and masters by default. However, you can position them elsewhere—for example, at the top—by switching to Slide view or Slide Master view, then dragging them to their new location.

Inserting footer information on a slide

Use the Header and Footer window to insert footer, date, and number information on one or more slides.

 MOS PowerPoint Exam Objective(s): 1.2.7

1. Select the slide on which you wish to include footer, date, and/or number information.
   This step is necessary only if you wish to apply the information to a single slide.
2. Click **Header & Footer**.
   On the Insert tab, in the Text group.

   The Header and Footer window opens with the Slide tab displayed.

   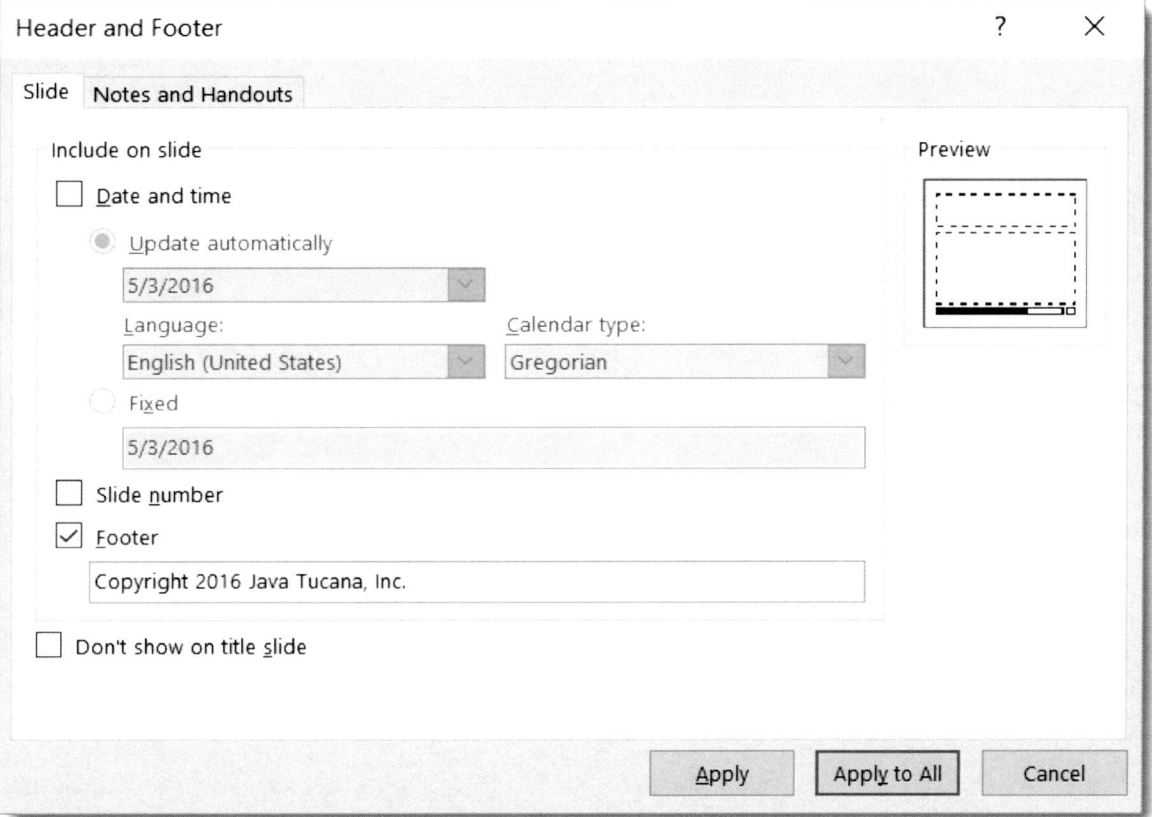

3. Click **Date and time**.
   Under "Include on slide."
   The option is now checked.
4. Click **Update automatically**, and select the date format from among the available choices.
   Under "Update automatically."

    Note: The *Fixed* format option allows you to type date and/or time information exactly as you would like it to appear. Keep in mind that doing so also prevents this information from automatically updating.

5. Select the Language and Calendar type (if available) from their respective fields.

6. Click **Slide number**.
   To display the slide number.

7. Click **Footer**.
   To display footer information.

8. Type the footer exactly as you'd like it displayed.
   In the footer box.

9. Check the **Don't show on title slide** option.
   The options you've set in the Header and Footer window won't appear on the title slide. To have this information appear on the title slide, simply click this option once again to uncheck it.

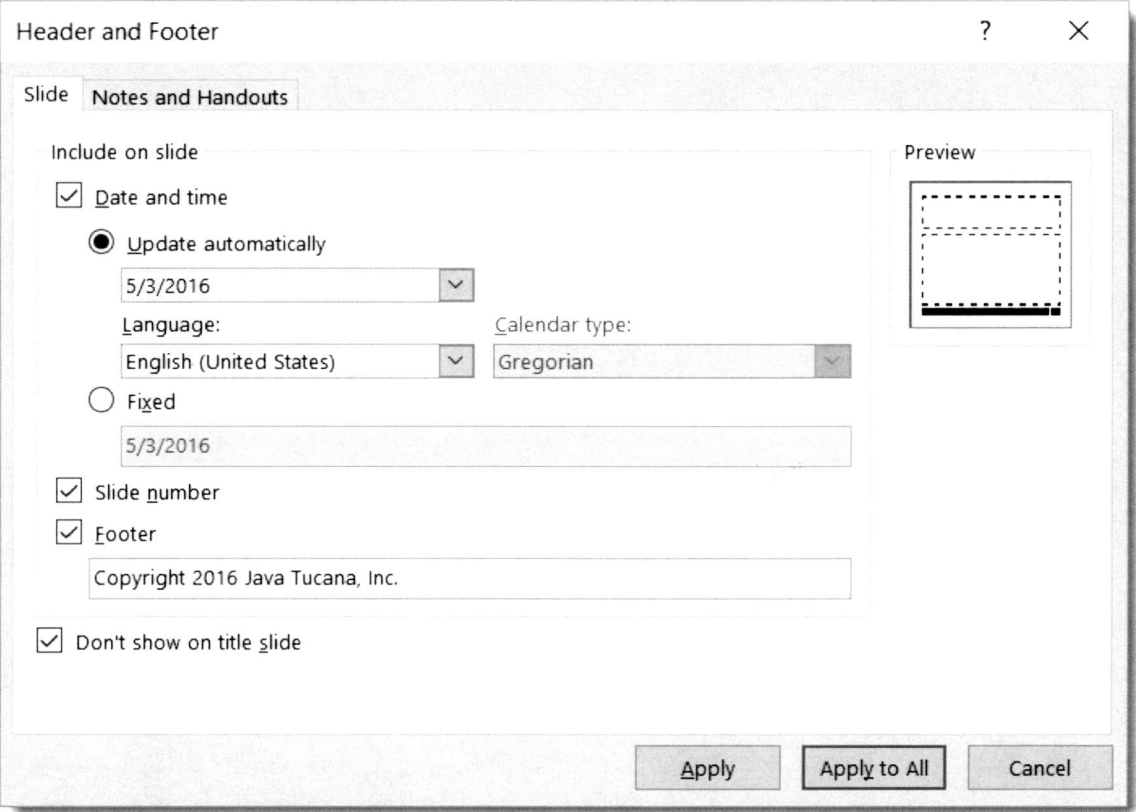

10. Apply the new settings.
    - To apply the settings to all the slides in the presentation, click **Apply to All**.
    - To apply them only to the current slide, click **Apply**.

    If you use the Apply to All option, and you later decide to suppress the display of this information on a slide, first select that slide, then use the Header and Footer window's Slide tab to deselect those options for that slide. Make sure that **Don't show on title slide** is selected (so that you don't alter its prior setting), then click **Apply**.

Headers and footers on handouts and notes pages

To add a header and/or footer to handouts and notes pages, use the Header and Footer window's Notes and Handouts tab. This tab contains essentially the same options as those on the Slide tab. However, the Notes and Handouts tab provides the additional option of adding a header at the top of each page. Once you've entered your settings, click **Apply to All**.

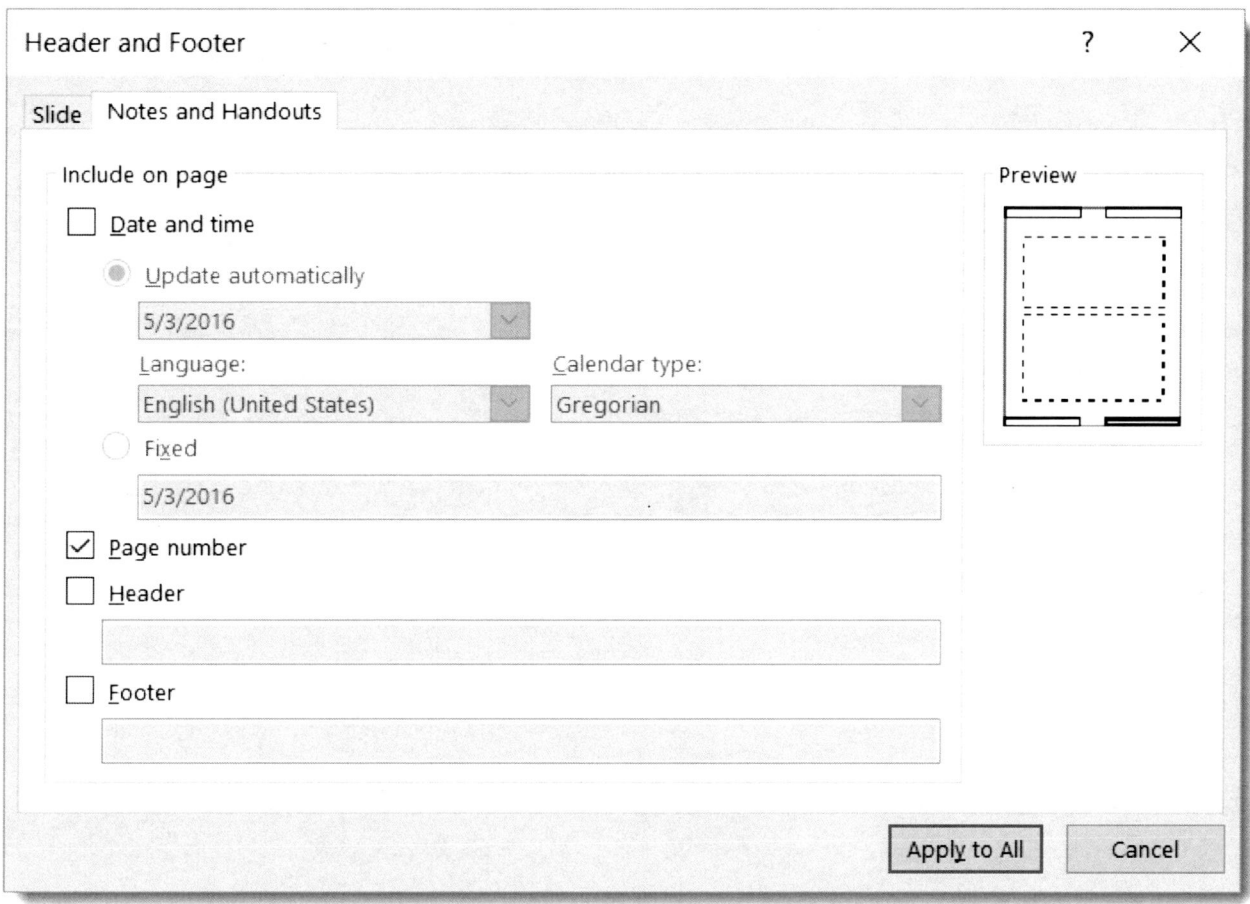

To edit text in header and footer placeholders directly, display the master containing the placeholder you wish to edit: Slide, Notes, or Handout. Then click in the placeholder and type or edit the text as you would normally.

 Note: Placeholders that you've set often contain special field codes that PowerPoint uses to display information. For example, <#> is the code for slide number. You can add text before and/or after these codes, but be sure to keep the codes themselves intact. Otherwise, the information they represent won't display properly.

Exercise: Adding and modifying a footer

Be sure to complete the exercise *Working with slide masters*.

Do This	How & Why
1. Open **JT Headers and Footers**, and save it as `My JT Headers and Footers`.	In the `Formatting` data folder.

2. Navigate through the presentation, and observe the footer information on each slide.

Every slide shows the same footer in the lower left, which currently consists of only a copyright statement. There's no date or slide number.

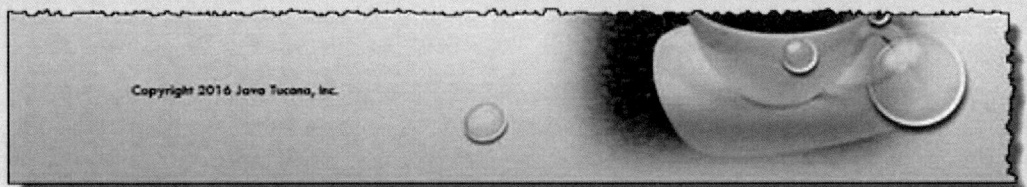

3. Display the presentation in Slide Master view.	On the View tab, in the Master Views group, click **Slide Master**. 
4. Select the slide master.	Scroll up and click **Droplet Slide Master** (as displayed in the tooltip), or press the up arrow key to move up to it.

5. Observe the master slide's footer placeholders.

On the left is the Footer area, on the right is the Number area, and between them is the Date area. Although the date and slide numbers aren't currently set to display in the presentation, they do have their own placeholders.

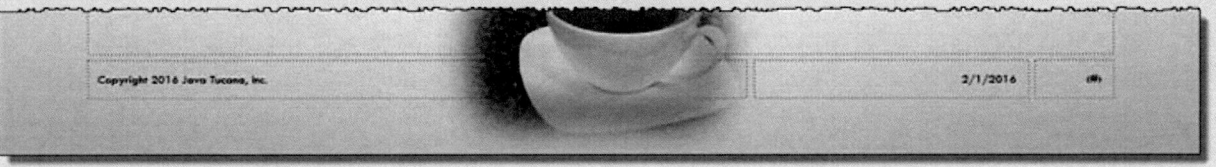

Do This	How & Why
6. Return to Normal view.	On the Slide Master tab, click **Close Master View**; or, in the status bar, click **Normal**.
7. Click the **Header & Footer** button.	On the Insert tab, in the Text group. The Header and Footer window opens, and the Slide tab is displayed.
8. Click **Date and time**.	Under "Include on slide," to check this option.
9. Click **Update automatically**.	Under "Date and time," to select its radio button.

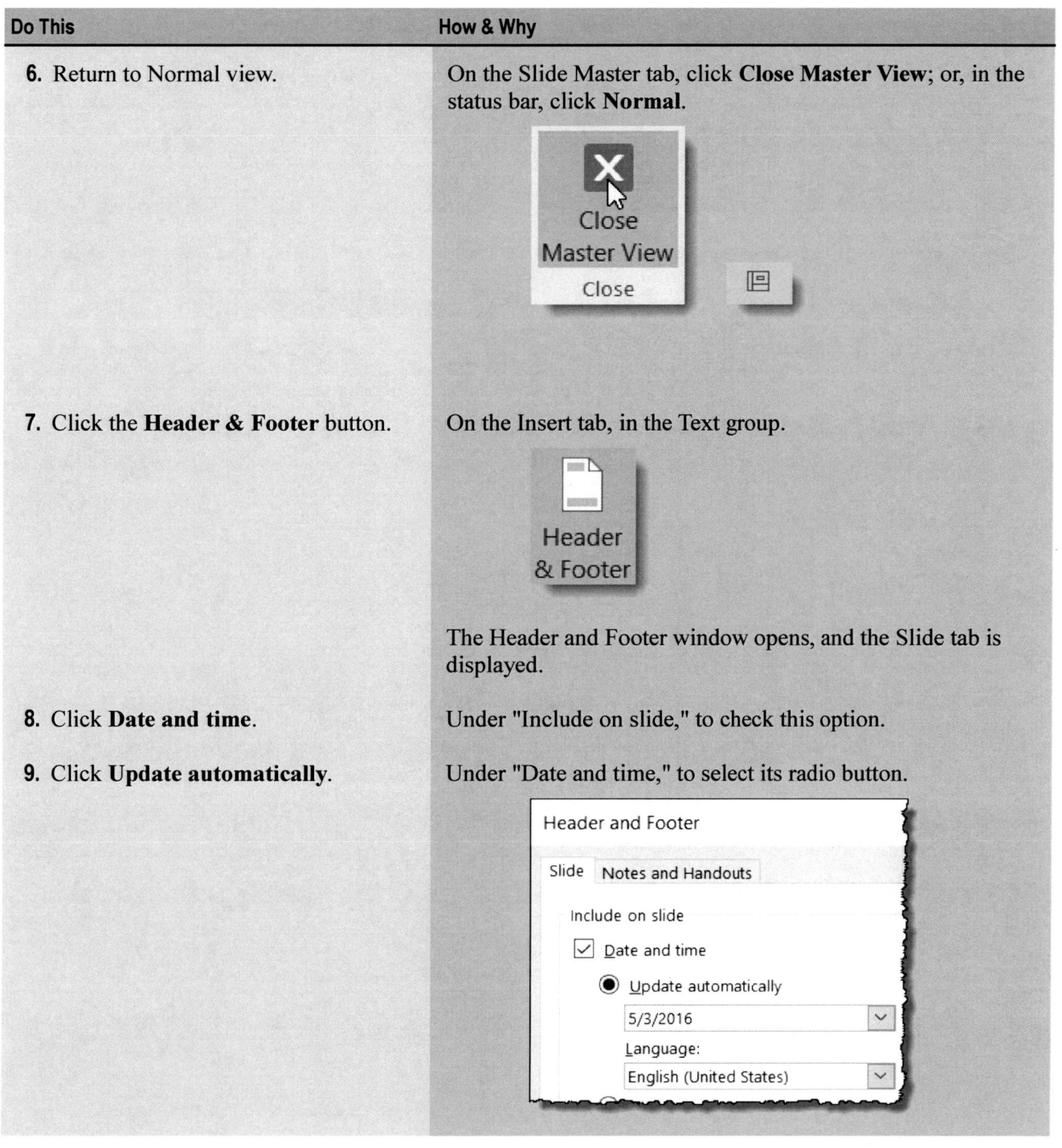

Do This	How & Why
10. Open the date format dropdown list, and select a date format.	Click ⌄ to display the choices, then click on a format to select it. 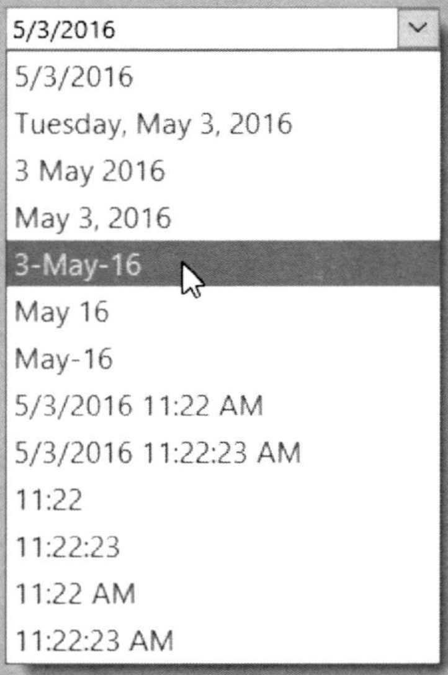 5/3/2016 Tuesday, May 3, 2016 3 May 2016 May 3, 2016 **3-May-16** May 16 May-16 5/3/2016 11:22 AM 5/3/2016 11:22:23 AM 11:22 11:22:23 11:22 AM 11:22:23 AM
11. Click **Slide number**.	Under "Include on slide," to have the slide number displayed on each slide.
12. Observe that the Footer option is checked.	This made the Footer area visible in the presentation when you first opened it.
13. Shorten the current footer to read `Copyright 2016 Java Tucana`.	In the Footer box.

14. Check the **Don't show on title slide** option.

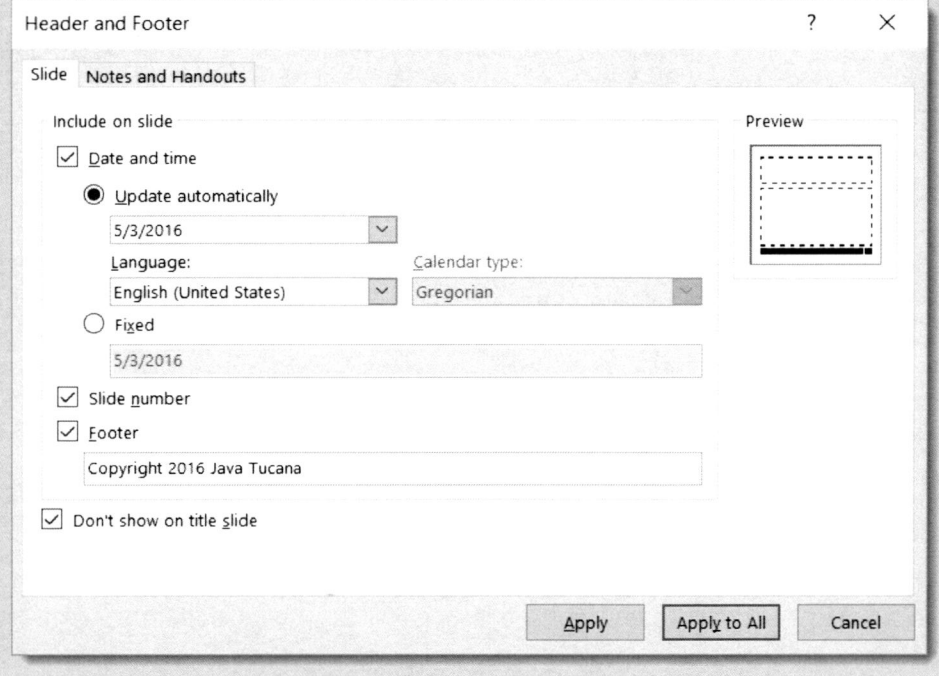

Do This	How & Why
15. Click **Apply to All**.	
16. Navigate the presentation.	
a) Observe slide 1.	No footer is displayed.
b) Observe the remaining slides.	

Slides 2 through 17 all display the same footer in the same way. The slide number changes with each slide.

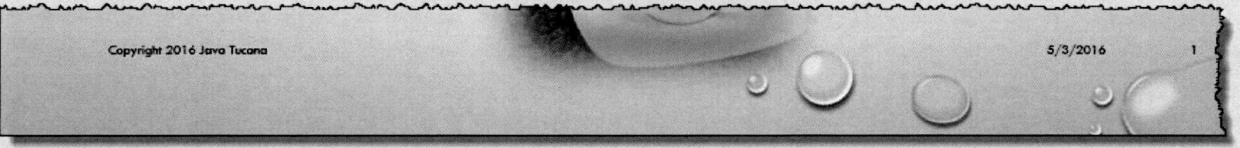

Do This	How & Why
17. Display Slide Master view.	On the View tab, click **Slide Master**.
18. Select the slide master.	Navigate to the Droplet Slide Master. You'll make the slide numbers larger and move the copyright statement closer to the lower-left corner of the slides.
19. Select the Date area of the footer.	In the Date area, click the <#> field code.

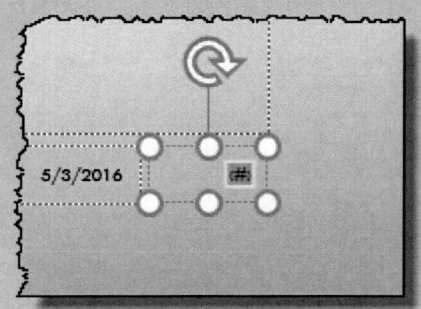

A rotation tool and sizing handles enclose the area.

Do This	How & Why
20. Change the size of the date display to **12** points.	
a) Display the Home tab.	
b) Open the Font Size box, and select **12**.	

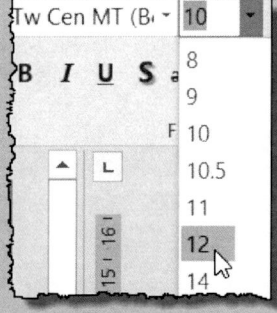

21. Drag the Footer area to the lower-left corner of the slide.

Do This	How & Why
a) Click on the text in the Footer area, and observe the mouse pointer.	An insertion point appears in the text, and sizing handles border the area.

b) Hover over the Footer area border, and observe the mouse pointer.

It becomes a four-headed arrow, indicating that you can click the area and drag it in any direction.

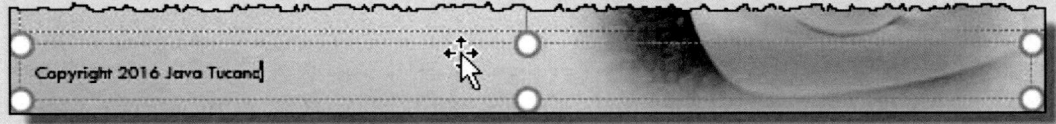

c) Press and hold the mouse pointer at this position, and drag the Footer area toward the lower-left corner of the slide.

When the left and bottom Footer area borders align roughly with those of the slide, release the mouse button.

22. Return to Normal view, and observe the completed footer.

Still visible only on slides 2 through 17. The slide number is now slightly larger, and the copyright statement now appears closer to the lower-left corner.

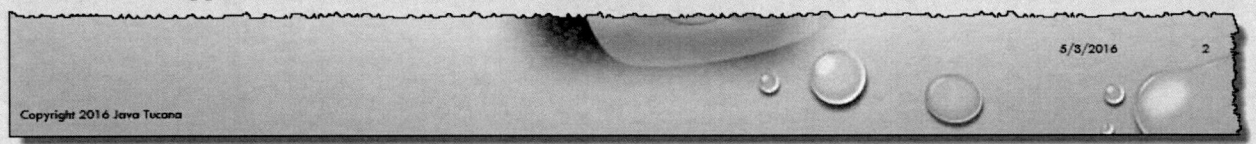

23. Save and close the presentation.

About layouts

In Slide Master view, by default, the Slides pane contains a single slide master, called the Office Theme Slide Master. Subordinate to it are 11 individual slide "layouts": Title Slide, Title and Content, Section Header, Two Content, Comparison, Title Only, Blank, Content with Caption, Picture with Caption, Title and Vertical Text, and Vertical Title and Text. By default, only the Title Slide layout is applied to an actual slide (slide 1).

Using the slide master to change a layout

You change a layout in Slide Master view.

 MOS PowerPoint Exam Objective(s): 1.3.3

1. Display Slide Master view.
   On the View tab, click **Slide Master**.

2. Select the layout you wish to change.
   In the Slides pane.

3. Add, remove, or alter any element you wish to change.
   To alter an element, first click in it to place the insertion point. Use the tools on the Slide Master tab to make your changes.

4. Return to Normal view.
   Click **Close Master View**, or click **Normal**.

   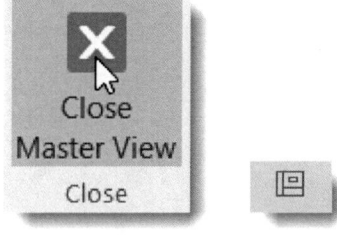

Applying a layout to a slide

You can apply any available layout to an existing slide or to a new slide.

 MOS PowerPoint Exam Objective(s): 1.2.1, 1.2.5, 1.3.4

1. Display the presentation in Normal view.
   In the status bar, click the **Normal** icon, if necessary.

2. Select a slide to receive the new layout.
   - Select the destination slide in the Slides pane.

- Add a new slide to receive the layout.
    i. In the Slides pane, select the slide that will precede the new slide.
    ii. On the Home tab, in the Slides group, click **New Slide**. The new slide appears and is automatically selected.

3. Click **Layout**.

    On the Home tab, in the Slides group.

    The Layout gallery opens.

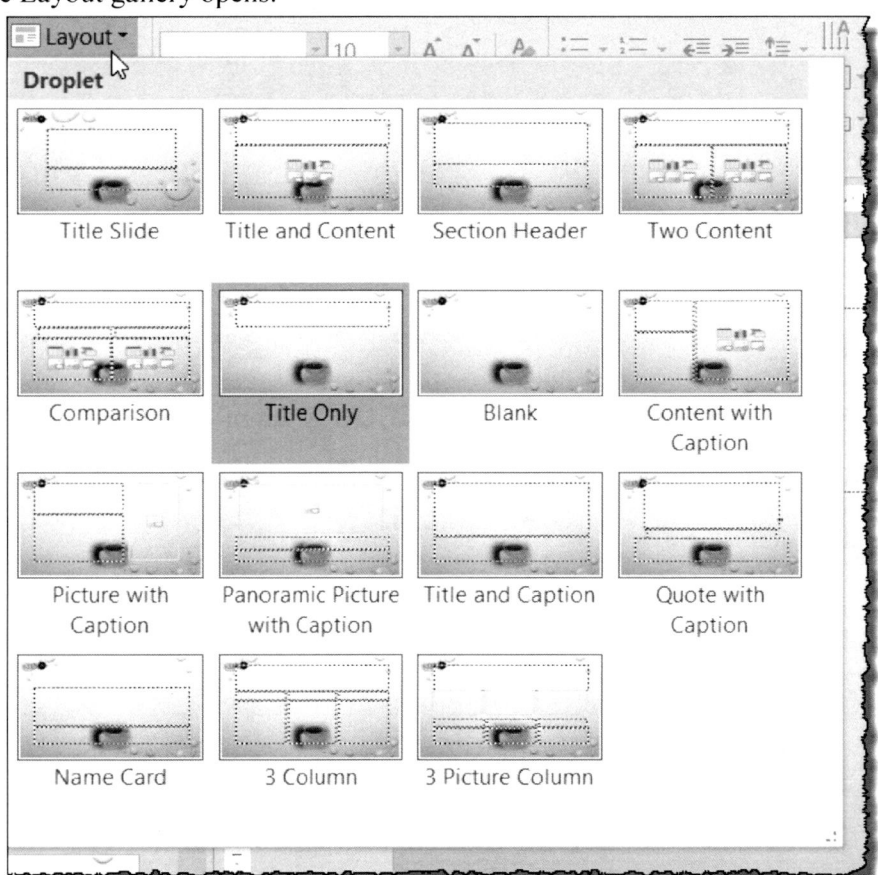

 Note: A slightly shorter method of applying a layout to a selected slide is to click the lower part of the New Slide button, which opens the Layout gallery. From there, you can choose a layout directly.

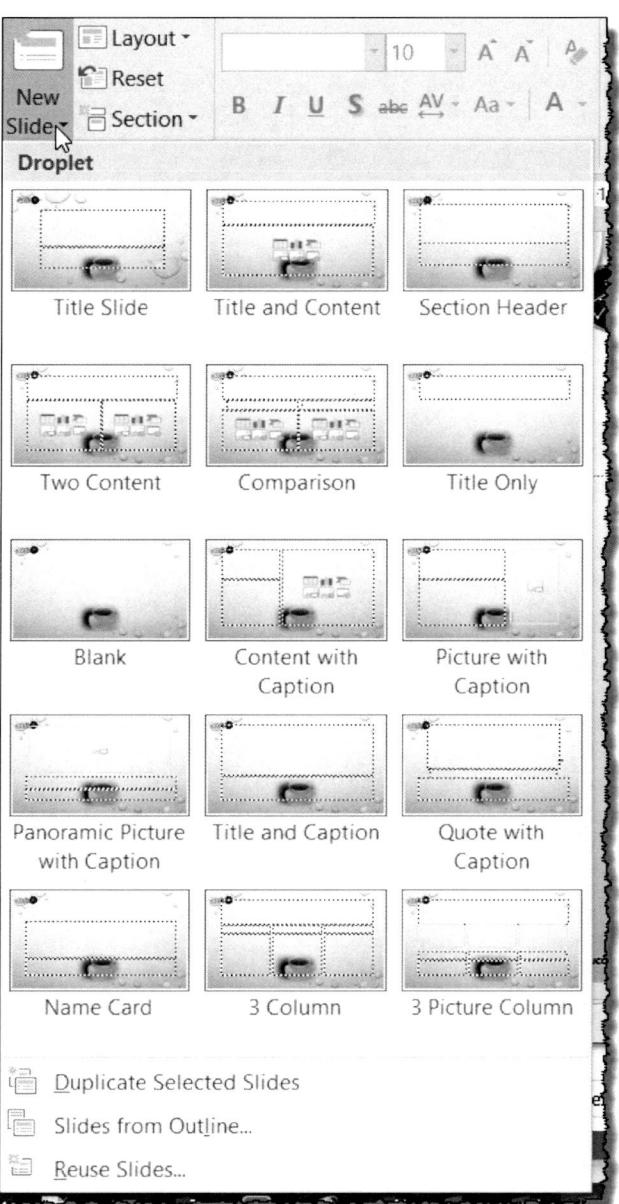

4. Click to select the layout for your slide.

   The layout is applied to the selected slide.

Exercise: Working with layouts

Do This	How & Why
1. Open `JT Layout.pptx`, and save it as `My JT Layout.pptx`.	From the `Formatting` data folder.
2. Scroll through the presentation's slides, and observe its theme, features, and layout. Notice also its title and text styles.	
3. Switch to Slide Master view.	On the View tab, in the View Masters group, click **Slide Master**.
4. Click on each of the various layouts provided.	Each type of layout can be used to control different features of a presentation, and each can be applied to specific slides.
5. Hover over the Title Slide layout.	The tooltip informs you that this layout is currently not in use by any slide.
6. Click to select the Title Slide layout.	

7. Select the text prompting you to edit the master title style.

In the main pane, triple-click **Click to Edit the Main Title Style**.

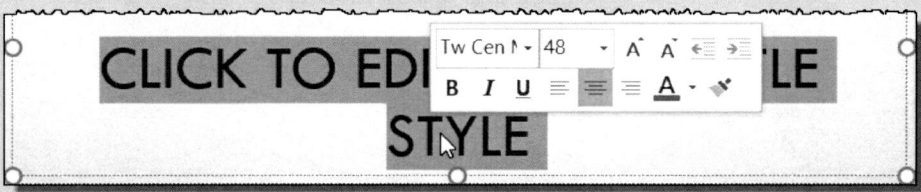

A text formatting toolbar is displayed.

8. Click the arrow to the right of the Font box. To display available fonts.

Do This	How & Why
9. Select the **Garamond** font.	
10. Change the type size to **54**.	The placeholder text reflects the formatting changes.
a) With the formatting toolbar still displayed, click the arrow to the right of the Font Size box.	
b) Select **54**.	
11. Return to Normal view.	On the Slide Master tab, click **Close Master View**, or click the **Normal** icon in the status bar. You'll add a new main title slide to the presentation.
12. Right-click slide 1, and select **New Slide**.	From the context menu. 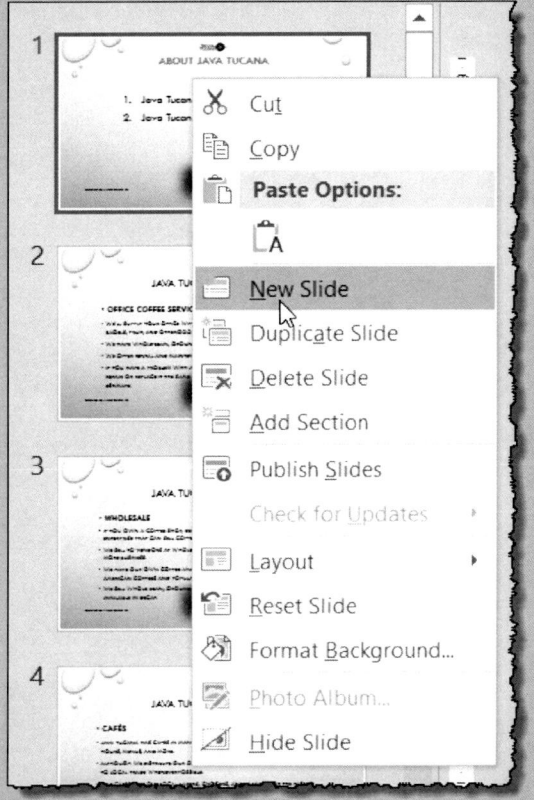 The new slide is inserted after the selected slide.
13. Click and drag the new slide 2 to place it at the top of the slides pane.	The new slide is now slide 1 of the presentation.
14. Click the **Layout** button.	On the Home tab, in the Slides group. To open the Layout gallery. Note that the layouts all fall under the Droplet theme, the current theme of the presentation.

Chapter 3: Formatting / Module A: Working with slide masters and layouts

Do This	How & Why

15. Select the **Title Slide** layout from the gallery.

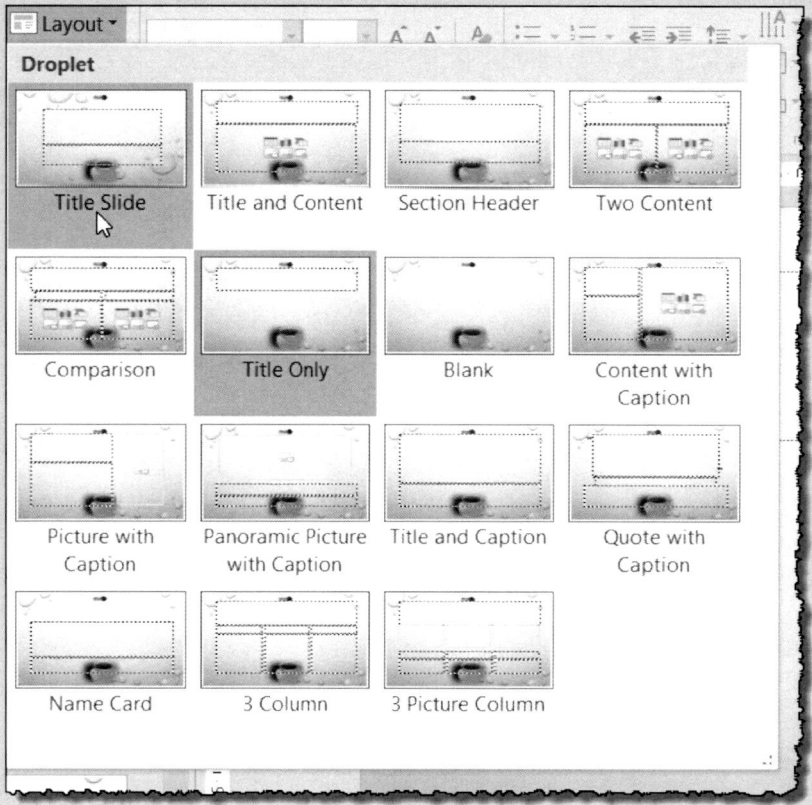

The layout is applied to the new slide, and placeholders for a title and subtitle are displayed.

16. Add the title `Java Tucana`.	Click in the title placeholder, then type the text. The new title is inserted in Garamond 54-point type. Note that although you typed the name in initial capitals, it appears in all capitals. This is because the titles in the Droplet theme were automatically formatted to appear in all capitals.

70   PowerPoint 2016 Level 1

Do This	How & Why
17. Add the subtitle `Only the Best`.	The subtitle also appears in all capitals.
18. Change the color of the slide's title to **Dark Red**.	
a) Select the title.	Drag over "JAVA TUCANA" or triple-click it.
b) Click the arrow next to the Font Color button.	To open the Font Color gallery.
c) Select **Dark Red**.	Under Standard Colors. 

19. Deselect the text boxes.

Click in a blank area of the slide outside the text boxes. The new title and subtitle are displayed on the slide.

20. Save and close the file.

Assessment: Working with slide masters and layouts

1. True or false? The easiest way to modify the formatting of all slides in a presentation at once is by modifying the slide master.

    - True
    - False

2. Which of these actions would you perform to change the theme of a presentation?

    - In Normal view, choose SmartArt on the Insert tab.
    - In Normal view, choose Outline on the View tab to open the gallery.
    - In Slide Master view, choose Themes on the View tab, and select a theme from the gallery.
    - In Slide Master view, choose Themes on the Slide Master tab, and select a theme from the gallery.

3. True or false? One of the benefits of Slide Master view is that you can change all layouts from a single slide master.

    - True
    - False

Module B: Formatting slides and text

You can change the appearance of text on one or more slides in your presentation. Also, even after you've applied a theme to your presentation, you can change the appearance of a slide background and apply effects such as textures.

You will learn how to:

- Format text and apply text styles
- Apply slide backgrounds and effects

About text styles

A text *style* is its font, size, color, spacing, alignment, and orientation. As you have seen, when you apply a theme to a slide master, the text style associated with it is automatically applied to all the slides governed by that master. Similarly, if you alter the master slide's text style, all slides that it governs will display the alteration.

You can, however, modify text styles of individual slides without affecting others in the presentation. But you can only do so in Normal view.

Changing master text styles

In Slide Master view, text style changes that you apply to a slide master affect all slides governed by that master.

 MOS PowerPoint Exam Objective(s): 2.1.2

1. Display your presentation in Slide Master view.
   On the View tab, in the Master Views group, click **Slide Master**.

2. Select the slide master.
   Not one of the layouts.

3. Edit the master title style.

   a) In the master title placeholder, select the text **CLICK TO EDIT MASTER TITLE STYLE**.

   b) To make changes in font, size, color, spacing, or alignment, use the context formatting toolbar; or, on the Home tab, use the tools in the Font and/or Paragraph groups.

   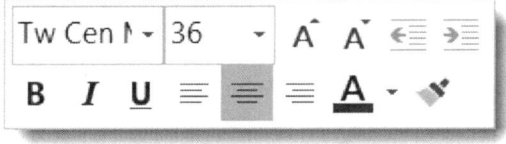

   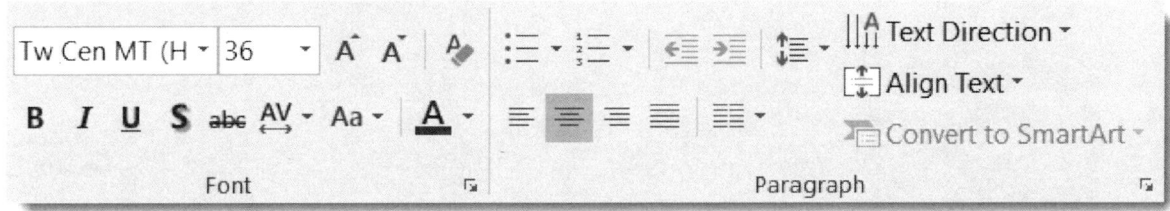

   c) For special text effects, such as text shape styles and WordArt styles, use the tools on the Drawing Tools Format tab.

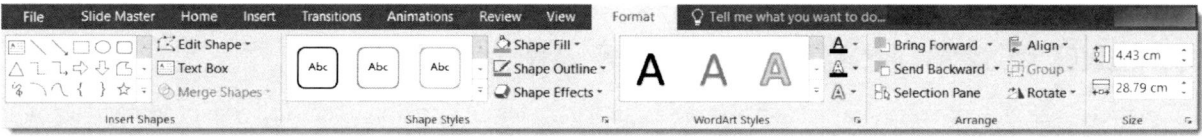

4. Edit the master text styles.

   a) Change the main text style.
      Select the placeholder text **CLICK TO EDIT MASTER TEXT STYLES**, then use one (or more) of the methods in step 3 to change the text format.

   b) Change the style of any subordinate text levels.
      Select the desired text level—for example, the **SECOND LEVEL** placeholder text—and use the formatting tools to change the text style as you wish.

In Normal view, the text on all presentation slides governed by the altered slide master appears in the new format.

Changing text styles of individual slides

You can change the style of text on individual slides without affecting any other slides.

 MOS PowerPoint Exam Objective(s): 2.1.6

1. Display your presentation in Normal view.
   If necessary, click [icon] in the status bar.

2. Select the slide containing the text you want to format.

3. Apply any formatting changes.
   Doing so overrides the master text style for only that slide.

In the event that you want to revert an individually formatted slide to the master style (determined by the slide master), in the left pane, right-click that slide to display a context menu. Then click **Reset Slide**.

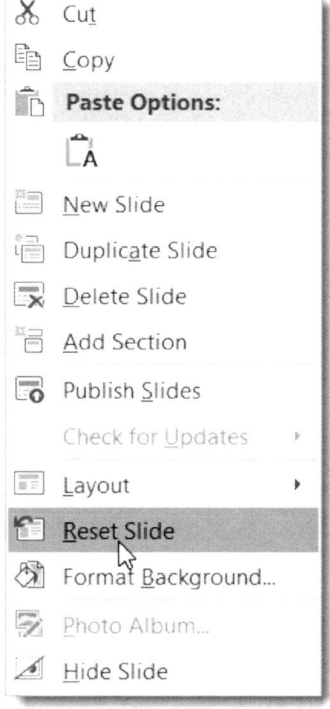

Creating bulleted and numbered lists

Creating bulleted and numbered lists in PowerPoint is quite simple.

 MOS PowerPoint Exam Objective(s): 2.1.5

1. Select the text you wish to convert to a bulleted or numbered list.
2. Click the **Bullets** or **Numbering** button.
    On the Home tab, in the Paragraph group.

3. You can further customize the bullet or number type.
    - To select another bullet type, click the arrow to the right of the Bullets button, and make a selection from the gallery. To further customize your selection, click **Bullets and Numbering**. On the Bulleted tab of the Bullets and Numbering window, you can change the size and/or color of an existing bullet type. In addition, you can click **Picture** to navigate to an image that you'd like to use as a bullet; or, click **Customize** to open the Symbol browser, from which you can select a symbol to use as a bullet.

    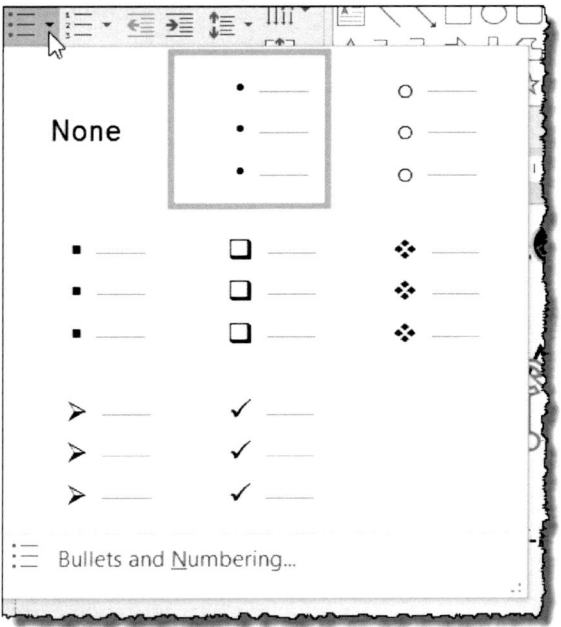

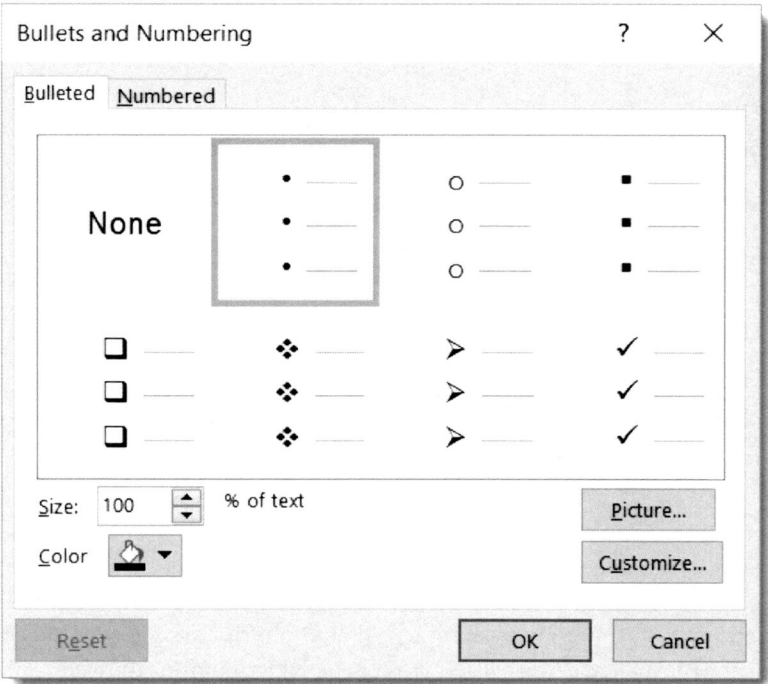

- To select another numbering type, click the arrow to the right of the Numbering button, and make a selection from the gallery. To further customize your selection, click **Bullets and Numbering**. On the Numbered tab of the Bullets and Numbering window, you can change the number style, as well as its size and color. In addition, you can specify the starting number for the first item in your list.

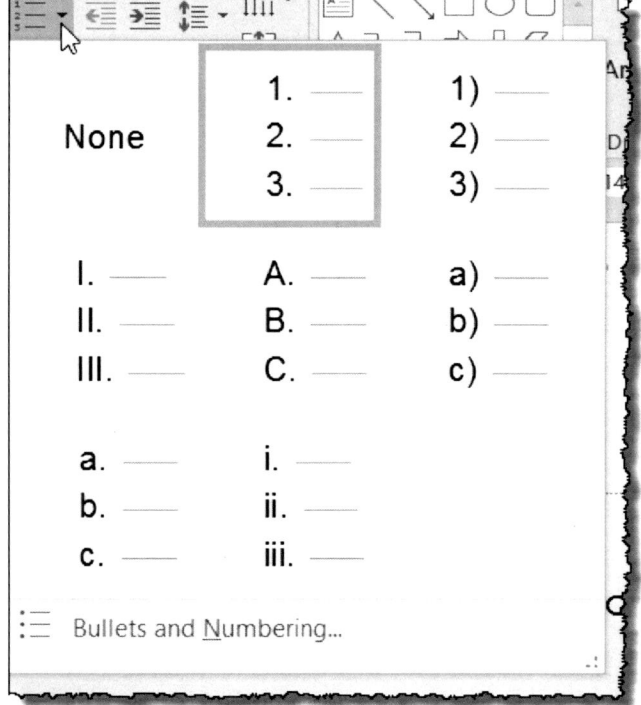

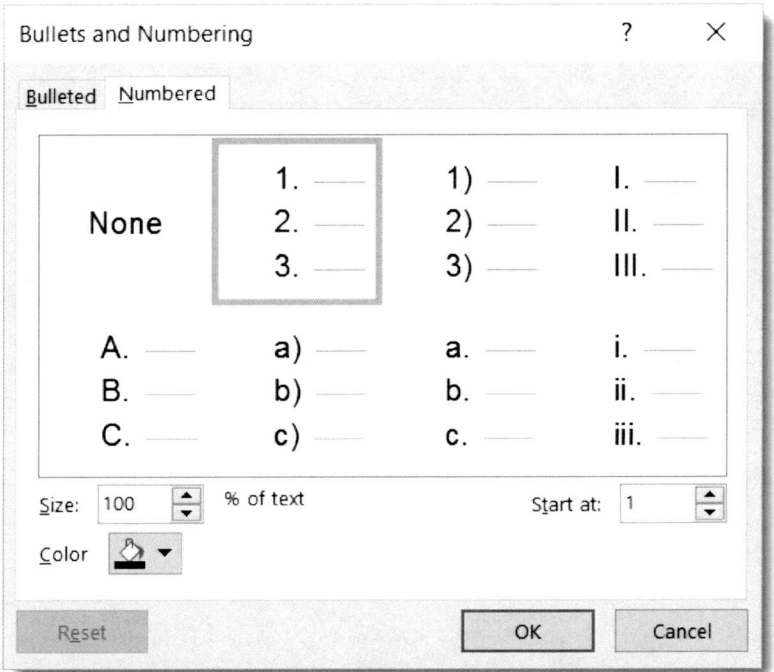

1. 2015 sales by region and product
2. Future prospects
   - Immediate
   - Long term

Exercise: Working with text styles

In this exercise, you'll change a master title style, and you'll format some text on individual slides.

Do This	How & Why
1. Open `JT Text Styles.pptx` and save it as `My JT Text Styles.pptx`.	In the `Formatting` data folder.
2. Navigate and observe the slides in the short presentation.	The titles of all the slides are currently very small and require enlargement. Also, a couple of the slides contain lists that could benefit from bullets and/or numbers.
3. Display Slide Master view.	On the View tab, click **Slide Master**.
4. Display the Retrospect Slide Master.	Select it in the left pane.
5. Select the text **Click to edit Master title style**.	
6. Change the size of the master title to 44 points.	Use the context formatting toolbar or the Home tab's Font group, open the Size list, and select **44**. 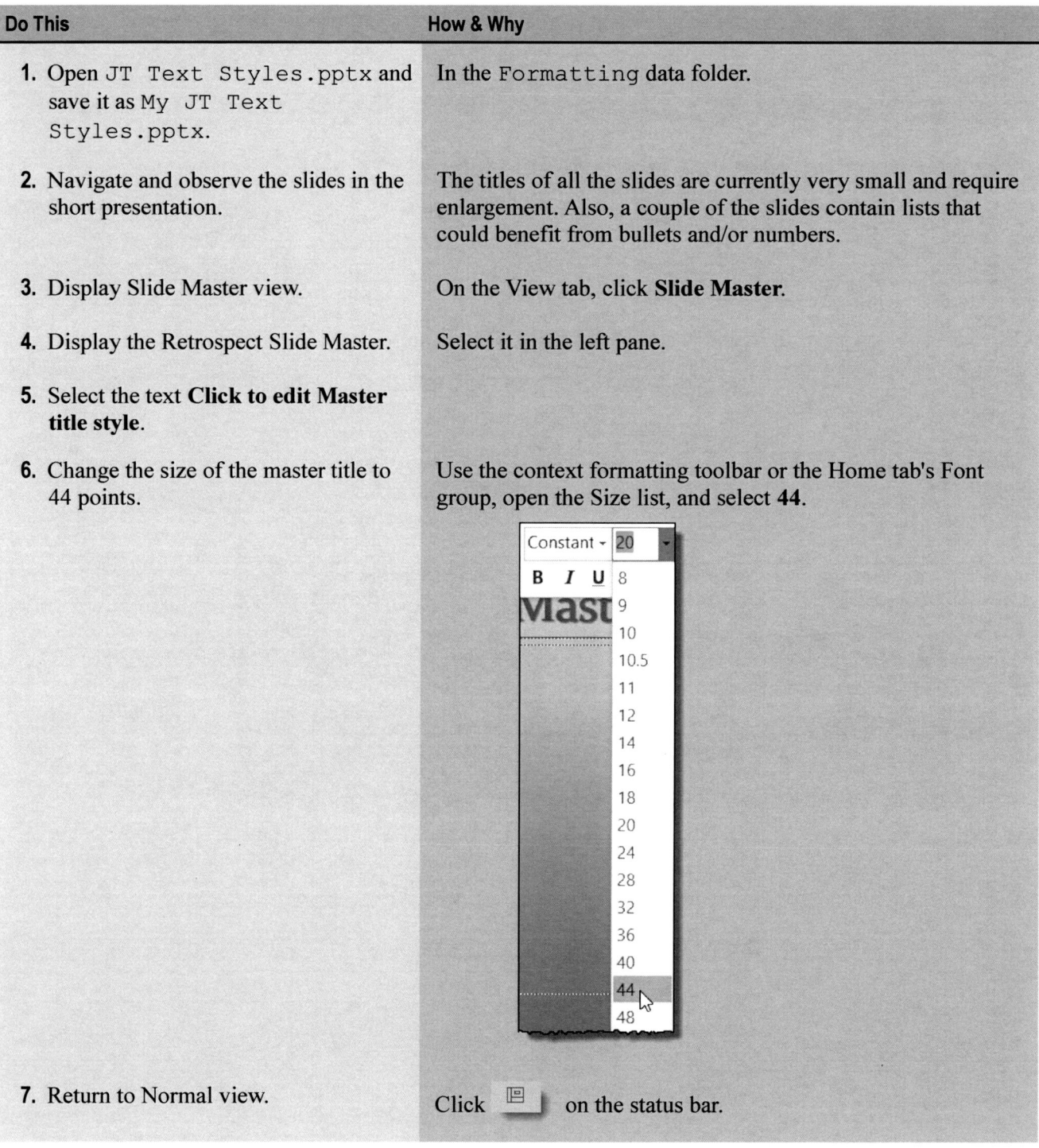
7. Return to Normal view.	Click [icon] on the status bar.

Do This	How & Why

8. View all the slides.

The title of each is enlarged. However, the slide 1 title is intended as the main one of the presentation, so it should probably stand out a bit more. You need to override the master title style for this slide to make its title appear different from the others, all of which are governed by the master title style.

9. Select the slide 1 title, **Java Tucana Sales Report**.

    You're still in Normal view.

10. Make the title bold.

    On the context formatting toolbar, or on the Home tab, in the Font group, click the **Bold** button.

11. Deselect the title, observe the result, and compare it to the other slides in the presentation.

Click a blank area of the slide outside the title text box to observe the title. Only the slide 1 title appears bold. Now, you need to make the other items on this slide stand out a bit more.

12. Enlarge the first two (main) list items to 36 points.

    Drag over **2015 sales by region and product** and **Future prospects**, open the Size list (in the context toolbar or on the Home tab), and click **36**. The two items are enlarged. Now, however, the indented list below them looks ridiculously tiny.

13. Enlarge the two indented items to 28 points.

    Select **Immediate** and **Long term**, and from the Size list, select **28**.

14. Deselect and observe the items on slide 1.

Do This	How & Why
15. Format the first two items as a numbered list.	
a) Select both items.	
b) Click the **Numbering** button.	On the Home tab, in the Paragraph group.
16. Format the indented items as a bulleted list.	
a) Select both **Immediate** and **Long term**.	
b) Click the **Bullets** button.	On the Home tab, in the Paragraph group.

17. Deselect the list, and observe the results.

The items appear as numbered and bulleted lists.

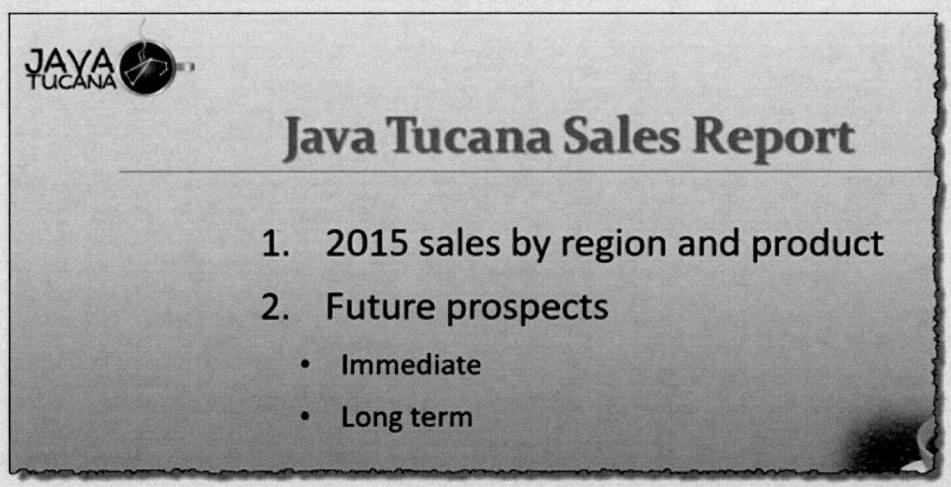

18. Observe slide 3.	The last three items aren't aligned properly in relation to the other text elements. Plus, they could use a bit of visual spice.
19. Format the last three items as a bulleted list.	The items begin **Within**, **We're**, and **In terms of**. Select all the items, then click the **Bullets** button.

Do This	How & Why
20. Deselect the list, and observe the results.	The items were indented slightly, but no bullets are displayed. You need to troubleshoot! **Immediate** We at Java Tucana are looking to futu Within each sales region, we're maki growing list of customer countries an We're building deeper, sustainable re partner with new growers, to expand shape and support their future growt In terms of end users, we are in the p into additional markets in all regions brand recognition and presence.
21. Select the three items again, then open the Bullets gallery.	Click the arrow next to the Bullets button. The Custom bullets option is selected, which, unfortunately for us, only indents the text slightly but does not actually display any bullets. You need to remedy this situation! 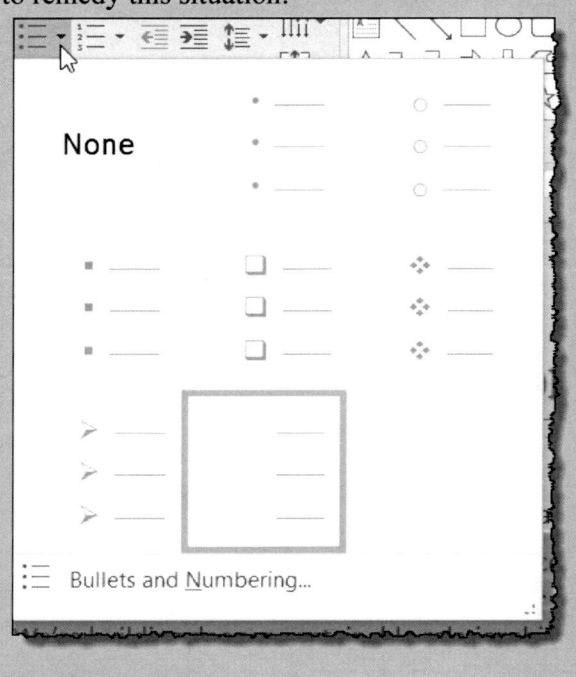
22. Select the **Filled Round Bullets** option.	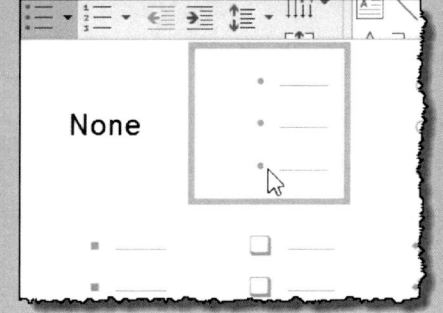

Do This	How & Why
23. Deselect the text, and observe the results.	**Immediate** We at Java Tucana are looking to future in a va Within each sales region, we're making a conc growing list of customer countries and clients. We're building deeper, sustainable relationship partner with new growers, to expand our inver shape and support their future growth. In terms of end users, we are in the process of into additional markets in all regions, to increa brand recognition and presence.
24. Save and close the presentation.	

About slide backgrounds

 MOS PowerPoint Exam Objective(s): 1.2.6

You can apply a slide background, then you can modify it to make it look the way you want. Simply select the desired slide and, on the Design tab, in the Customize group, click **Format Background**. This opens the Format Background pane, which is context sensitive, and makes available many different kinds of settings, depending on whether you've selected a slide, clicked in a text box, clicked an object, and so on.

When you select a slide in the left pane of Normal view, only the Fill settings are visible in the Format Background pane. These settings control the background fill effects, and those in the lower part of the pane change, depending on whether you've selected a *Solid*, *Gradient*, *Picture or texture*, or *Pattern* fill. The settings for each fill type allow you to tweak it in many ways.

- *Gradient*: Provides fill settings such as Presets; Type, such as Linear, Radial, and Rectangular; Direction; Color, Position, and Transparency; as well as Gradient stops, which allow you to specify a precise gradient using three sliders.

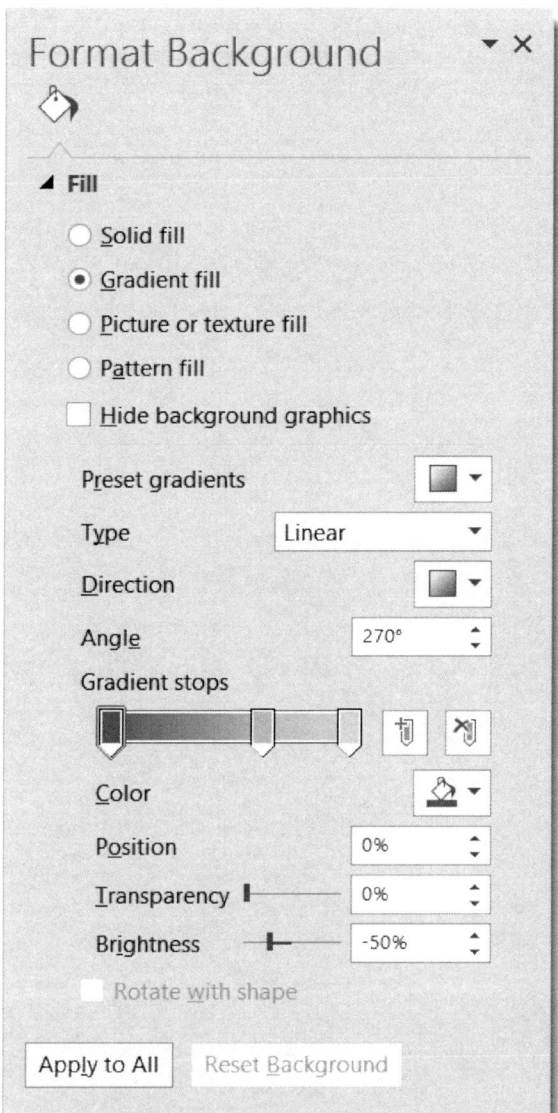

- *Solid*: Provides Color and Transparency settings.

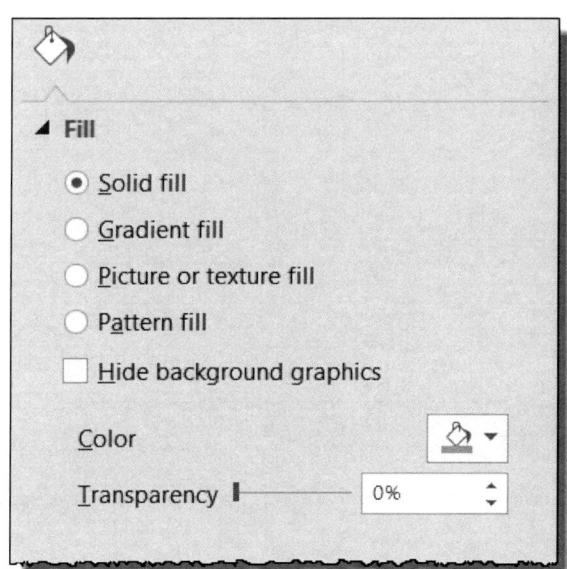

- *Picture or texture*: Allows you to use a suggested texture, or open or download a picture file to use as a background. Included are additional options, such as Texture; Transparency; and orientation offset, size, and alignment settings.

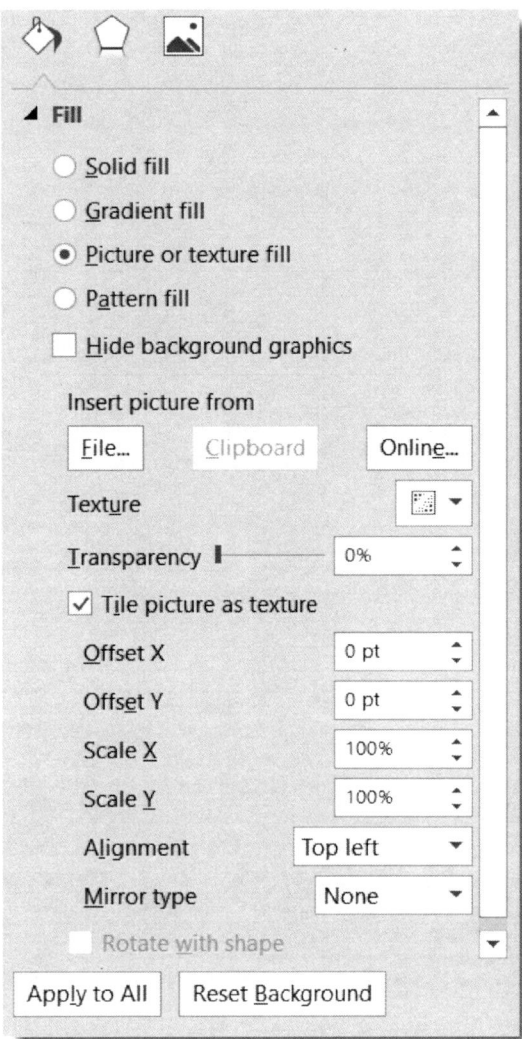

- *Pattern*: Allows you to select a fill pattern, and modify foreground and background pattern colors.

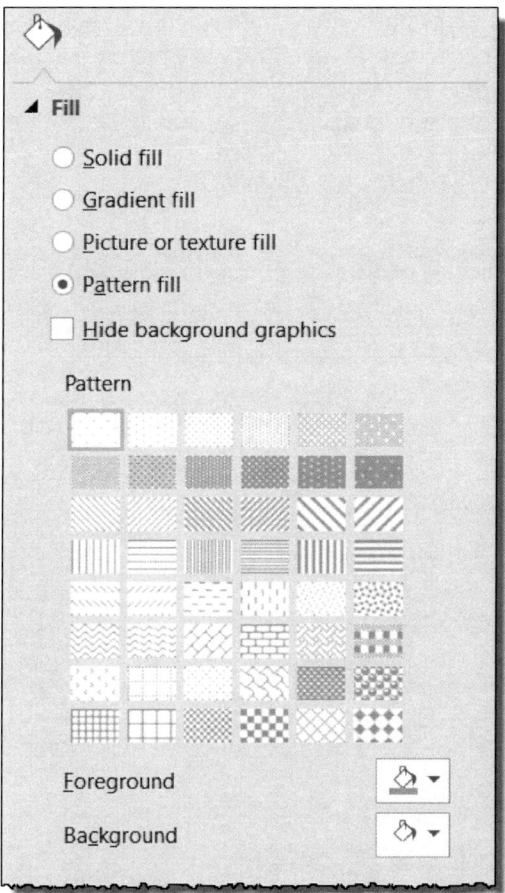

- The **Hide background graphics** option removes any background pictures from view. Keep in mind that doing so also removes the graphics from the final presentation.

Besides affecting the selected slide, any changes you make can be applied to all slides in the presentation. To do so, once you've made your changes, click **Apply to All**.

Once you change settings, the **Reset Background** button serves as a kind of "panic button" that allows you to revert the background to its original settings, should your artistic impulse have taken you to unwanted territory.

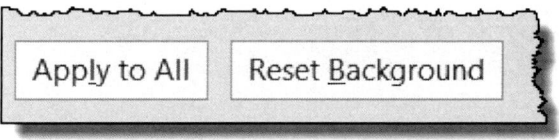

Gridlines

When you're working with the many visual elements available in PowerPoint, the rulers can help you to assess relative sizes and positions of objects, and so on. But especially when moving objects around on slides, some people find it helpful to display gridlines. *Gridlines* are evenly spaced horizontal and vertical dotted lines that provide a visual reference. You can view them in Normal, Outline, or Notes view. Gridlines don't display in the final product, however—they're merely a kind of preview.

  MOS PowerPoint Exam Objective(s): 2.3.4

To display gridlines, on the View tab, in the Show group, click **Gridlines** to check the option. To remove the gridlines, click **Gridlines** again to uncheck it.

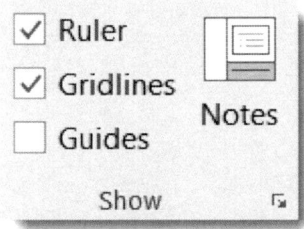

Exercise: Working with slide backgrounds

Do This	How & Why
1. Open `JT Background.pptx`, and save it as `My JT Background.pptx`.	In the `Formatting` data folder.
2. Navigate through this short presentation, and observe the appearance of slide text and graphics in relation to backgrounds.	The presentation looks pretty good, but the text and bullets could stand in better contrast to their background. This is especially noticeable in slides 3 and 4, which contain more text than the others. The lack of contrast compromises their readability.
3. Select slide 2.	
4. Open the Format Background pane.	On the Design tab, in the Customize group, click **Format Background**.

Do This	How & Why
5. Click the Preset gradients box, and select the **Top Spotlight - Accent 2** preset. 	

The chart background on slide 2 is a little brighter, making the chart figures more readable.

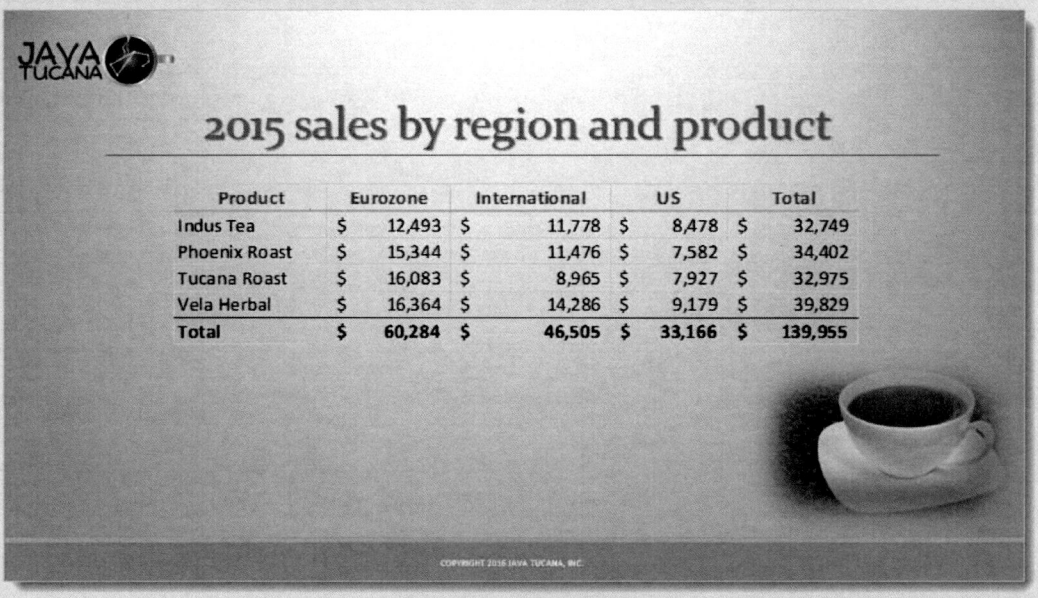

Do This	How & Why
6. Select slide 3.	The Format Background should still be open; if not, click **Format Background**.
7. Click the **Picture or texture fill** option.	
8. Select a texture.	
a) Click on the **Texture** box.	The Texture gallery opens.

Do This	How & Why

b) Click a texture.

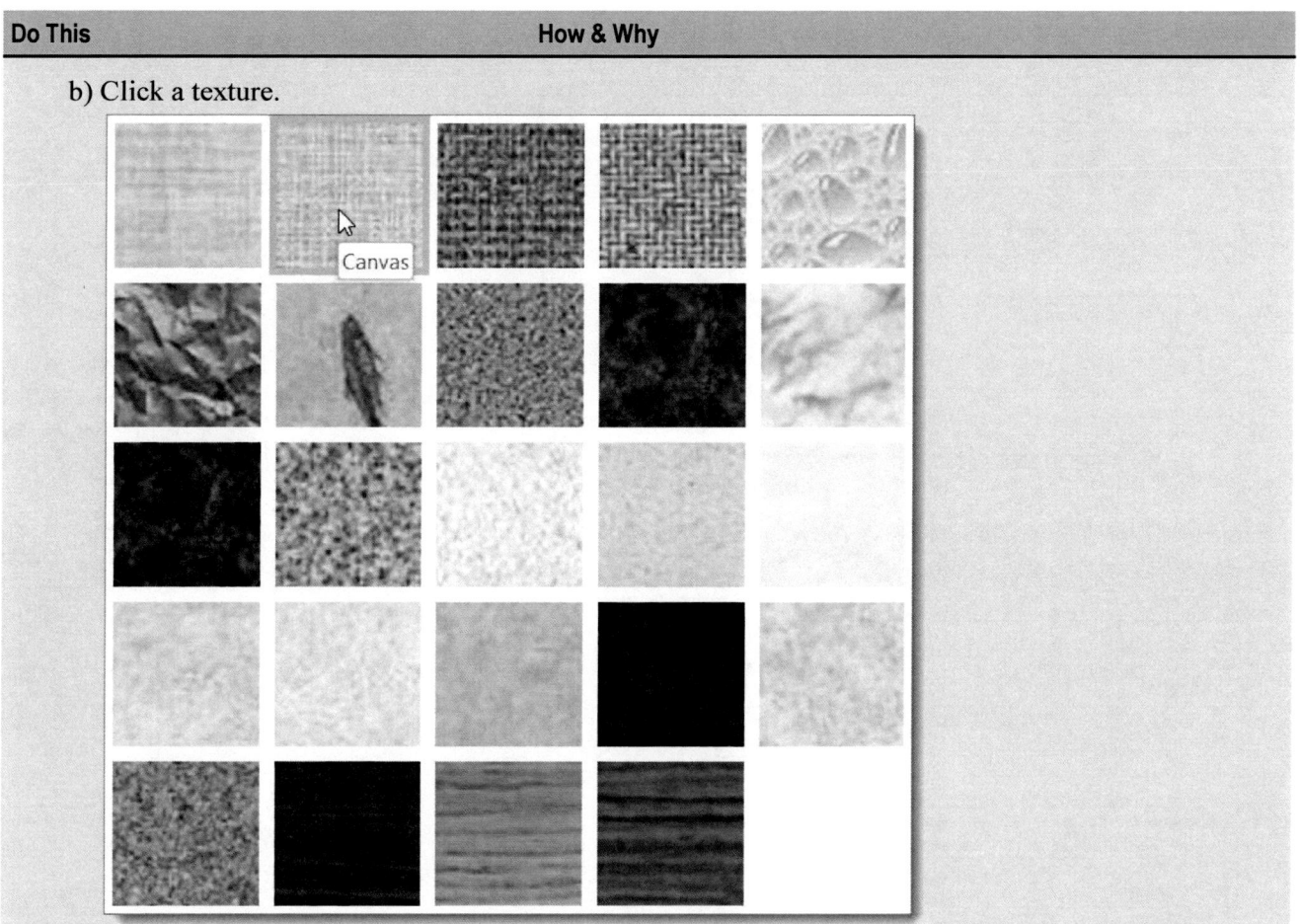

Do This	How & Why
9. Adjust the transparency of the textured background, so that the text is easily readable. • Drag the Transparency slider left to decrease texture transparency, or drag it right to increase transparency. 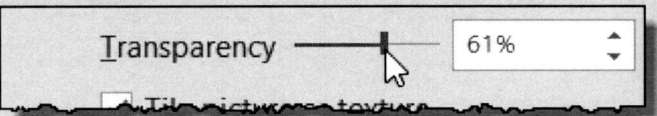 • Next to the Transparency percentage box, use the increment or decrement arrow buttons to increase or decrease texture transparency, respectively. 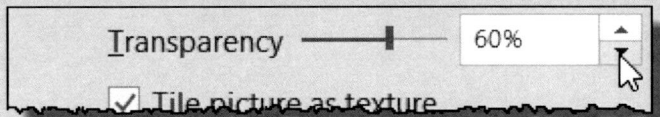 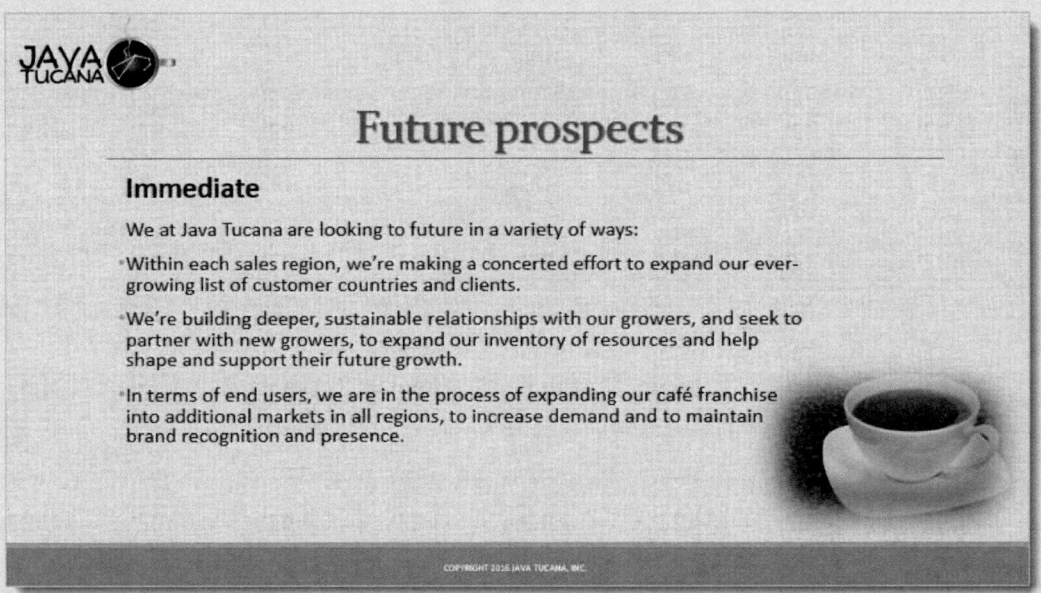	
10. Select slide 4, and click **Picture or texture fill**.	In the Format Background pane. The appearance of this slide might be too "busy." A preset texture is already applied to the slide, but you'll change this option shortly.
11. Check the **Hide background graphics** option.	The logo and coffee cup images are removed from the slide.
12. Select the **White Marble** texture from the gallery. a) Click the **Texture** box.	

Do This	How & Why

b) Click **White Marble**.

Use the tooltips as a guide.

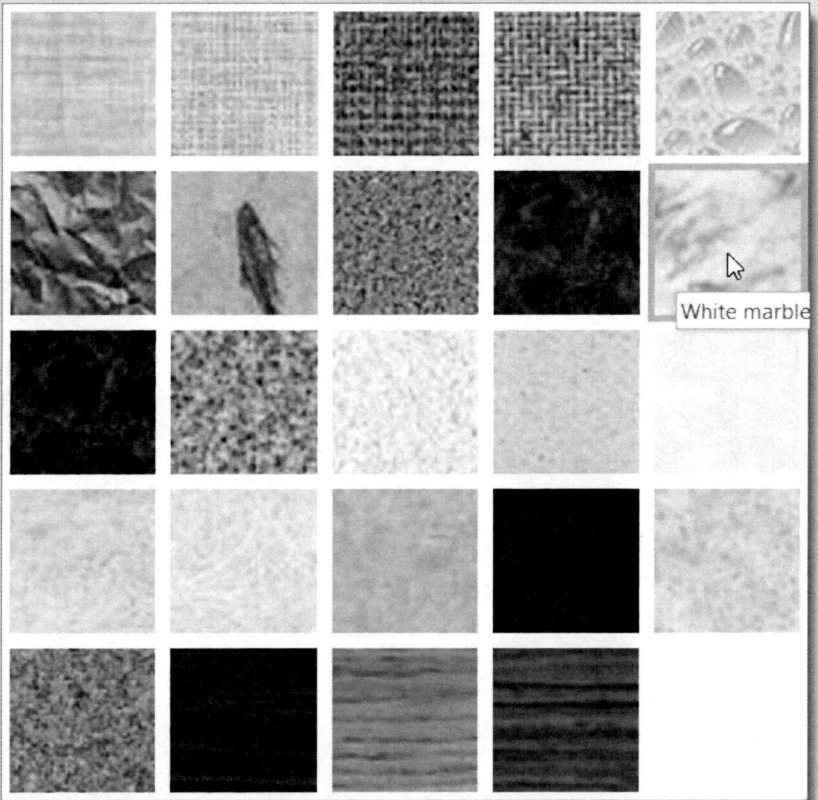

The White Marble background texture is applied. However, it doesn't appear to aid readability of the text, and it looks rather hideous. You'd better fix that!

Do This	How & Why
13. Click the **Reset Background** button.	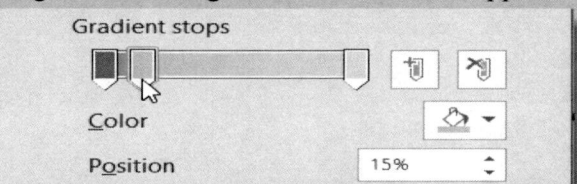 The slide background reverts to its original gradient fill. However, the "Hide background graphics" option remains checked. In this context, "resetting" refers to background color and texture but does not affect certain additional options.
14. Drag the Gradient stops central slider to the left, until the value in the position box reads **15%**.	To lighten the background where the text appears. 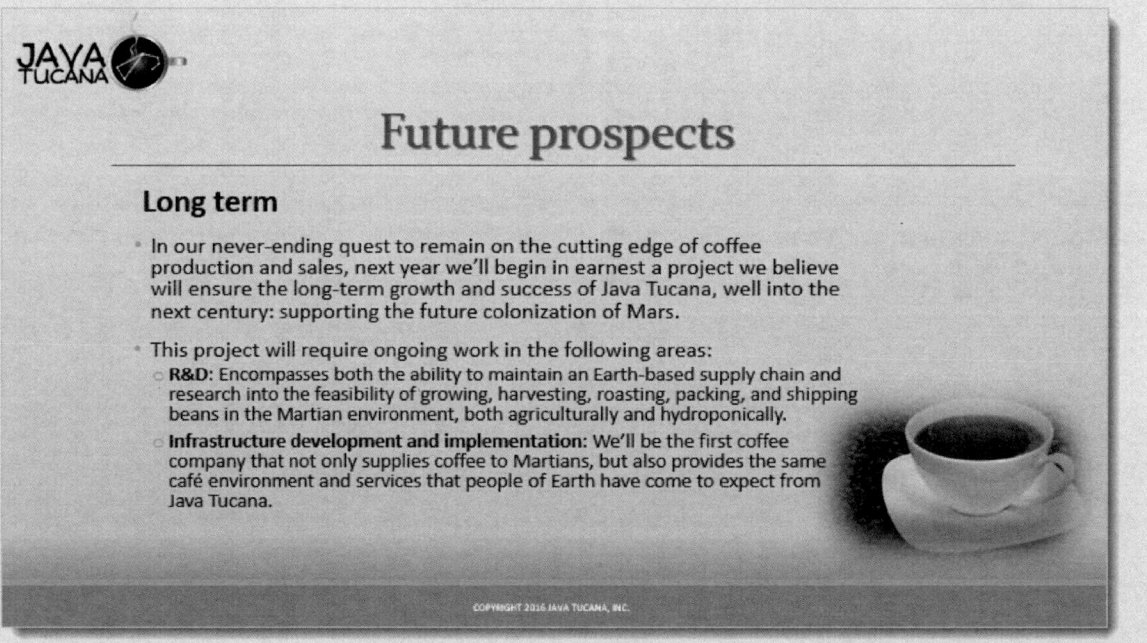 The text appears considerably more readable. Perhaps you can display the background graphics after all.

15. Uncheck **Hide background graphics**.

The graphics don't seem to detract from the overall look of the page, and the logo seems necessary on this last slide.

16. Save and close the file.

Assessment: Formatting slides and text

1. Where can you change text styles so that all slides in a presentation will have identically formatted text.

    - On the Slide Title layout, in Slide Master view.
    - On the slide text, in Master view.
    - On the slide master.
    - On the Text Master, in Slide Master view.

2. True or false? You can change the text style of a slide by unchecking Slide Master Layout option in Slide Master view.

    - True
    - False

3. How can you create a numbered list that doesn't begin with the numeral 1?

    - Select the appropriate numbered list style in the Numbering gallery.
    - Specify the starting number of the list on the Numbering tab of the Bullets and Numbering window.
    - In the Bullets and Numbering pane, uncheck the Start at 1 option.
    - In the Numbering window, select the Customize option.

4. True or false? If you've made all your changes to a slide background, including hiding the background graphics, you can restore the graphics by clicking Reset Background.

    - True
    - False

Summary: Formatting

You should now know how to:

- Apply and modify slide masters, headers and footers, and layouts
- Modify text styles of all or individual slides, create bulleted and numbered lists, display gridlines, and modify backgrounds of all or individual slides

Synthesis: Formatting

1. Open `JT Formatting Assessment.pptx`, and save it as `My JT Formatting Assessment.pptx`.
2. Format the two lines of text under the title as a numbered list.
3. On slides 2 through 9, make all the text items (other than introductory phrases) bulleted lists.
4. Apply a theme to the whole presentation.
5. Add a new title slide to begin the presentation, and assign it the Title Slide layout.
6. Give the title slide the title `Java Tucana`. Subtitle it `Only the Best`.
7. Insert footer information.
   a) Edit the copyright statement to read `Copyright 2016 Java Tucana`. Then move it to the lower-left corner of the slide and resize it, as necessary. If you like, display gridlines as a visual reference.
   b) Select a date format to display.
   c) Display slide numbers.
   d) Have the footer display on all slides except for the title slide.
8. Change any (or all) master text styles to affect all the slides in the presentation.
9. Format the title slide text styles to make them unique.
10. Choose at least one other slide, and make its text style(s) different from all the others.
11. Apply a single background to all the slides in the presentation. Apply any formatting—including colors, textures, and other effects—that you like.
12. Make the title slide background unique, and suppress the background images on it.
13. Create another background for the slides that begins each major section. They can either all be the same or completely different from one another. Apply any formatting you like. Feel free to include one or more images, from either a file or downloaded from the Web.
14. Save and close the presentation.

Chapter 4: Working with shapes and images

You will learn how to:

- Create and format shapes
- Insert and work with images

Module A: Creating and formatting shapes

In PowerPoint, you can create shapes that provide visual impact and can help to convey information. There are many tools for drawing and working with basic shapes, and you can change shapes, move them, resize them, and even layer them as you wish.

You will learn how to:

- Draw, modify, and layer shapes on your slides

About shapes

PowerPoint provides some powerful tools that allow you to create and work with shapes on your slides. The easiest way to add a shape to a slide is by using the Shapes gallery. To open the Shapes gallery, on the Insert tab, in the Illustrations group, click **Shapes**.

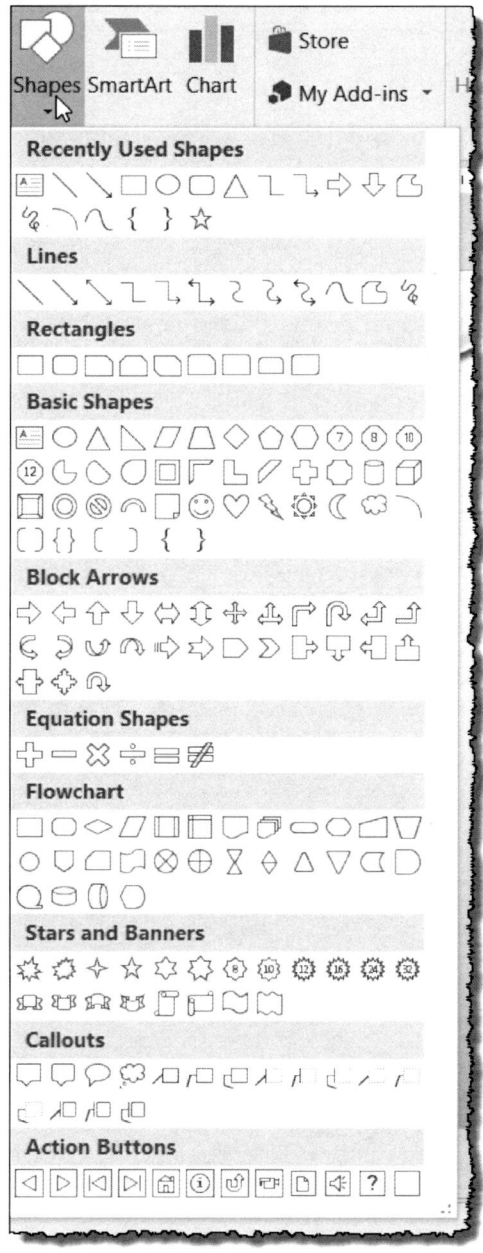

The Shapes gallery is arranged by shape type, making it easier for you to select the shape you want.

- *Recently Used Shapes*: Each time you create/draw a new shape, that shape subsequently appears here. Up to 24 shapes display here; after that, each new shape replaces the oldest one.
- *Lines*: Every type of line, from completely straight to free form.
- *Rectangles*: Every type of "rectangle," even those with one or more corners "cut off."
- *Basic Shapes*: A potpourri of common shapes of various types.
- *Block Arrows*: Straight and curved "hollow" arrows.
- *Equation Shapes*: Used for simple arithmetic.
- *Flowchart*: Used for creating flowcharts.
- *Stars and Banners*: Used primarily for grabbing attention.
- *Callouts*: Speech and text balloons like those used in comics.
- *Action Buttons*: Used primarily for slideshow navigation.

Click a shape in the gallery to select it. Once you've clicked a shape, click to place the shape on the slide. You then "draw" the shape from that point. However, keep in mind that the techniques for drawing shapes vary slightly by type. For example, drawing a straight line is different than drawing a circle or polygon.

Even after you've selected and placed a shape on a slide, you can change it to another shape. To do so, first select the shape you wish to replace, then display the Drawing Tools Format tab. In the Insert Shapes group, click **Edit Shape** to open a menu, and select **Change Shape**, then select the new shape. The selected shape is placed at the position of the one it replaces.

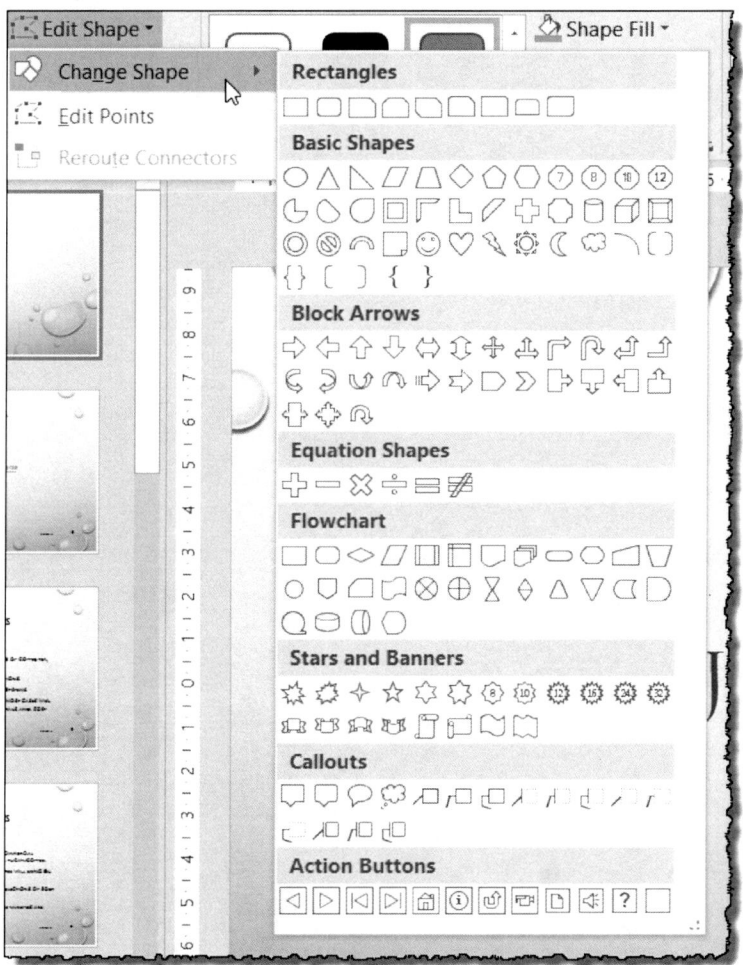

Once you create any open shape, it can serve as a text box as well, in which you can enter text. The effect is the same as clicking **Text Box**. Either way, you drag it to define its area.

Drawing shapes

In PowerPoint, *shapes* are lines—including straight and freehand ones—and open shapes, such as circles, ovals, polygons, and so on.

 MOS PowerPoint Exam Objective(s): 2.2.1, 2.2.2

1. Click **Shapes**.
   On the Insert tab, in the Illustrations group.

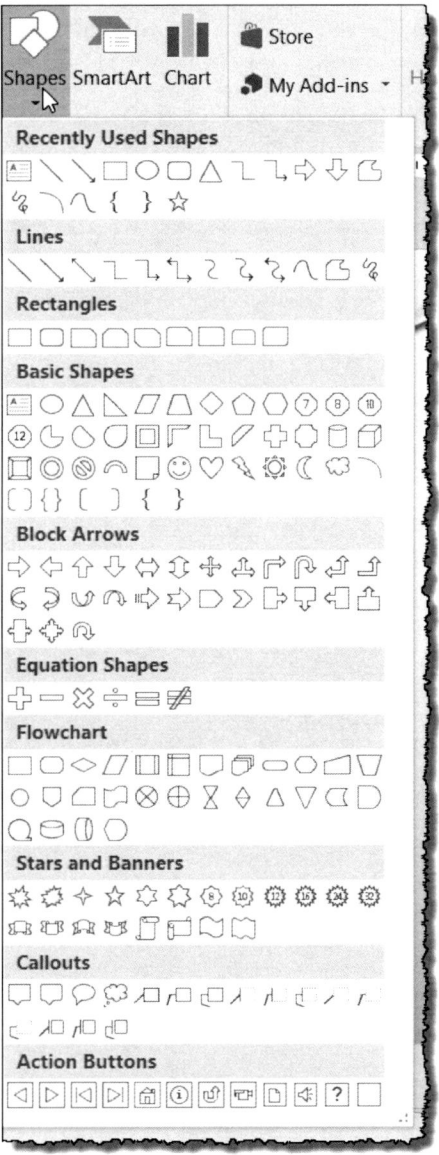

2. Select a shape.

   Click the shape to select it.

3. Click on the slide to place a point of origin for the shape, and drag to a destination point.

   To define the length of the line or the area to contain the open shape. When you click, press and hold the mouse button, so that you're ready to drag. To draw a perfectly straight line, press and hold the **Shift** key before you drag. Dragging up/down or left/right results in a vertical or horizontal line, respectively. However, if you press **Shift** and drag on a diagonal, the straight line is drawn at a 45-degree angle.

 Note: You can insert text within (or over) a shape. Once your shape is drawn, on the Insert tab (or the Drawing Tools Format tab), click **Text Box**. Then drag inside (or over) the shape to define the text box, and type the text.

Curved shapes

If you select the Curve shape from the Line group in the Shapes gallery, you can specify exactly how many curves you'd like in the shape and exactly where you'd like those curves placed along its length.

First, select the **Curve** shape.

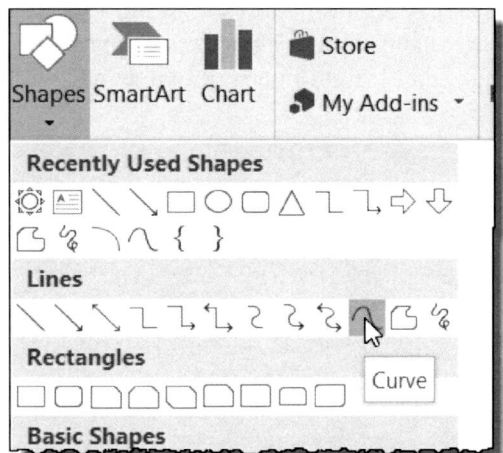

Next, click to place the origin point of the curve. (In this case, you don't press and hold, as there's no need to drag to draw the shape.) Then, click anywhere else that you want the next (and subsequent) curves to appear. To end the shape, double-click a destination point. If you place the destination point at the point of origin, the shape becomes a closed loop.

Useful tools for working with shapes

Besides the rulers and gridlines, another very useful tool for helping you to position, size, and align shapes (as well as other slide elements) is PowerPoint's guides. The *guides* are horizontal and vertical crosshairs that meet at the exact center of a slide. Thus, for a visual reference, you can use either crosshair as a center line, or the crosshairs formed by both. Rulers, gridlines, and guides displayed in conjunction can be powerful aids in helping you create well-designed slides.

To display the guides, on the View tab, in the Show group, click **Guides**.

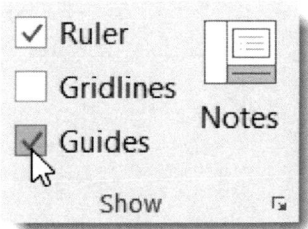

The guides align at the zero points on their respective horizontal and vertical rulers. Whenever you work with drawn shapes, PowerPoint zero-centers the rulers.

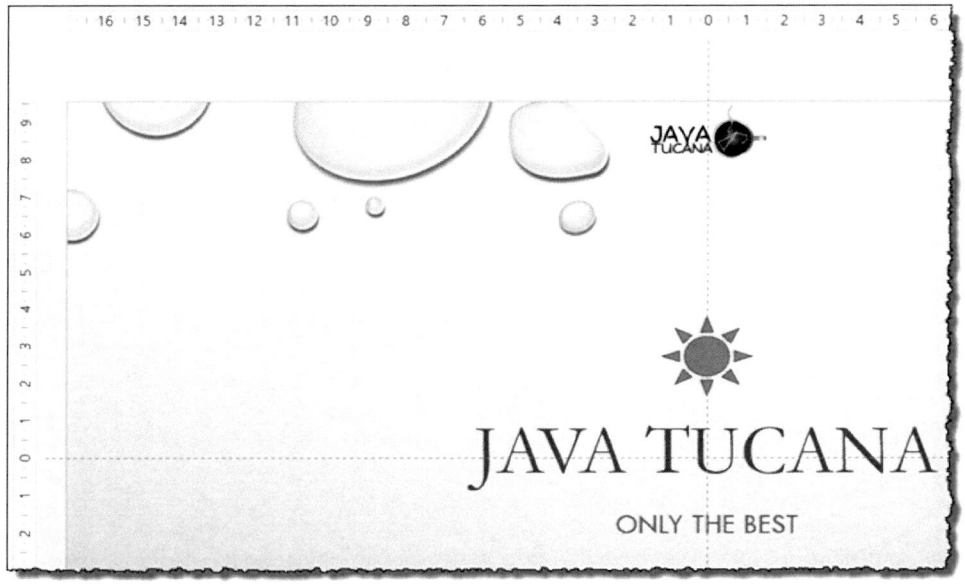

 Note: Once you click on a text object, the rulers measure horizontal and vertical distance and denote tab stops, margins, and so on. Also, if you wish to change the position of one or both guides—and thus were they intersect—just drag them to the new location. For example, this can be useful to center an object on a point that isn't the center of the slide.

For further control of gridlines and guides, click ▫ (the launcher) in the View tab's Show group. This opens the Grid and Guides window. Here, you can adjust features such as grid spacing, and you can specify exactly what displays. The **Snap objects to grid** option is useful when you want to make sure objects are perfectly aligned to the grid: as you move an object close to the grid, the object "snaps" to the gridline as if connected to it by a rubber band.

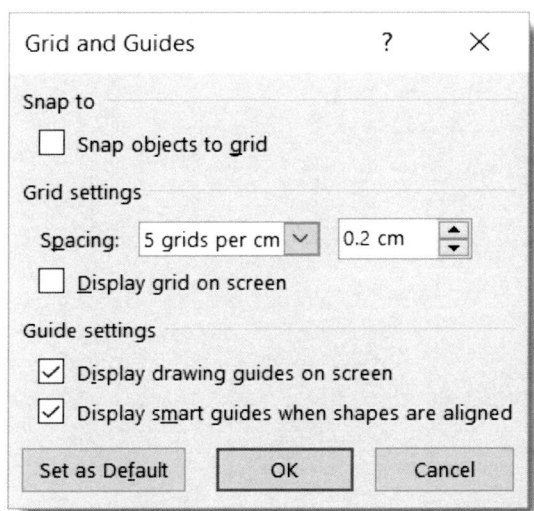

The *zoom slider*, near the right edge of the status bar, can be extremely useful, particularly in helping you size and align smaller shapes at precise locations on your slides. Drag the slider to the right to zoom in or to the left to zoom out. The value displayed is the percentage of zoom. A value of 100% is normal size. Thus, for example, 50% would be half the normal size, and 300% would be three times the normal size.

In the Drawing Tools Format tab's Arrange group, the **Align** button contains many options for aligning a shape (or any object) on a slide.

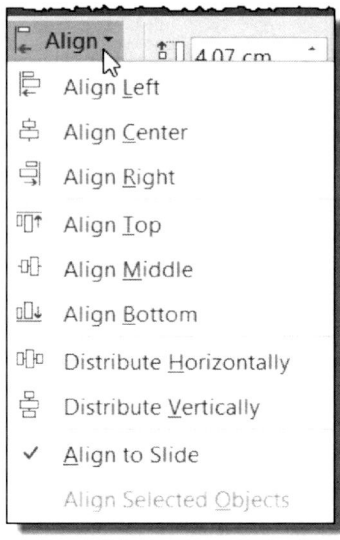

- *Align Left*, *Align Center*, and *Align Right* are used to position shapes (objects) horizontally.
- *Align Top*, *Align Middle*, and *Align Bottom* are used to position them vertically.
- *Distribute Horizontally* and *Distribute Vertically* are for evenly spacing selected shapes (objects) in their respective directions. *Align to Slide* is selected by default; however, selecting multiple shapes activates the *Align Selected Objects* option. The two outermost shapes in the selection determine the area of distribution.

A very important tool in the presentation design arsenal is the **Undo** command, available on the Quick Access toolbar or by pressing **Ctrl+Z**. Even if you're not fond of keyboard shortcuts, it's highly recommended that you remember this one, as it comes in very handy—and not just in PowerPoint.

To undo your last action, click on the Quick Access toolbar, or press **Ctrl+Z**. To display a list of your most recent actions, click the arrow at the right of the button. A list of actions, from most recent to least recent, is displayed. Thus, you can undo your most recent action or multiple ones.

```
Move Object
Move Object
Move Object
Insert Shape
Clear
Move Object
Resize Object
Move Object
Resize Object
Resize Object
Move Object
Resize Object
Move Object
Bring Forward
Bring Forward
Shape Style
Shape Style
Resize Object
Send to Back
Insert Shape
Undo 8 Actions
```

Note: When you undo multiple actions, you can't "skip over" actions in the list. Thus, using this method, selecting the fifteenth most recent action also "undoes" the 14 actions that followed it.

Resizing shapes

When you select a shape, resizing handles become visible. These handles work the same way as those on text box borders. In addition, shapes display a special handle that allows you to change the shape symmetrically.

MOS PowerPoint Exam Objective(s): 2.2.3

1. Click the shape you wish to resize.
   To select it and display its resizing handles.

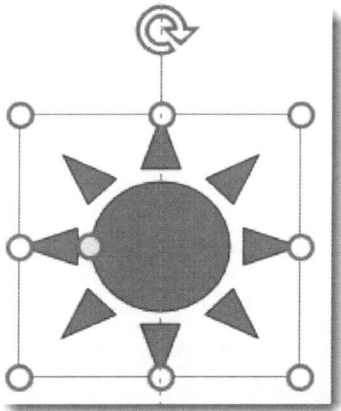

2. Drag the resizing handles as you would to resize a text box.
3. Drag the special yellow sizing handle toward the center of the shape.
   The shape's proportions are altered symmetrically.

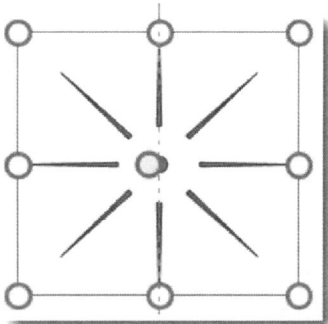

4. Drag the yellow handle back out past its original position, to the outer edge of the shape.

The shape's proportions are again altered, but this time its central area is enlarged and its outer edge is diminished in size.

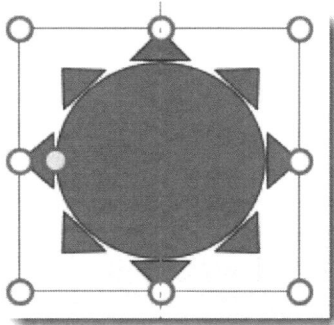

Shape styles

 MOS PowerPoint Exam Objective(s): 2.2.4, 2.2.5

You can format shape styles using the Shape Styles group on the Drawing Tools Format tab. Another—and perhaps more powerful—way is via the Format Shape pane, which you open by clicking the Shape Styles group (launcher) button. Either way, you have the choice of setting fill options, outlines, and shape effects, including 3-D, reflections, and shadows. Besides being able to set all these options individually, PowerPoint provides many different kinds of presets that group these effects to good advantage, which can take some guesswork out of the process, particularly for non-artists.

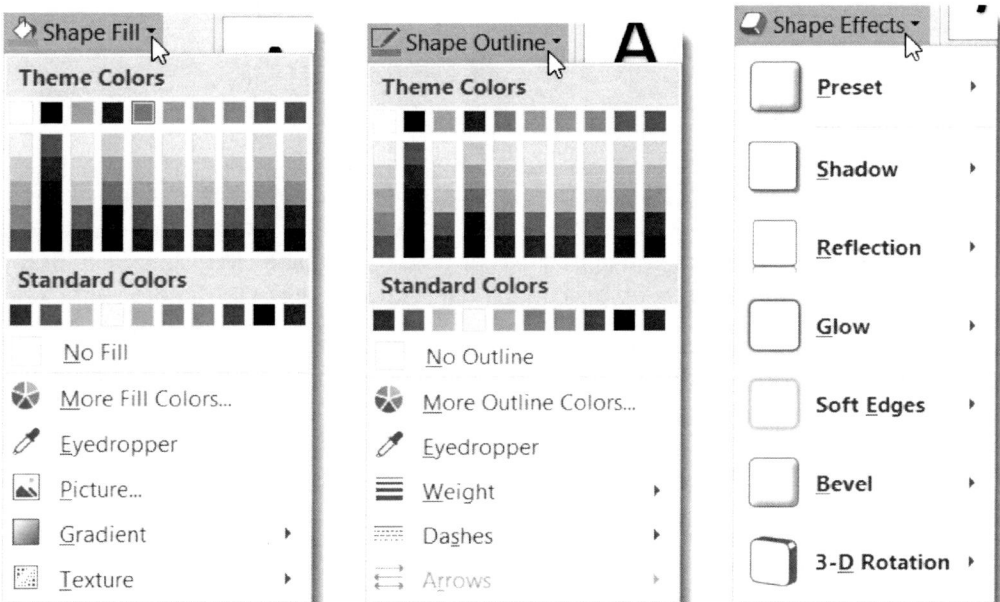

- *Shape Fill is the color, texture, or pattern you can use to fill a closed shape. Use these options in the same way you would when working with slide backgrounds. Many of the same tools apply to both.*
- *Shape Outline is the outline, or border, of a shape, or, if the shape is a line, the appearance of the line.*
- *Shape Effects allows you to apply effects such as shadows, reflections, and 3-D.*

The Format Shape pane provides all these options as well, but they're combined in one location and are more easily fine-tuned. Plus, you have access to precise Size & Properties options.

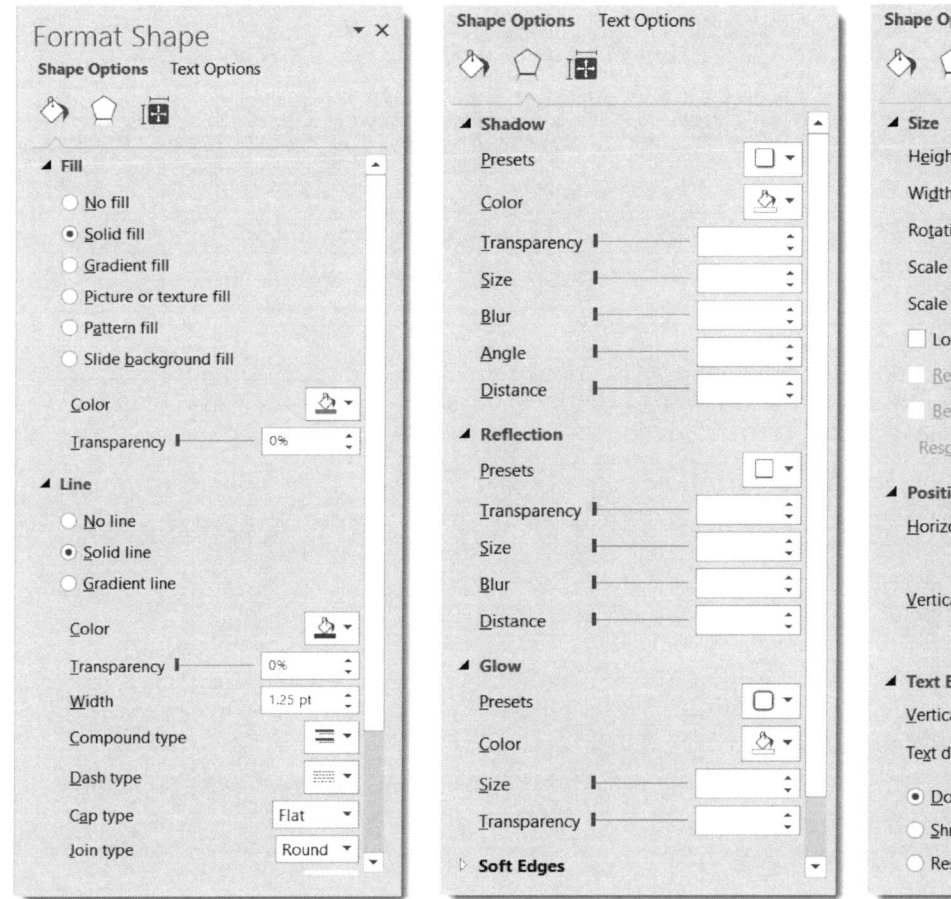
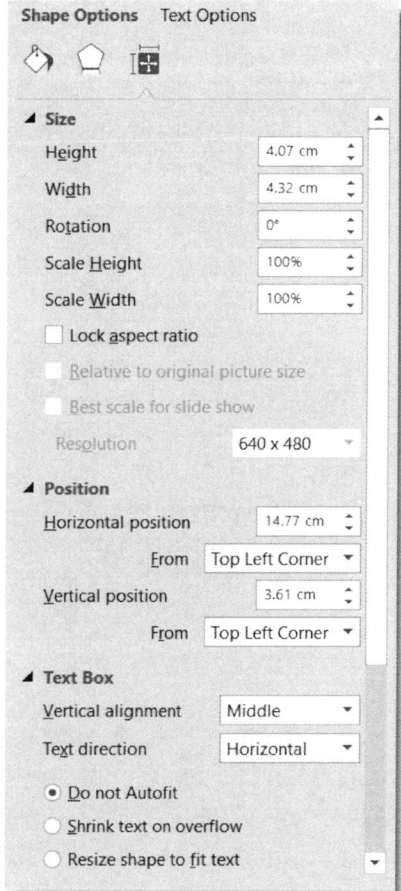

Layering, aligning, and grouping shapes

It's possible to add many different shapes, text boxes, and other objects to a slide. But when you do so, you run the risk of them running into each other in ways that are neither pleasant nor helpful. Fortunately, you can control this slide "traffic" by working with objects as *layers*.

When you add a shape to a slide, it's considered one object layer. If you add another object, whether or not the objects overlap to any extent, the new object is treated as another layer laid on top of the first one, and so on. Thus, you run the risk of having objects that you added earlier covered up, at least to some extent, by those added later. This is especially important when objects added later have an opaque fill color, for example.

Fortunately, PowerPoint allows you to endlessly shuffle the stacking order of layers to your heart's content. You can also align slide layers to position them where you want. Once you've finished working with the layers, you can then group them, so that you can then move the group of layers without altering their relative positions and alignment.

 MOS PowerPoint Exam Objective(s): 2.4.1, 2.4.2, 2.4.3, 2.4.4

1. Select an object layer that you wish to move among the stack.
   Click the object. Its layer is automatically selected.

2. Move the layer to the front (top) or back (bottom) of the stack.
   Using the tools in the Drawing Tools Format tab's Arrange group.

   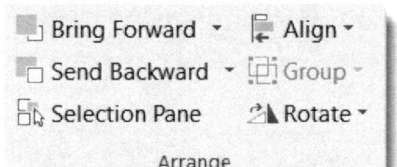

   - To move the layer one layer forward, click **Bring Forward**. Each time you use this command, it brings the object forward one layer.
   - To move the layer to the front, click the arrow next to the Bring Forward tool, and select **Bring to Front** from the menu.

   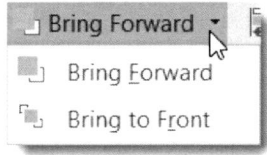

   - To move the layer one layer backward, click **Send Backward**. Each time you use this command, it sends the object back one layer.
   - To move the layer to the back, click the arrow next to the Send Backward tool, and select **Send to Back** from the menu.

   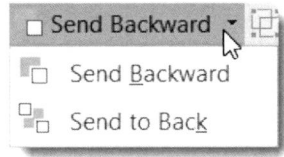

3. To align objects, select the objects, and then click **Align**.
   Use **Ctrl** to select multiple objects. On the Drawing Tools Format tab or Picture Tools Format tab, depending on the objects selected.

   A list of alignment options is displayed.

4. Select an alignment option.

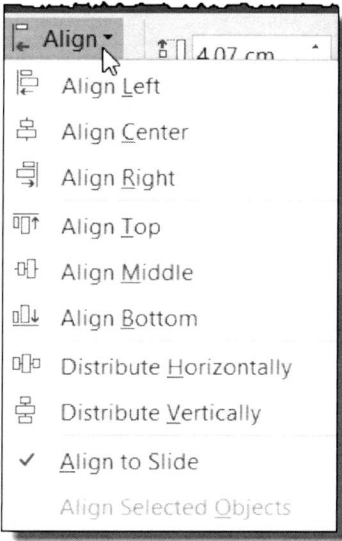

5. To group objects, select them, and then click **Group**.

   To display a list of Group options. Before the objects are grouped, the Group option is the only one available.

6. Click **Group**.

   In the list of Group options.

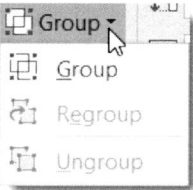

Exercise: Working with shapes

In this exercise, you'll create and work with shapes.

Do This	How & Why
1. Open JT Shapes.pptx, and save it as My JT Shapes.pptx.	In the Working with shapes and images data folder.
2. Make sure that rulers, gridlines, and guides are displayed.	All three options are available on the View tab, in the Show group. Make sure that each is checked.
3. Make sure slide 1 is selected.	

Do This	How & Why
4. Select the **Line** tool from the Shapes gallery.	In the Insert tab's Illustrations group. 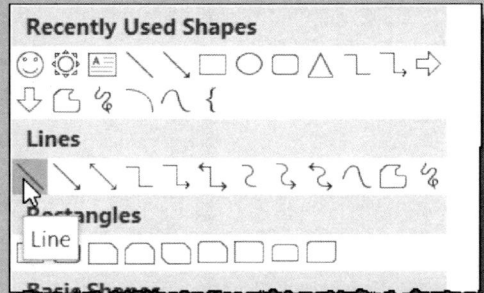 The mouse pointer becomes a crosshair. 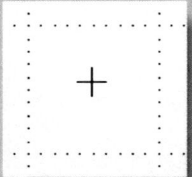
5. Create a perfectly horizontal line, and center it vertically between the lines of text, and horizontally using the vertical guide.	
a) Press and hold **Shift**, and about midway between "JAVA TUCANA" and "ONLY THE BEST," and left of the vertical guide, click to place the mouse pointer, and drag to the right, roughly past the vertical guide.	
b) Click to set a destination point.	A straight, horizontal line appears.
c) Drag to center it between the lines of text.	As you drag the line up and down, at a certain position, fine horizontal guides on either side of the line indicate that it's perfectly centered between the lines of text.

d) Now, carefully center the line horizontally as well.

The guides for centering vertically appear The horizontal guides (for centering vertically) appear above and below the line, and the vertical center guide (for centering horizontally) becomes bolder, indicating that the line is properly centered.

Do This	How & Why
e) If necessary, resize the line to make it roughly the size shown in the figure.	Use the sizing handles. Afterward, double-check to make sure it's still centered, and adjust it, as necessary.
6. Apply a shape outline to the line.	
a) If necessary, click to select the line.	
b) Click **Shape Outline**.	On the Drawing Tool Format tab, in the Shape Styles group.
c) Select a Weight of **1 pt**.	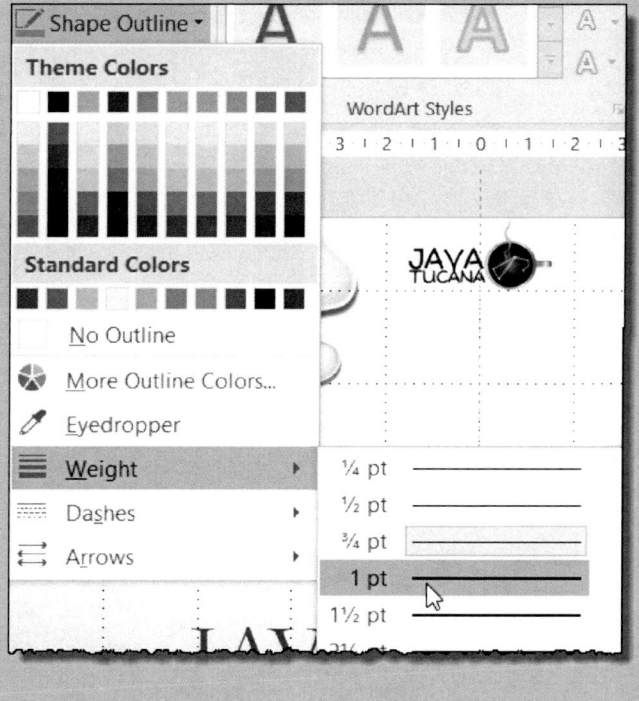
d) Click Shape Outline, and apply the color named **Black, Text 1**.	
7. Place a roughly vertical, curved shape at both ends of "JAVA TUCANA."	

Do This	How & Why
a) Select the Curve shape from the Shapes gallery. 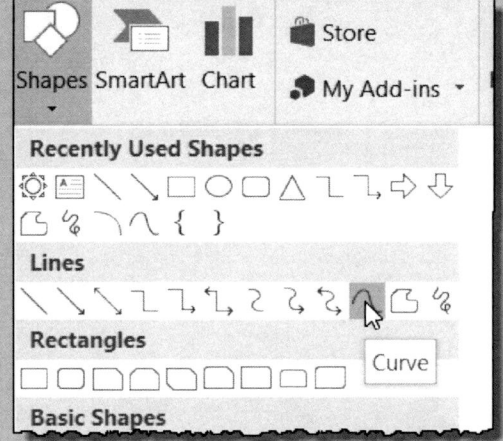 b) Click to place its origin point. Then click a few points along the way to create a roughly vertical wave shape. Double-click to place a destination point and complete the shape. c) Repeat steps 7a and 7b to create a similar curved shape at the other end of the text. d) Move the curves, as necessary, to roughly match the figure. 	
8. Select both curves.	Select one curve, then press and hold **Ctrl**, and click to select the other curve.

Do This	How & Why

9. Apply the **Green, 5 pt glow, Accent color 2** shape effect.

Click the **Shape Effects** tool in the Shape Styles group to open the Glow gallery.

10. Add an open shape on the slide, enclosing the existing shapes and text. | Typical open shapes include rectangles, ovals, and other geometric shapes. The shape is displayed filled by default, and it now covers all the other work you've done! Don't worry, you'll fix this shortly.

Do This	How & Why
11. First, apply the **Recycled paper** fill texture to the new shape.	Click **Shape Fill**, point to Texture, and use the tooltip to find and click **Recycled paper**.  The fill texture is applied to the shape, but you still can't see what's behind it.
12. Send the front layer back one layer. a) If necessary, select the textured shape.	

Do This	How & Why
b) Click **Send Backward**.	To send the front layer back one layer. 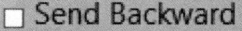 Not exactly the result you'd like! Only the curve last added appears in front now. The other shapes all remain hidden behind the filled shape. It's clearly time for some extreme layering. 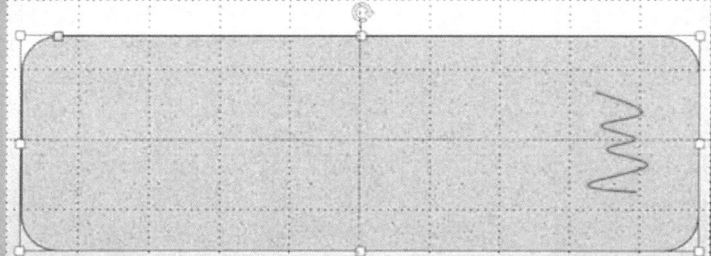
13. This time, send the filled shape to the back of the stack.	
a) Click the arrow next to Send Backward.	To open the Send Backward options.
b) Click **Send to Back**.	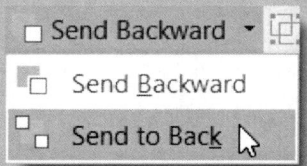 Now, all your new shapes and the text are visible and appear to sit on the textured surface of the back layer.
14. Remove the shape outline.	Use the figure as a guide. 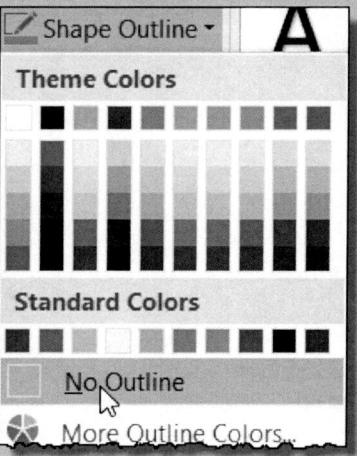

Do This	How & Why
15. Apply the **Preset 3** shape effect.	Use the figure as a guide. 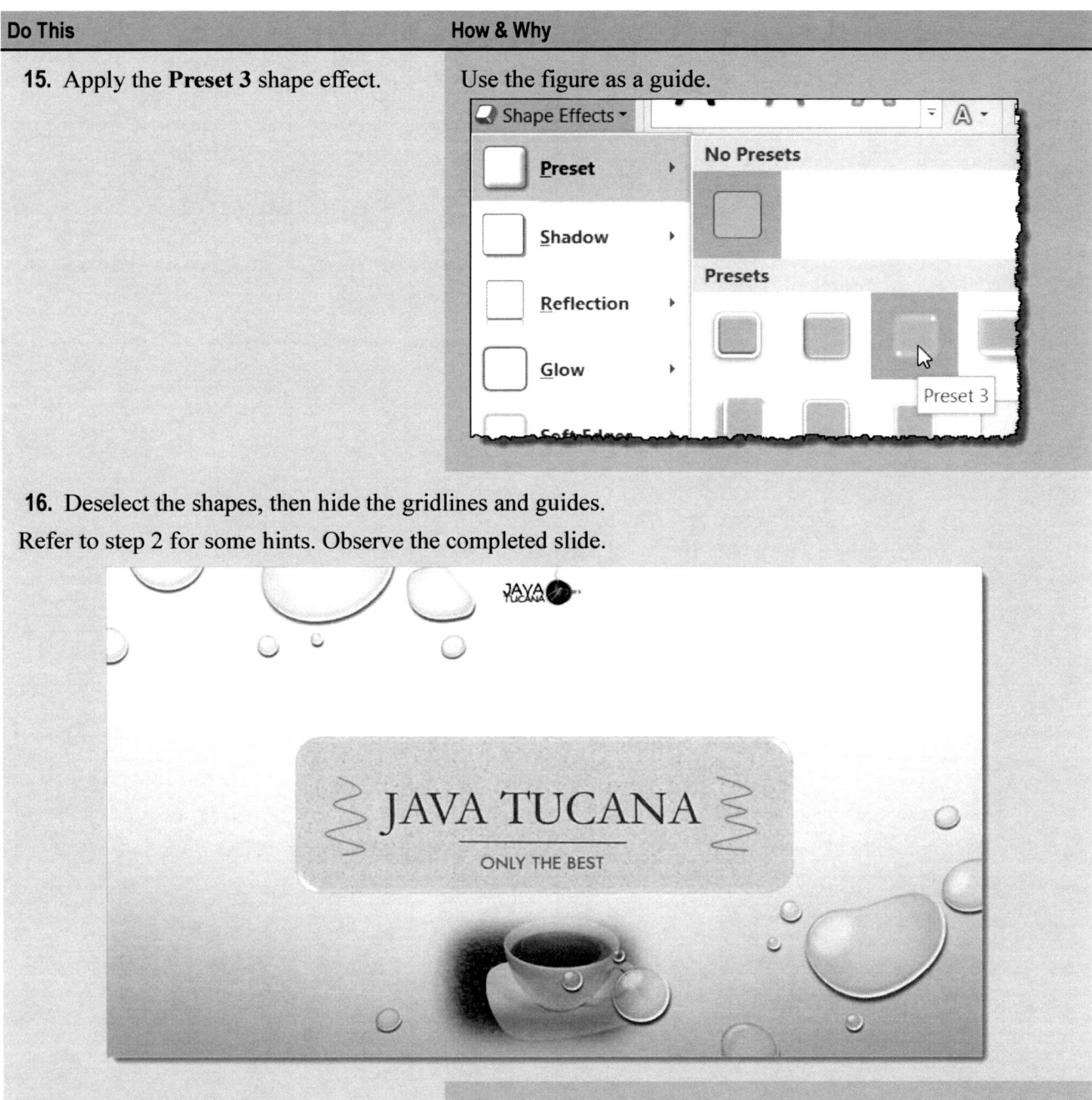
16. Deselect the shapes, then hide the gridlines and guides. Refer to step 2 for some hints. Observe the completed slide.	
17. Save and close the file.	

Assessment: Creating and formatting shapes

1. True or false? The Shapes gallery allows you to create multiple shape layers at once.
   - True
   - False

2. Which of the following statements about creating curved shapes is true?
   - To create each curve in a single curved shape, click and drag in a rounded manner to avoid sharp angles.
   - It's important to click at the destination point to complete the shape.
   - Double-click at the destination point to complete the shape.
   - You're allowed up to 24 curves in a single curved shape.

3. True or false? Pressing and holding the Shift key while drawing a line allows you to create perfectly straight diagonals.
   - True
   - False

4. Which of the following statements about shape layers is true?
   - To bring the backmost layer to the front, you must click Bring to Front multiple times, especially if there are several layers or more.
   - In a shape group of five layers, if the third layer contains important text, and all other layers are opaque, the text layer could be brought to the front to render it readable.
   - In a shape group of five layers, if the third layer contains important text, and all other layers are opaque, the text on the third layer could be formatted as bold to make it show through the other layers.
   - Always send the front-most layer to the back of the stack if it obscures the layer behind it.

Module B: Working with images

Just as with shapes, you can enhance your presentation by inserting images on your slides. Because PowerPoint treats images as objects, you can modify them, add effects, and layer them to achieve your aims.

You will learn how to:

- Insert, resize, crop, add effects to, and add styles to images

About images

Images can be a great way to enhance and clarify your presentations. An *image* can be a photograph or other graphic represented as a digital file, including scanned art. There are two main types of image files that can be used in PowerPoint: bitmap images and vector graphics.

- A *bitmap* image is composed of millions of tiny dots, or *pixels*, that taken together form an image, like photos in a printed newspaper or magazine. Bitmap images such as photographs and scanned images are commonly used on web pages. The quality of a bitmap image is determined by two factors: its resolution and its size. *Resolution* refers to how many pixels per unit area the image contains—the higher the value, the greater the resolution. This value is variously represented, but one common way is as pixels per inch (ppi). A high-resolution bitmap image will reproduce well when enlarged. However, it does so at the cost of file *size*. Thus, multiple high-resolution bitmap files in a single presentation can result in a huge file. On the other hand, if the image won't be greatly enlarged, and it covers only a small area, its file size need not be overly large. Some common bitmap image file extensions used in PowerPoint presentations are .bmp, .gif, .jpeg, and .png.

- A *vector* graphic is a high-quality image file. It can be as simple as a line drawn using a Microsoft application, or an elaborate graphic drawn using a specialized application such as Adobe Illustrator. In a vector file, information about the precise geometry of every shape contained in the image is encoded with it. The result is a high-resolution image, regardless of size. Thus, a vector graphic can be reduced or enlarged without loss of image quality. Some common vector graphic file extensions used in PowerPoint presentations are .cdr, .cgm, .drw, and .eps.

Once you import an image, you can modify and work with it in countless ways, using many of the same tools used to work with shapes and other objects.

Inserting images from a local file

 MOS PowerPoint Exam Objective(s): 2.3.1

You can insert images from local files via the Insert Picture window.

1. Select a destination for the image.

    You can insert images onto individual slides. However, if you wish to display the exact same image on every slide, you can select the slide master as the destination. There, you can also set it as a background image.

2. Click **Pictures**.

    On the Insert tab, in the Images group.

    The Insert Picture window opens.

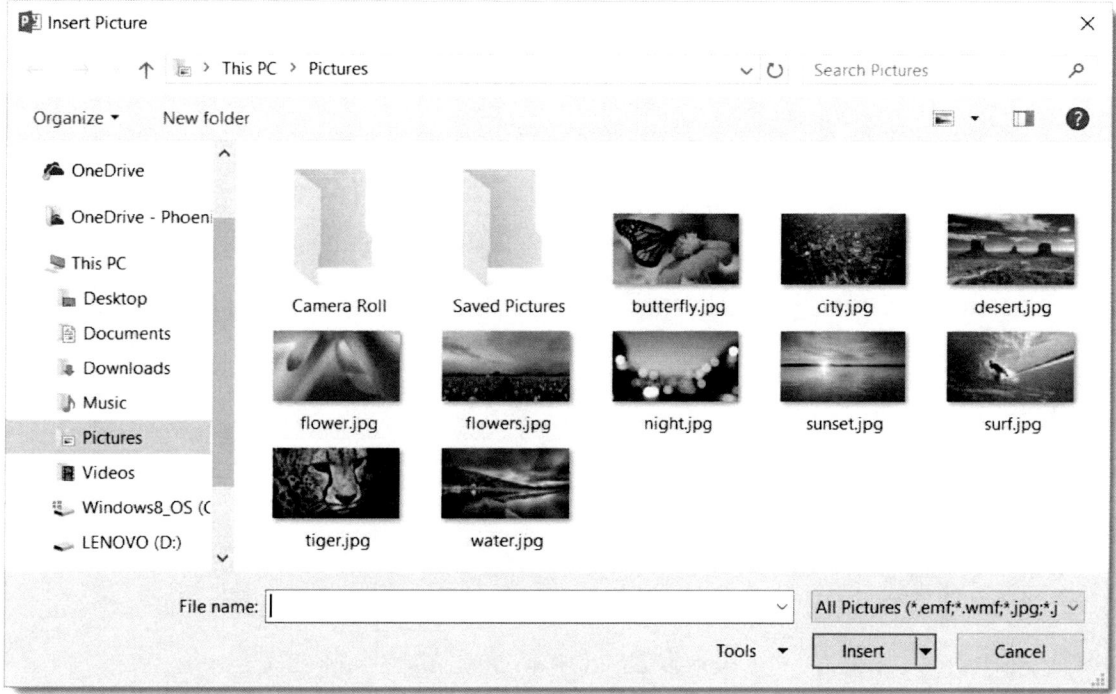

3. Navigate to the location of the image file you wish to insert.
4. Select the file, and click **Insert**.

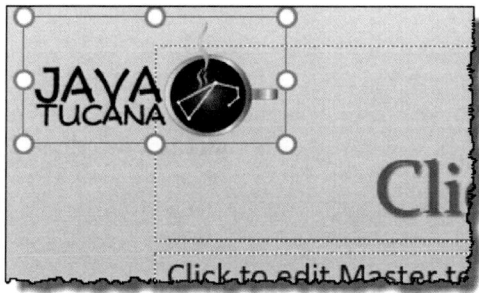

Inserting online images

A whole world of images is available from online sources. You use the Insert Pictures window to locate online images.

 MOS PowerPoint Exam Objective(s): 1.2.4

1. Select a destination for your online image.
   You can insert images onto individual slides. However, if you wish to display the exact same image on every slide, you can select the slide master as the destination.
2. Click **Online Pictures**.
   On the Insert tab, in the Images group.

   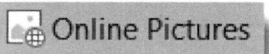

   The Insert Pictures window opens.

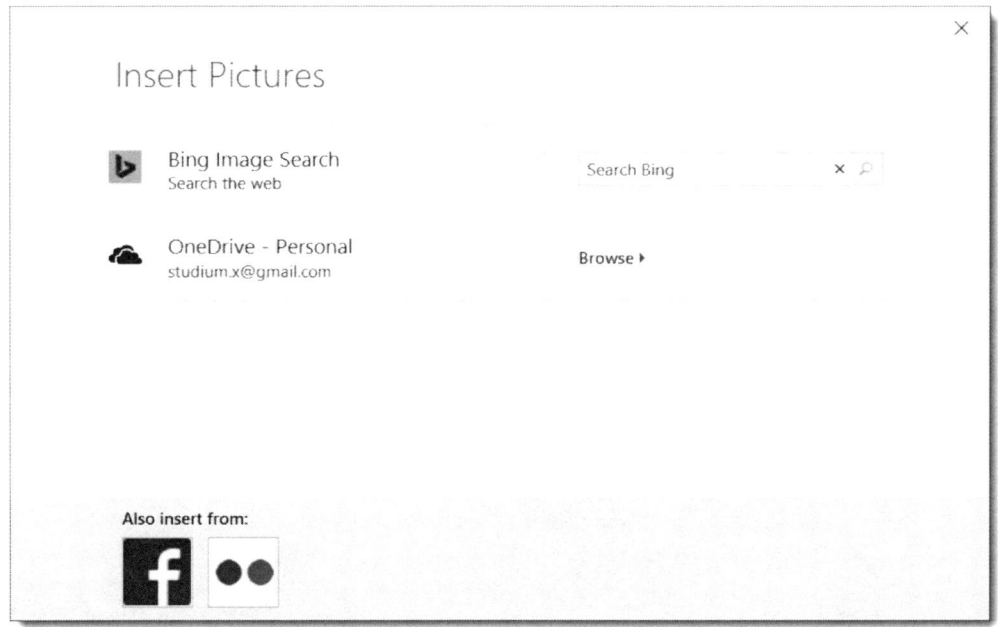

3. Click in the Search Bing box, and type a search word or string. Then press **Enter**.

   Next to Bing Image Search. Unless you have a specific web destination in mind, this is an excellent portal for image searches. When typing a search string or keyword, try to be as precise as possible. For example, if you're looking for images of coffee beans, that's an excellent search string to type. Typing "beverage" or "hot drink" would result in too broad a search.

   The Bing Image Search results are displayed in the window. Often, when searching for online images, a warning message like the one shown in the figure is displayed. This is a reminder to be careful about downloading and using images that might be protected by copyright. It can be alright to download copyrighted images for your own private use, but it's often better to be safe and not use them at all, unless you request and receive permission from the copyright owner. You can search specifically for images available in the public domain. In the figure, the *Show all web results* option displays all images, regardless of their copyright status.

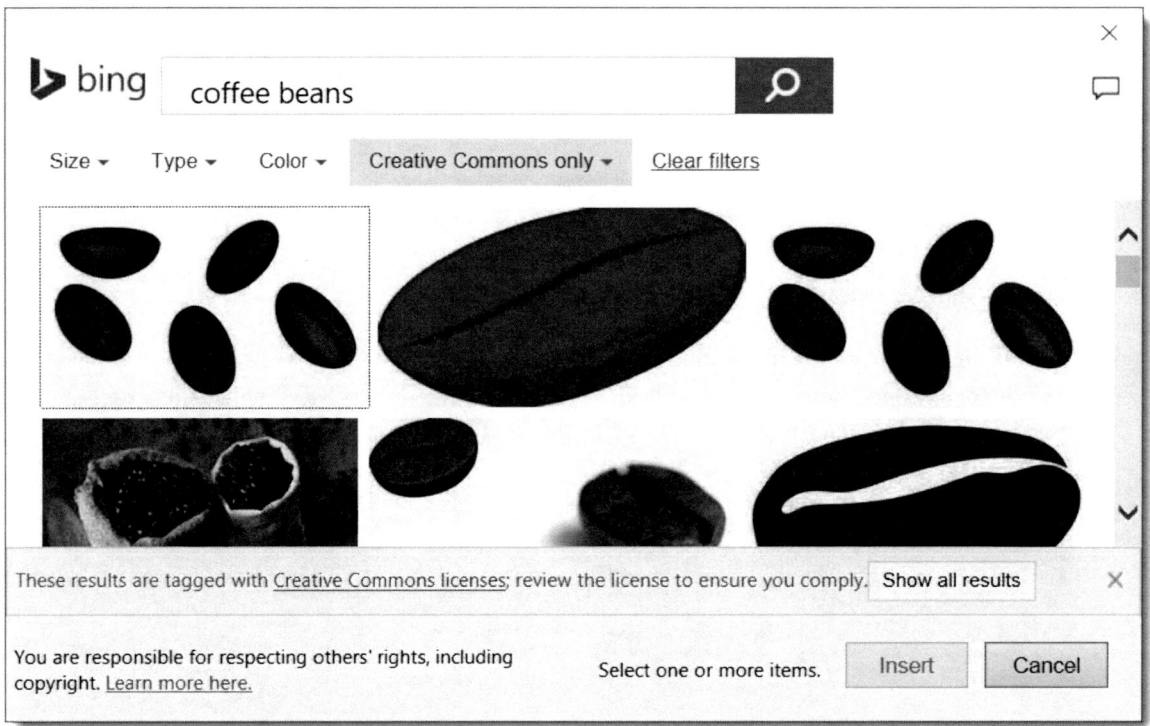

4. Scroll through the images displayed, and hover over images to view their size information.

This is a quick way to glean information about a specific image. For example, the tooltip in this image lets you know that it's a vector graphic.

5. Select the image you wish to insert, and click **Insert**.

To select multiple images, click each image's checkbox, which appears in the upper-left corner when you hover over it. Then click **Insert**.

Depending on the size of the inserted image, it can cover the larger part of a slide, which means that some adjustments are usually necessary before the image appears exactly as you want it.

 Note: To use an inserted image as a background image for all slides in a presentation, first open Slide Master view, and select the slide master. Then insert the image onto the slide master, resize and position it as needed, display the Send Backward options, and click **Send to Back**.

Sizing and moving images

In PowerPoint, text boxes, shapes, and images are all considered objects. As such, many of the same controls are available to all types of objects. Thus, sizing and moving images works in the same way as with other objects.

 MOS PowerPoint Exam Objective(s): 2.3.2

1. Select the image.

    Image handles appear on the image border. For rectangular images, handles appear on each side and at the corners.

2. Resize the image.

    - Drag a handle on any side of the image to increase/decrease its size in that dimension. However, keep in mind that doing so distorts its *aspect ratio*—the ratio of width to height.
    - Drag a corner handle to increase/decrease the size of the image diagonally. Doing so retains the original aspect ratio.
    - Press and hold **Ctrl** and drag a handle to make the above changes, but with the object centered at the same point on the slide. So, if you've already picked the perfect position for your masterpiece and don't wish to move it, using Ctrl resizes the object while keeping it centered in the same spot.
    Sometimes, however, you might need to move the image even after you've carefully resized it.

3. Drag the image where you'd like it to appear on the slide.

    Whether an image is selected or not, you can still move it. Images are a bit different than some other objects, in that when an image is selected, you don't have to carefully hover over the border to see the four-headed arrow. Instead, hovering anywhere over the image makes it visible.

Cropping images

When you select an image, the Picture Tools Format tab becomes available. It contains many powerful tools for working with images. The tools in the Size group are the ones used for cropping and sizing.

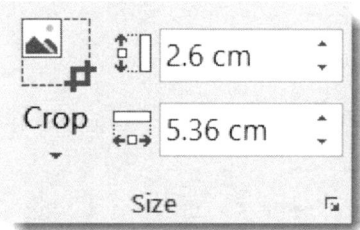

 MOS PowerPoint Exam Objective(s): 2.3.2

1. Select the image to be cropped.

    The Picture Tools Format tab is displayed.

2. Click the **Crop** tool.

    Not the downward-pointing arrow below it.

    Next to each sizing handle, a cropping handle appears.

3. Drag any crop handle to crop the image as desired.

You can use cropping handles in much the same way you use sizing handles. However, when cropping, you're actually removing a portion of the image, not resizing it.

Plainly visible within the cropping handles is the area of the image left intact. Faintly visible is the image area from which the image itself was cropped. This provides a helpful aid to seeing what's been cropped from the image.

4. Deactivate the Crop tool.

Clip **Crop** again, or press **Esc**.

The cropping handles are removed, and the image area that held the removed part of the image is now also removed.

5. If necessary, move the image to its original location, prior to cropping.

Applying styles and effects

The Picture Tools Format tab provides you with many powerful tools for changing the appearance of images. To apply styles to an image, use the tools in the Picture Styles group. Here, you can apply all the same kinds of stylistic effects to your image as you would to shapes, including shadows, reflections, borders, and 3-D effects.

 MOS PowerPoint Exam Objective(s): 2.3.3

The preset styles in the Picture Styles gallery provide a great way to quickly apply combinations of effects. Even if you end up customizing your formatting, a preset can provide a great starting point from which to orient yourself in terms of formatting an image in the most meaningful way. However, keep in mind that when applying effects to images, more is often not better. At its best, overindulgence distracts viewers from the point of a slide; at its worst, it could undermine a whole presentation.

1. Select the image, if necessary.

    The Picture Tools Format tab is displayed. Let's take a look at all the style presets.

2. Display the full Picture Styles gallery.

    In the lower right of the Picture Styles gallery, click the **More** button.

The full Picture Styles gallery opens.

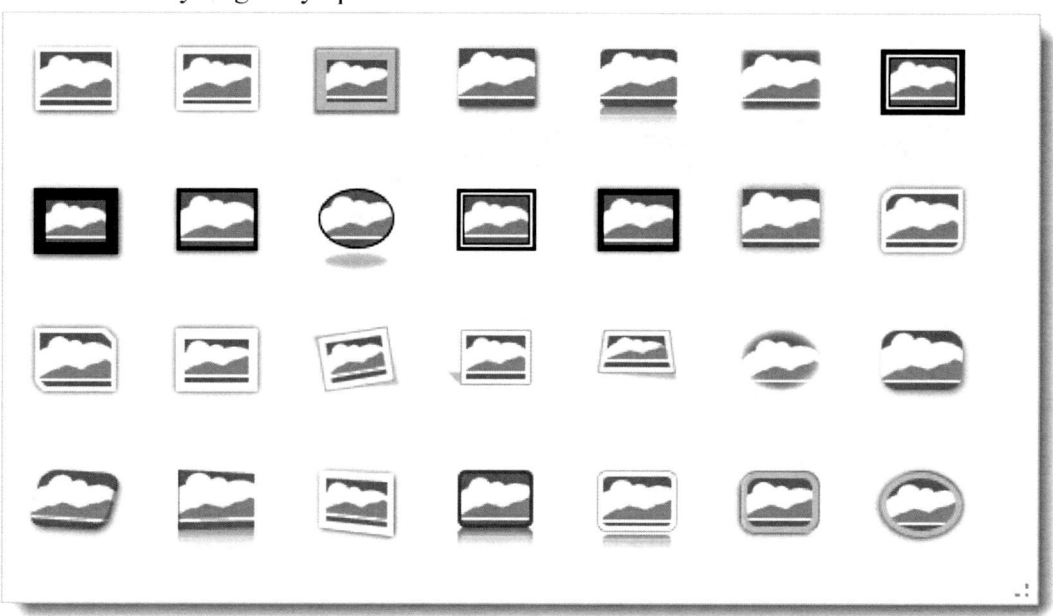

3. Hover over each preset. Observe the image as you do so.

   The image previews the effect of applying each preset.

4. Select a preset.

   The preset style is applied to the image.

5. Click **Picture Effects**.

   In the Picture Styles group.

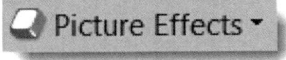

The Picture Effects gallery opens, displaying many of the same effects options available when working with shapes and other objects.

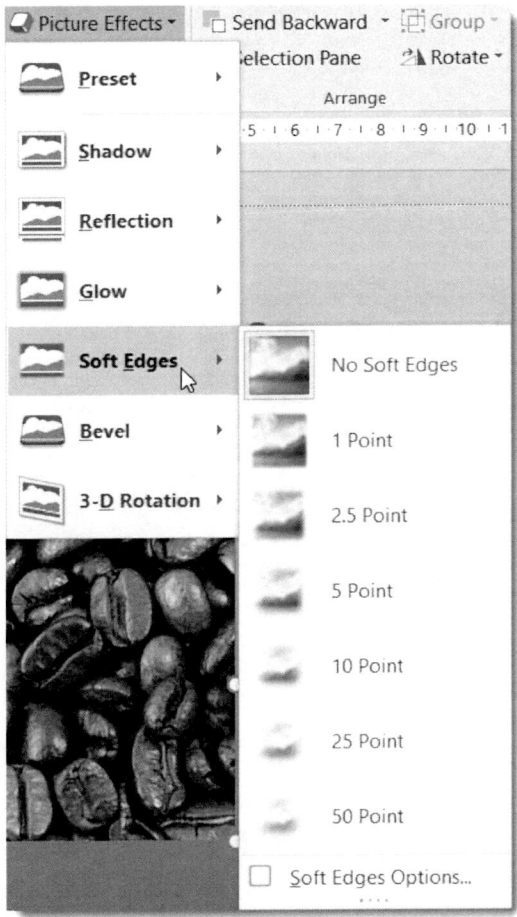

6. Use the Picture Effects tool to apply an effect.

In case you come to a point where you realize that you've seriously ruined a precious image you're working on, you can always choose from the Reset Picture options in the Adjust group of the Picture Tools Format tab. Clicking the **Reset Picture** button itself removes any formatting, such as styles and effects, that you've applied. However, to remove all formatting and sizing and return the image to its original, pristine condition, click the arrow next to Reset Picture, and click **Reset Picture & Size**.

Exercise: Working with images

In this exercise, you'll insert, adjust, and work with images.

Do This	How & Why
1. Open `JT Images.pptx`, and save it as `My JT Images.pptx`.	From the `Working with shapes and images` data folder.
2. Observe the slides in this short presentation.	They are all lacking a logo and at least one other image.
3. Open Slide Master view, and select the slide master.	On the View tab, click **Slide Master**. Navigate up to the slide master.
4. Insert the Java Tucana logo onto the slide master.	

Do This	How & Why

a) Click **Pictures**.
On the Insert tab.

The **Insert Picture** window opens.

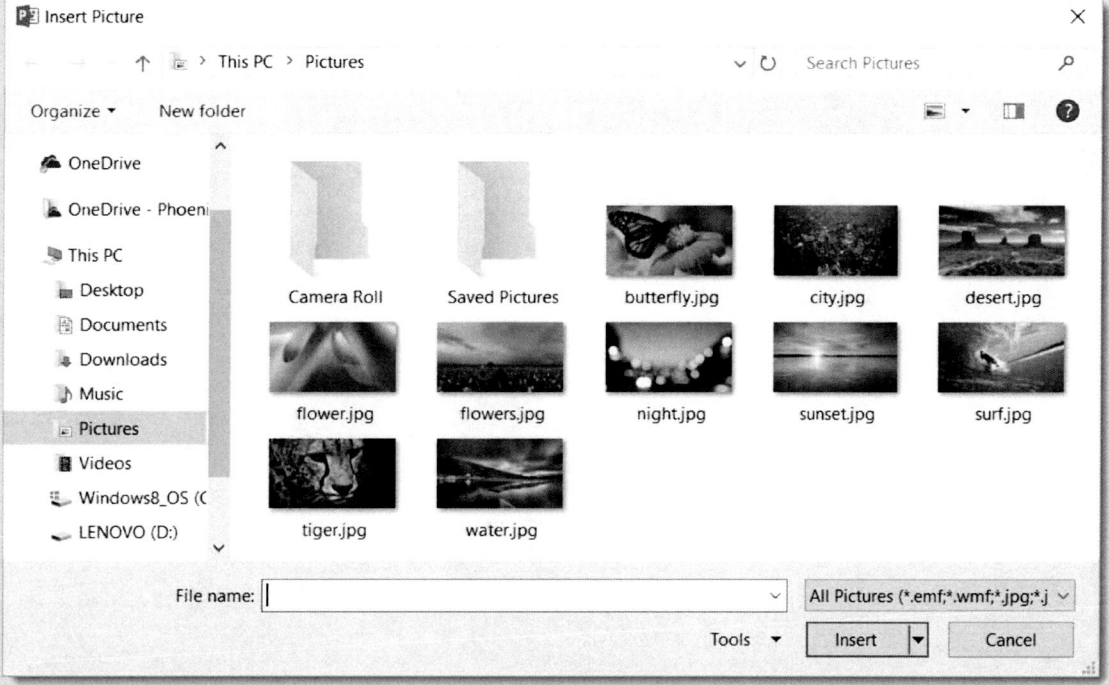

b) Navigate to the `Working with shapes and images` data folder.

c) Select **JT Logo - Trans Back.png**, and click **Insert**.

The Java Tucana logo appears on the master slide.

5. Size and position the logo to match the figure. Try to maintain the original aspect ratio of the image.

Use the sizing handles to resize it. One way to maintain the aspect ratio is to drag a corner handle, rather than a side handle.

Do This	How & Why
6. Insert the **coffee cup.jpg** image onto the slide master.	Use step 4 as a guide.
7. Crop the image to match the figure.	
a) On the Picture Tools Format tab, click **Crop**.	The cropping handles are displayed at the image border.
b) Drag the cropping handles to roughly match the figure. 	
c) Click **Crop** or press **Esc**.	To complete the cropping.
8. View all the presets in the Picture Styles gallery.	Click the **More** button. 
9. Select a preset style from the gallery.	
10. Apply any other effects to the image.	Remember that you can always click **Reset Picture** or **Reset Picture & Size** to start over. Likewise, **Undo** is especially good to use for undoing your most recent artistic transgressions.
11. Position the image on the slide where you think it should go, then set it as the back layer.	To ensure that it doesn't cover any other slide objects. Click **Send to Back**.
12. Return to Normal view, and navigate through the presentation to observe your handiwork.	
13. Save and close the file.	

Assessment: Working with images

1. Which of the following statement is true when sizing images?
    - Dragging a corner sizing handle is one way to preserve an image's aspect ratio.
    - Pressing and holding Ctrl before moving a sizing handle maintains an image's aspect ratio.
    - Dragging a corner sizing handle keeps the image centered in its original position.
    - Pressing and holding Ctrl and moving any sizing handle is the only way to preserve image resolution while enlarging or reducing it.

2. True or false? When repositioning an image, care must be taken not to slide the image between object layers.
    - True
    - False

3. What happens to the image area after cropping is completed?
    - It's reduced to the newly cropped image size.
    - Nothing happens; the original image area border retains its position.
    - The cropped image expands to fill it.
    - Its center remains anchored to the same point on the slide.

4. Even after you've applied a preset style from the Picture Styles gallery, you can continue to apply individual effects to images.
    - True
    - False

Summary: Working with shapes and images

You should now know how to:

- Draw straight lines and freehand curves; create open shapes; and resize, apply styles to, and layer shapes
- Insert images from local and online sources; use them as slide backgrounds; size, reposition, and crop them; and apply styles to them

Synthesis: Working with shapes and images

1. Open `JT Shapes-Images Synthesis.pptx`, and save it as `My JT Shapes-Images Synthesis.pptx`.
   From the `Working with shapes and images` data folder.
2. Ensure that rulers, gridlines, and guides are all displayed; and use the zoom tool, as necessary.
3. Draw three types of straight lines in the presentation: horizontal, vertical, and diagonal. Make at least one of them a feature on all slides of the presentation. Make at least one of the three a feature of only one slide.
4. Create one shape with multiple curves that's displayed on all slides.
5. Create an open shape that contains a text object.
6. Carefully size and position the shapes. Use the Align feature to place shapes, where appropriate.
7. Apply styles to the shapes.
8. Layer the shapes, where appropriate, so that all layers are visible.
9. Insert the `JT Logo - Trans Back.png` image file to display on every slide.
   From the data folder.
10. Size and position it in a good spot, so that it doesn't cover up any essential elements on any slide.
11. Apply any effects to the logo that will keep it clearly readable.
12. Insert the `coffee cup.jpg` file so that it's also a feature of every slide, and crop it to show only the part of the image that you want.
13. Apply a style to it, and add any effects that you like.
14. Set it as the background image for all slides in the presentation.
15. Return to Normal view, then navigate the presentation to observe the results.
16. Save and close the presentation.

Chapter 5: Working with charts and tables

You will learn how to:

- Create and modify charts
- Create and format tables

Module A: Working with charts

PowerPoint allows you to create charts on your slides. Charts are simply a pictorial representation of your data. Sometimes, a picture really does say a thousand words or, more accurately, conveys what a thousand numbers can't.

You will learn how to:

- Create and modify charts in your presentations

About charts

A *chart* shows you, in one of many ways, pictures of *series* of numbers. In a *pie chart*, for example, a series of numbers appears as slices of a pie that represents a whole.

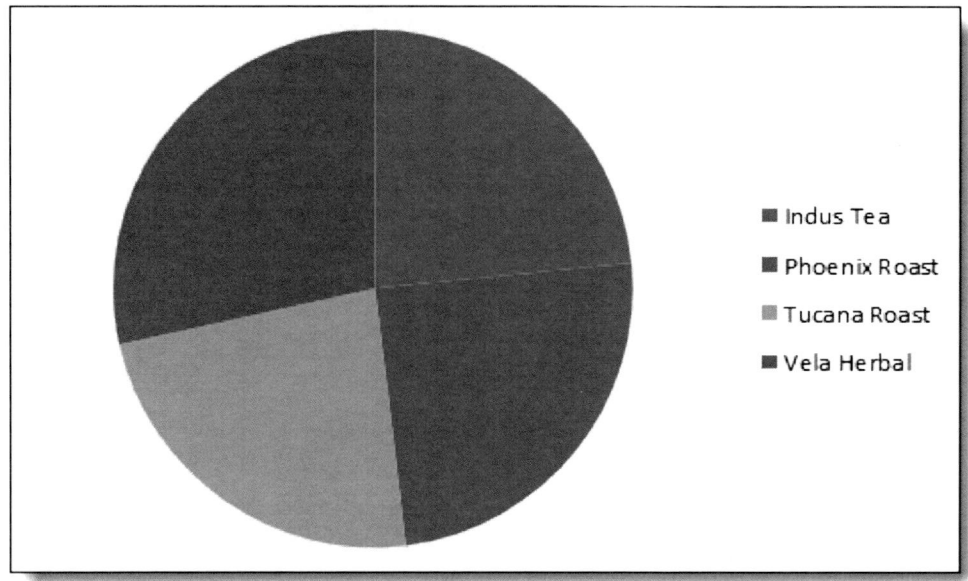

In a *line chart*, on the other hand, each series is a line, with points representing each individual value.

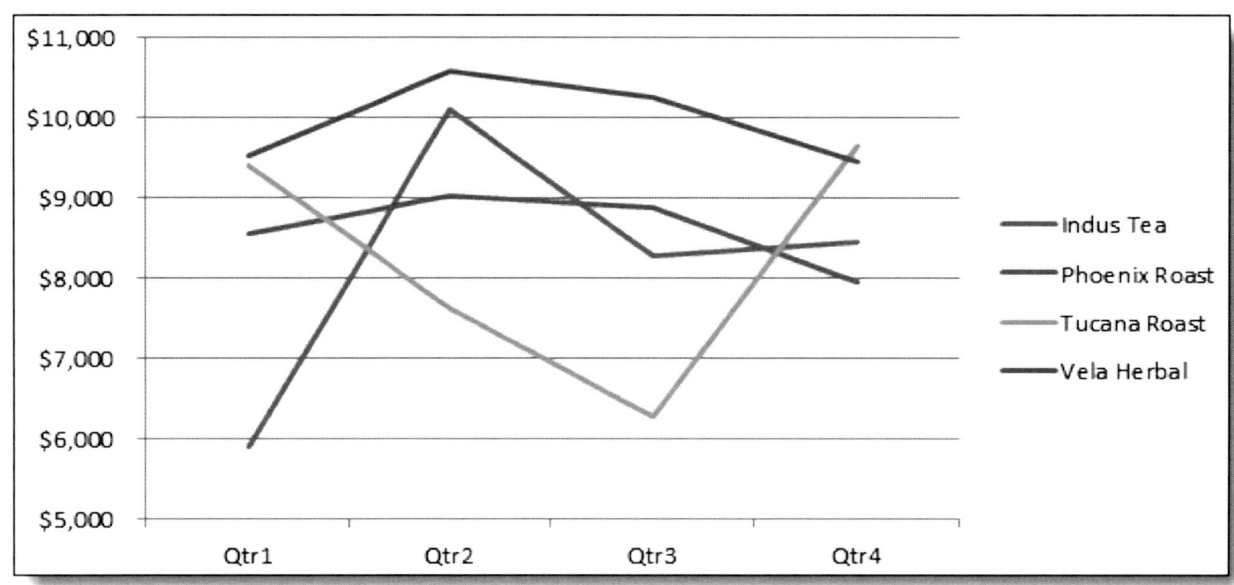

PowerPoint makes it easy to create simple charts like these. But you also have the power to make complex charts that compare different kinds of data, combine different chart types, and highlight the point you want to make.

Chart types

PowerPoint offers many chart types that you can use for representing various kinds of data, and thus make various points to an audience. Within each type, there are also many sub-types.

- *Column charts* show data as columns, either single columns for each value, or stacked to show how individual values relate to totals for a particular category. They are useful for showing magnitude in an obvious way.
- *Line charts* show series of values as points along a line. They are great for showing trends.
- *Pie charts* show how values relate to a whole. The data you select for a pie chart should have only one series of values.
- *Bar charts* are really the same as column charts, with the bars running horizontally (as opposed to columns, which run vertically).
- *Area charts* combine line charts and columns by filling in the areas below the lines.
- *X Y (scatter) charts* show coordinates, and are useful for looking at how two related variables are distributed.

PowerPoint also has a few other chart types that are useful for other types of data.

Adding a chart to a presentation

In PowerPoint, there are a few ways to add a chart to your presentation. Whatever method you choose, it's easiest to do so by first adding a new slide to your presentation to serve as the chart's destination.

 MOS PowerPoint Exam Objective(s): 3.2.1

1. Add a new slide to your presentation.
   - On the Home tab, click the upper part of the **New Slide** button.

   - Click the lower part of the New Slide button to display layout options, and select a layout that includes a Content area.

   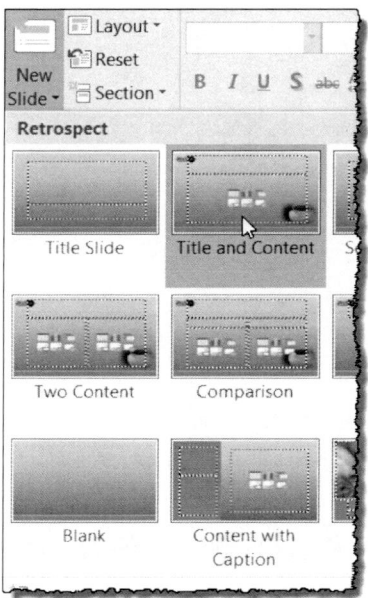

2. Click the **Insert Chart** icon.
   In the content placeholder of the new slide. Or, on the Insert tab, in the Illustrations group, click **Chart**.

The Insert Chart window opens. The left pane of the All Charts tab displays all the main chart types that are available in PowerPoint. Selecting one displays a series of sub-types across the top of the tab, to help you refine your chart selection. The larger area previews the appearance of the select chart type and sub-type. The Recent option displays recently used chart types, and Templates displays any saved chart templates.

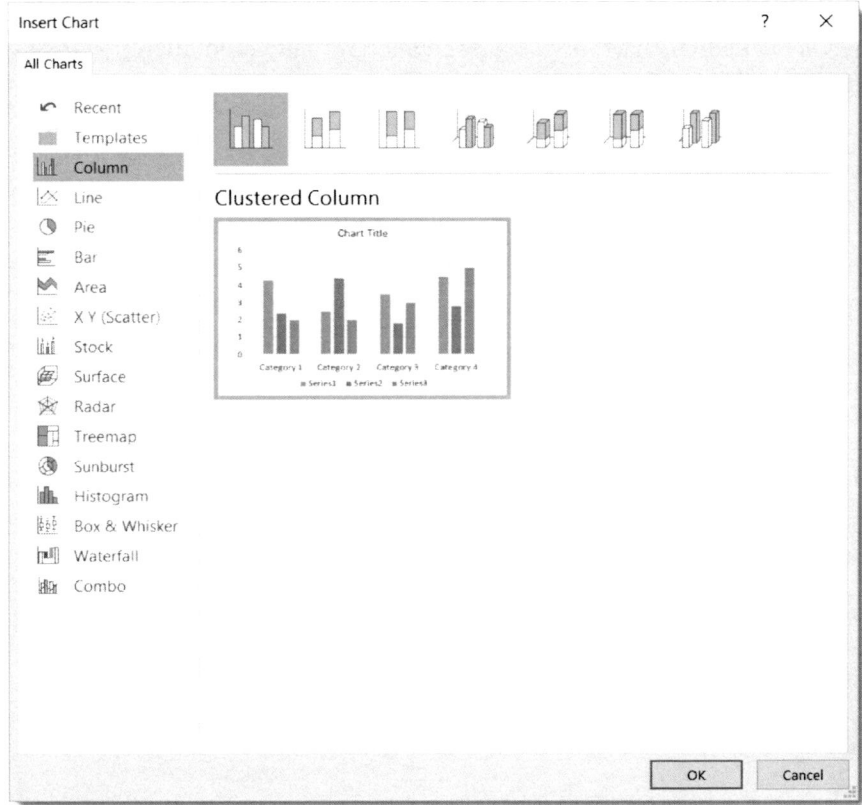

3. Select a main chart type.
   In the left pane.

4. Select a sub-type, if you wish.
   In the upper pane, to further refine your selection.

5. Click **OK**.
   The new chart appears on the slide. The chart's selected, and above it an Excel spreadsheet contains data placeholders in cells, columns, and rows.

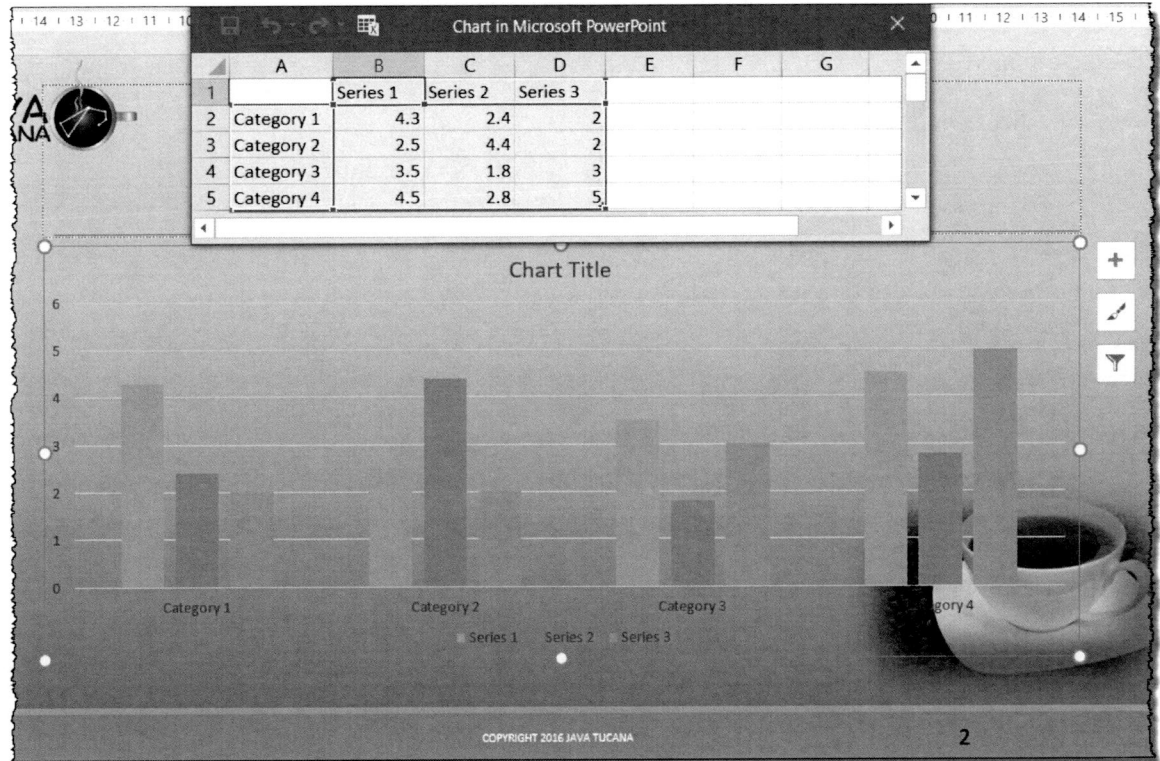

6. Enter the data that you intend the chart to represent.
    In the spreadsheet cells.
    As you enter data, the chart changes to reflect them.

Note: When you add a chart to a slide that already contains other objects, use your knowledge of moving, resizing, aligning, and layering them to achieve the look you want, and to make sure that everything that should be seen can be seen.

7. Close the Excel spreadsheet.

   When you've finished entering data and want to get a better look at the chart, click in the spreadsheet window.

   > **Note:** The spreadsheet data are saved as part of your presentation, so even though you close the spreadsheet, the data remain intact. Just remember to save your presentation.

8. Add a chart title.

   Click in the Chart Title text box, and enter a title for your chart.

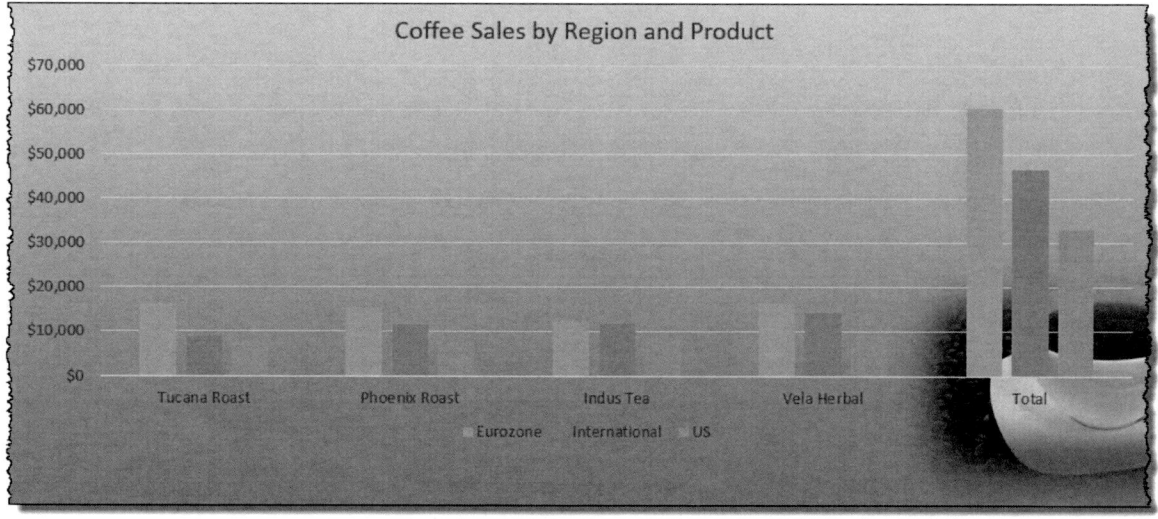

Changing the chart type

After you set the type of a chart, you can very easily change its layout and style.

 MOS PowerPoint Exam Objective(s): 3.2.3

1. Select the chart.
2. On the Chart Tools Design tab, click **Change Chart Type**.
   To display the Change Chart Type window.

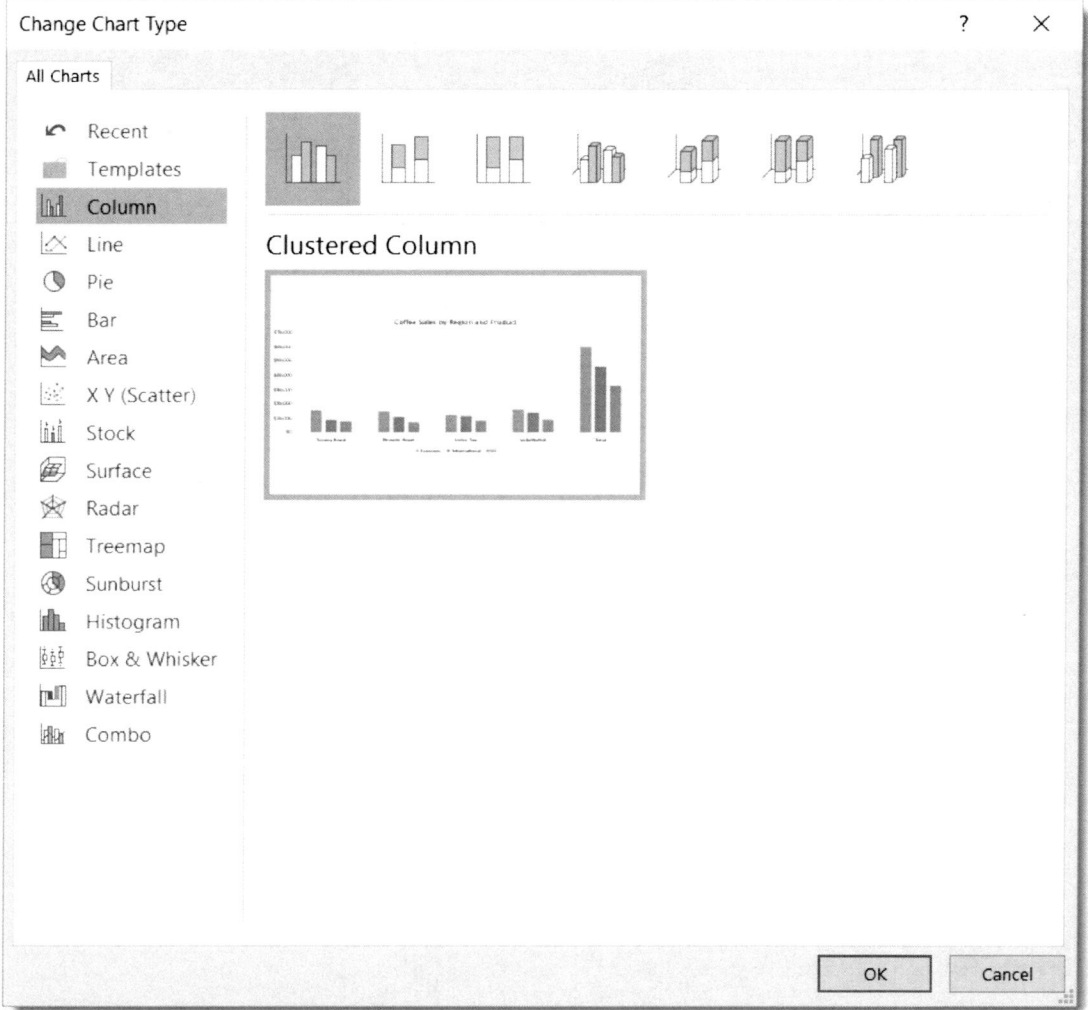

3. Select a type on the left, then a sub-type, and click **OK**.
   You can get a preview of what your data will look like in a particular chart type by hovering over it.

The chart type changes, and now the Chart Tools Design tab gives you many options for layout and style that are specific to the new type. Simply click **Quick Layout** and choose an option, or select a style to see what it will look like.

Chart elements

Charts come from the data you select when you make them. And each element of the chart represents either something in that data or something you can add to the chart and control.

 MOS PowerPoint Exam Objective(s): 3.2.4

Figure 1: Chart elements

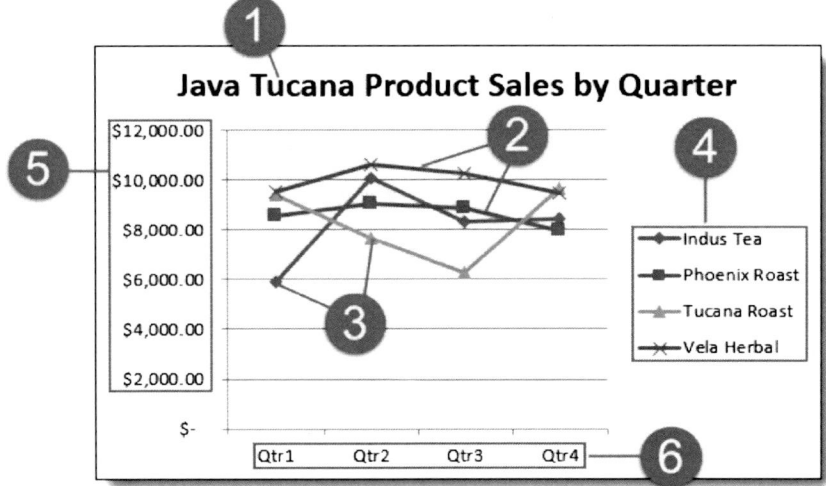

① The *chart title* is usually something you will add to the chart, rather than something that comes from the selected data.

② *Data series* are the series of values that show up in lines, columns, or other ways in your charts.

③ *Data points* represent the individual values within data series.

④ The *legend* identifies the data series in the chart.

⑤ The *value axis* shows the scale for what the chart is measuring. You can exercise enormous control over how the value axis appears and works. It is often plotted vertically, as in this example, but it does not have to be.

⑥ The *category axis* shows the categories of information within the data series. It is usually the horizontal axis, but not always.

Changing the chart layout

A chart's *layout* is the arrangement of its elements. PowerPoint makes it very easy to change the chart layout.

 MOS PowerPoint Exam Objective(s): 3.3.5

1. Select the chart.
2. On the Chart Tools Design tab, click **Quick Layout**.
    In the Chart Layouts group.
    The Quick Layout gallery opens.

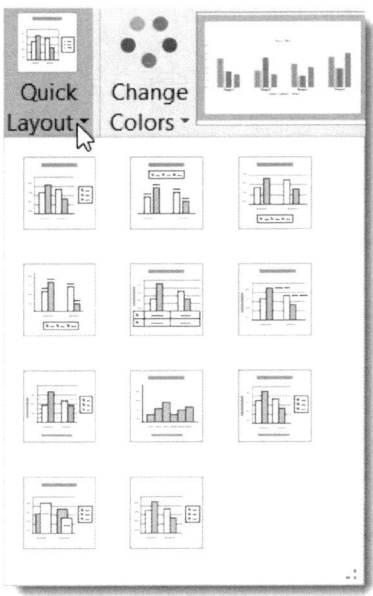

3. Hover over each layout in the gallery, and observe your chart.
   The chart previews each layout as you hover over it.
4. Select a layout from the gallery.
   Click to select it.
   The chart is updated with the new layout.
5. Click the **Chart Elements** button.
   To the right of the selected chart. To further refine your layout selection.

A checklist of Chart Elements options is display. Check an option to have it displayed with the chart; uncheck to hide it.

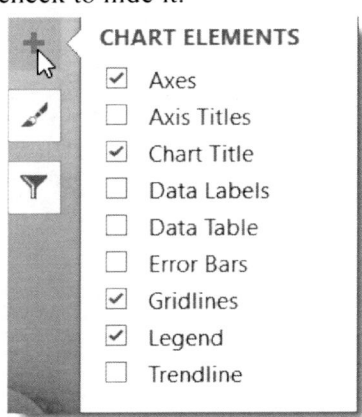

Applying chart styles

PowerPoint provides many different chart styles that you can apply to your charts. A chart *style* is a preset combination of color and other formatting options.

 MOS PowerPoint Exam Objective(s): 3.2.5

1. Select the chart.
2. On the Chart Tools Design tab, select a style preset from the Chart Styles gallery.
   You can display all the gallery options at once by clicking the gallery's **More** button.

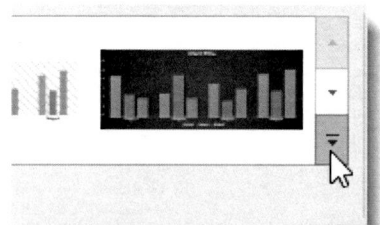

The full Chart Styles gallery displays all the styles appropriate to the current chart type.

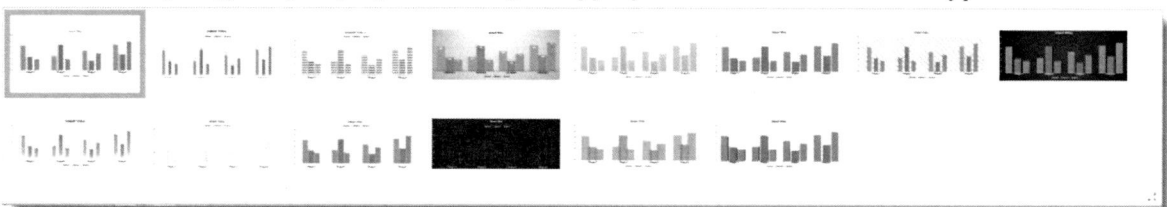

3. Select a style from the gallery.
   The new style is applied to the chart.

Inserting an Excel chart

PowerPoint makes it easy to import an Excel chart into PowerPoint.

 MOS PowerPoint Exam Objective(s): 3.2.2

1. Copy the Excel chart.
   Excel is running, and the workbook containing the chart is open. On the Home tab, in the Clipboard group, click the **Copy** button; or press **Ctrl+C**.

   The chart is copied to the Clipboard.
2. Switch to PowerPoint, and select the destination slide.
3. Paste the chart onto the slide.
   Click **Paste**, or press **Ctrl+V**.
   The Excel chart appears on the slide, and a Paste Options button appears at the lower-right corner of the chart.
4. Click the **Paste Options** button.

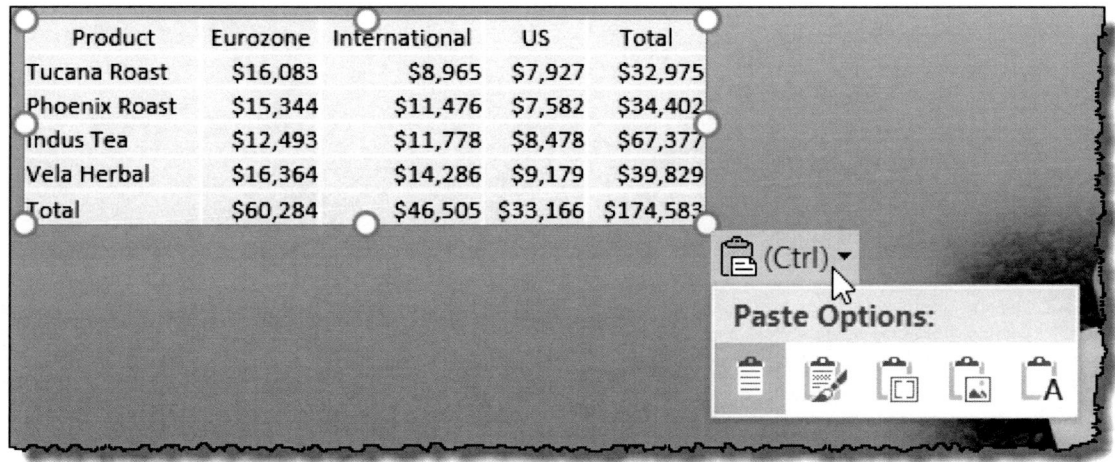

5. Select a Paste option.

Paste icon	Function
	Use Destination Styles pastes the raw data using the destination styles and becomes a PowerPoint table in the current presentation format. This is the default option.
	Keep Source Formatting retains source formatting to copy the data to PowerPoint.
	Embed uses the destination theme and links data to the workbook. Any subsequent data changes are made in Excel.
	Picture uses only the chart image, which can't be updated in either PowerPoint or Excel.
	Keep Text Only pastes the text as a single text box.

Editing chart data

Once you've created a chart with embedded or linked data, you can update the data whenever you like. When you do so, the chart automatically updates as well.

1. Select the chart containing data you wish to edit, then choose an Edit Data option.

    On the Chart Tools Design tab, in the Data group.

    - To edit the data in PowerPoint, click **Edit Data**. An Excel spreadsheet containing the data opens above the chart.

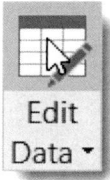

- To edit the data in Excel, click the lower part of the Edit Data button, and select **Edit Data in Excel**. The original workbook opens in Excel.

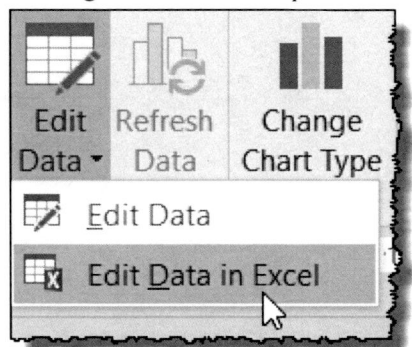

2. Edit the data, as necessary.

   To change the value in a spreadsheet cell, click the cell, type the new value, and press **Enter**. The chart itself updates automatically after you enter the new value.

    Note: If source values are changed in their Excel workbook, you can update the corresponding chart within PowerPoint by selecting the chart, then clicking **Refresh Data** on the Chart Tools Design tab.

Exercise: Working with charts

You'll create a chart, change its type and layout, apply styles, and import a chart directly from Excel.

Do This	How & Why
1. Open **JT Charts.pptx**, and save it as `My JT Charts.pptx`.	From the `Working with charts and tables` data folder.

2. Navigate to and observe slide 2.

It contains a table that's an embedded Excel spreadsheet.

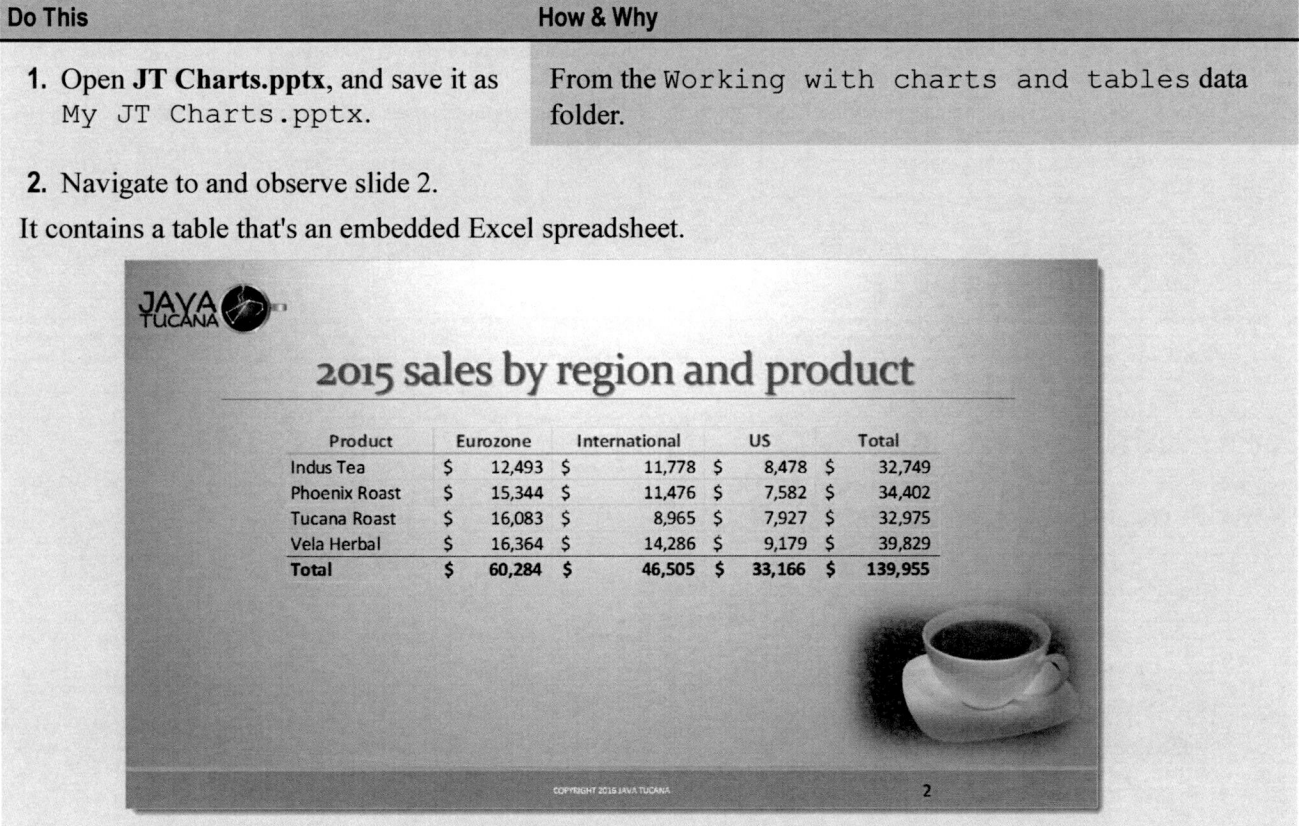

Do This	How & Why
3. Double-click the table.	

The PowerPoint window shudders, then mutates into a hybrid PowerPoint-Excel window, giving you access to many of Excel's powerful commands and options. In the Excel table, the data are already selected.

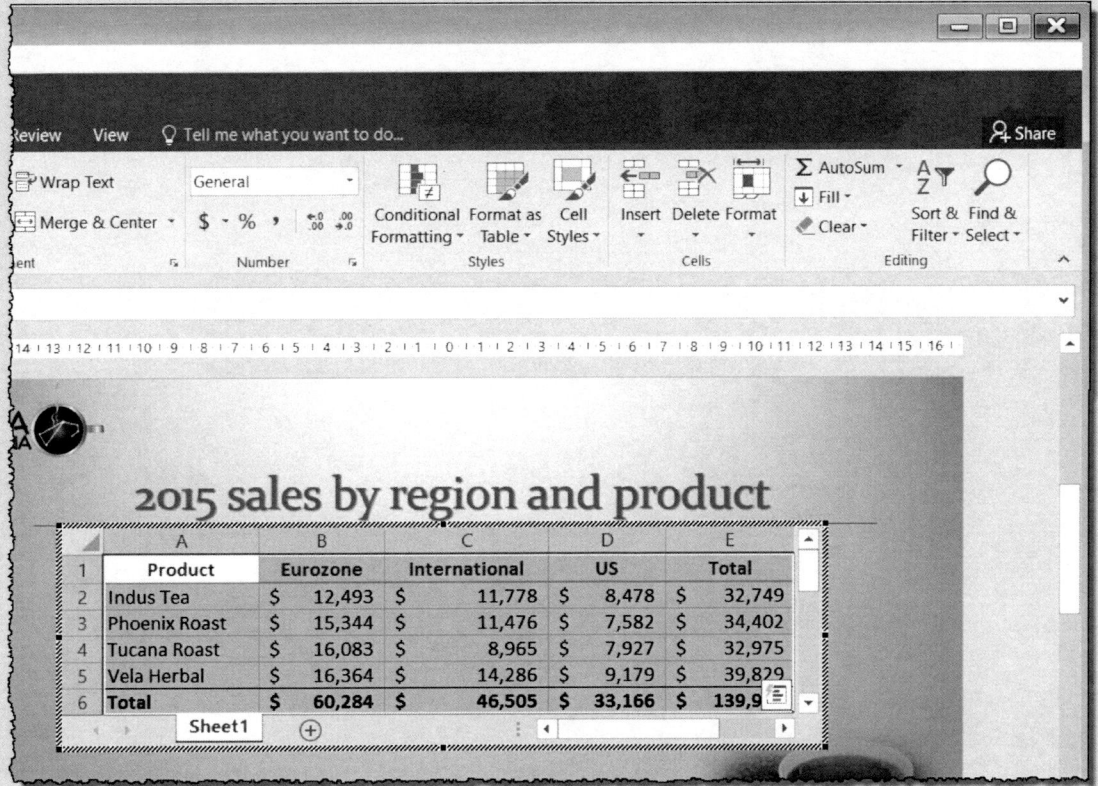

Do This	How & Why
4. Copy the selected table data to the Clipboard.	Click **Copy** or press **Ctrl+C**.
5. Press **Esc** *twice* to return to the PowerPoint presentation.	The first press deselects the data, the second closes the hybrid view and returns to PowerPoint.
6. Add a new slide to the presentation.	With slide 2 still selected, on the Home tab, click **New Slide**. A new, blank slide 3 appears.

Do This	How & Why

7. On slide 3, in the Content placeholder, click the **Insert Chart** icon.

The Insert Chart window opens.

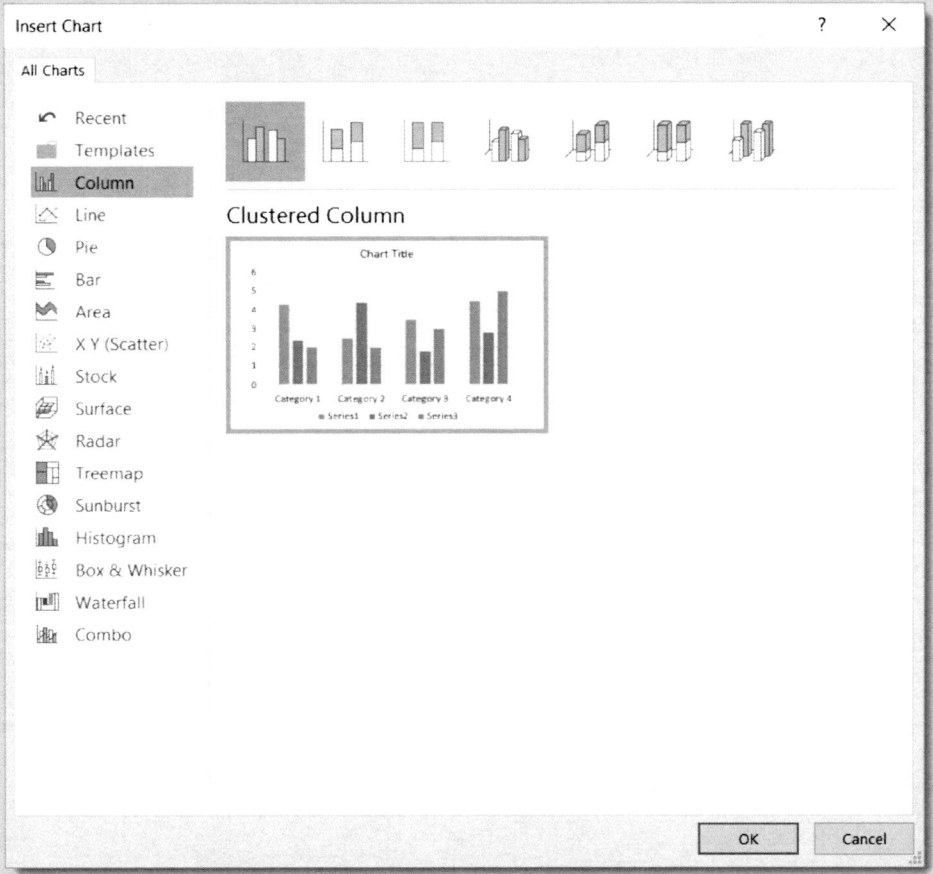

8. Navigate to view some of the available chart types and sub-types, and observe the results in the displayed preview.

9. Click the **Column** chart type, click **Clustered Column**, and click **OK**. | The leftmost Column sub-type. The chart appears on the slide with the Excel spreadsheet above it, but it contains only placeholder data.

Do This	How & Why
10. On the spreadsheet, click in cell A1, and paste the contents of the Clipboard.	Click **Paste** or press **Ctrl+V**. The spreadsheet is populated with the pasted data, and the chart updates to illustrate the data.

Note: If a warning message displays regarding pasting formulas, click **OK** to close it.

11. Close the spreadsheet.	Click the 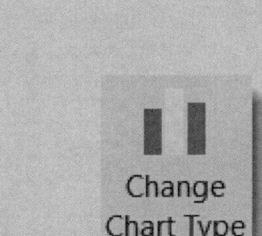 button.
12. If necessary, select the chart on slide 3.	
13. On the Chart Tools Design tab, click **Change Chart Type**.	The Change Chart Type window opens. This is essentially the Insert Chart window renamed.
14. Select a different chart type and sub-type, then click on **OK**.	The same data are illustrated in a different way. With some chart types, certain chart features aren't included by default, while others are.

Do This	How & Why
15. Click **Quick Layout**, and hover over the different layouts available. As you do so, observe the results on the chart.	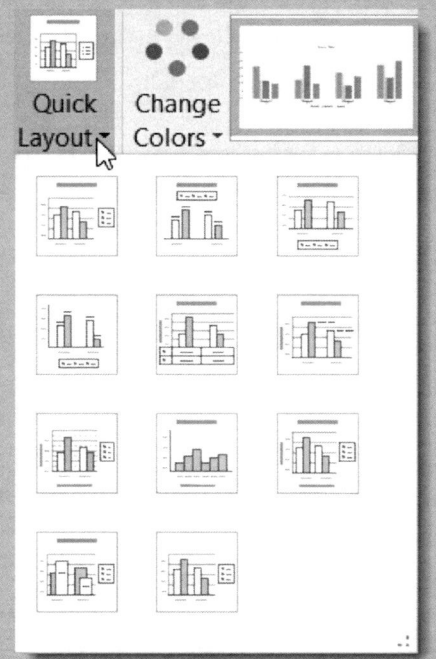
16. Select a layout from the gallery, and observe your results.	
17. Click the **Chart Elements** button.	
18. In the Chart Element options checklist, uncheck the **Chart Title** option, and include/exclude other elements.	Try to keep the important options checked. However, you can always go back and change what's displayed, should things not work out as you intend. You won't need the Chart Title option, as you'll use the Title area of the slide instead.
19. Apply a chart style of your choice.	Select a style from the Chart Styles gallery on the Chart Tools Design tab. You can use the More button to display all styles at once. 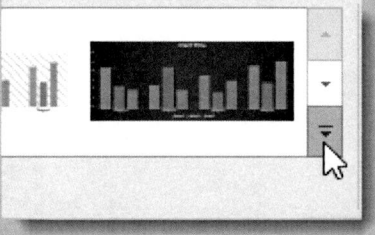
20. Edit the chart data. a) Click **Edit Data**.	 The Excel spreadsheet containing the data opens.

Do This	How & Why
b) Change a few values in the spreadsheet, and observe the chart as you do so.	The chart reflects each change in the data.
21. When you're finished changing data, close the spreadsheet and observe the completed chart.	
22. In the slide Title placeholder area, type `2015 sales by region and product`.	
23. Save and close the presentation.	

Assessment: Working with charts

1. True or false? When charting your data, once you've decided on a chart type, if you decide to change the type later, you can only pick one from the same type.

    - True
    - False

2. Which statement about chart elements is correct?

    - The chart title is usually something you add to the chart, rather than something that comes from the selected data.
    - A data series is the collection of chart data used in a single presentation.
    - A chart legend tells the story behind the data.
    - The category axis shows the types of data you can use for a specific type of chart.

3. True or false? When you edit the data in an embedded Excel spreadsheet in PowerPoint, the resulting chart is updated automatically.

    - True
    - False

Module B: Working with tables

In the same way that a picture can be worth a thousand words, displaying values can be a powerful way to deliver information. One great way to do this in a presentation is to display values in a table.

You will learn how to:

- Create and work with tables in your presentation

About tables

A table is a series of rows and columns of data. A *cell* is the intersection of a row and column. Each cell in a table contains a singular data item, consisting of either text, numbers (quantities, currency amounts, dates, and measurements), or formulas to perform calculations.

Expense	Year1	Year2	Year3	Year4	Year5
Rent	24000	24000	24000	25200	25200
Remodeling	12000	2000	2000	2000	2000
Legal	5000	500	500	500	500
Equipment	9000	1000	2000	2000	1000
Supplies	12000	13200	0	16000	17600
Advertising	4000	1000	1200	1400	1600
Payroll	60000	65000	80000	90000	100000
Miscellaneous	10000	11000	12000	13000	14000
Totals:	$136,000	$117,700	$135,200	$150,100	$161,900

1 *Text*, which you use to label information. Here, the text identifies what is in the rows (categories of expenses) and the columns (yearly figures).

2 *Numbers*, which can be of various kinds (quantities, currency amounts, dates, and measurements). Here, the numbers represent dollar amounts in the budget.

The other important thing you can enter in tables is formulas. The totals in this figure are calculated using formulas. Of course, the types of tables you might use in PowerPoint can be much less or much more complicated.

Creating tables

In PowerPoint, there are a few different ways to create a table. One way is to use the Insert Table icon in a Content placeholder. Another way is to use the Table button on the Insert tab, from which you can use a grid to specify your table's dimensions, draw a table using Draw Table, or create an Excel spreadsheet. However, the simplest and most direct of these methods is to use the Insert Table icon.

Inserting a table

To use the Insert Table icon in a Content placeholder, it's easiest to do so on a fresh slide.

 MOS PowerPoint Exam Objective(s): 3.1.1, 3.1.2

1. On a new slide, click the **Insert Table** icon.
   In the Content placeholder.

   The Insert Table window opens. Here, you set the number of columns and rows you want in your table.

   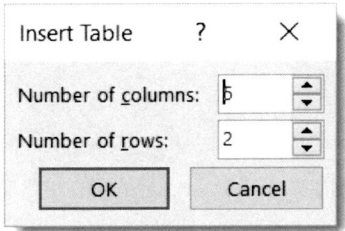

2. Specify the number of columns and rows in their respective boxes.
   You can select the value in each box, and type a value directly, or you can use the ▲ (increment) and ▼ (decrement) buttons to change the values. Be sure to account for a header row (for column headings).

3. Click **OK**.
   The table is inserted onto the slide. Notice that the top row is shaded. PowerPoint assumes the top row of the table will contain column headings and thus sets it off from the rest of the table.

   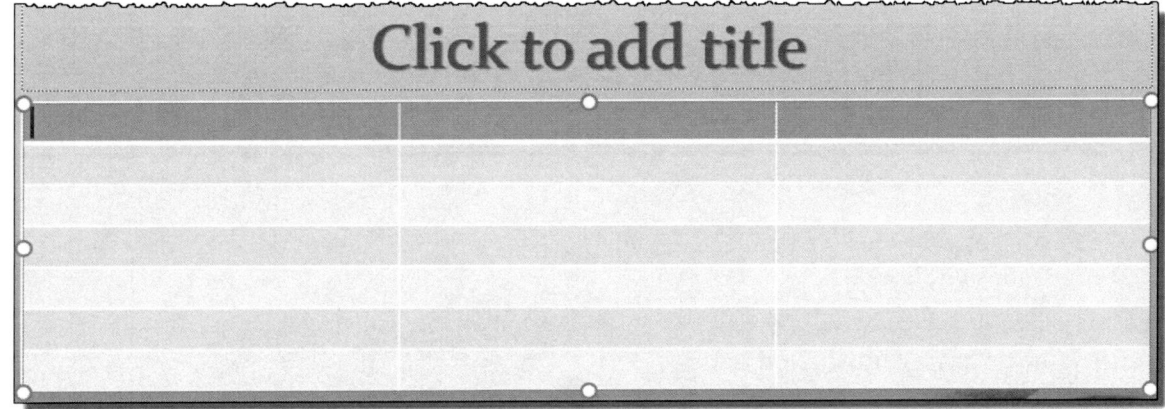

    Note: Even after you've created a table, you might need to add/delete rows and/or columns to your table. To do so, use the tools in the Rows & Columns group on the Table Tools Layout tab.

   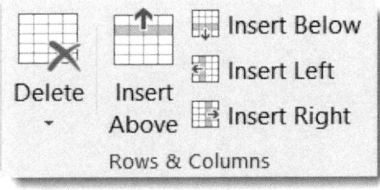

Entering data

Entering and editing data is most of what you do in a table. There are many kinds of data: numbers, text, dates, and formulas, for example. But the basics of entering data are always the same.

1. Select the cell where you want to enter data.
2. Type the data you want to enter.
3. Press **Enter**.

    If you're entering data in a PowerPoint table using an Excel spreadsheet and the formula bar is visible, you can press **Enter** or click the Enter box (the check mark) on the formula bar.

Applying styles

 MOS PowerPoint Exam Objective(s): 3.1.3

PowerPoint's Table Tools Design tab offers many options for applying styles and formatting to your tables. And don't forget, you can also use the many formatting options on the Home tab. For more structural changes to your tables, there's the Table Tools Layout tab.

You can apply style and formatting options to a table either before or after you've entered the table data. However, whenever possible, it makes sense to have at least some of your data in place before you experiment with styles and formats. With the data in place, it's often much easier to get a sense of how particular data should be emphasized, for example.

When considering style and formatting options, it's a good idea first to apply a preset style from the Table Styles gallery to your table, and then to make any additional "minor" changes using some of those other style and formatting tools.

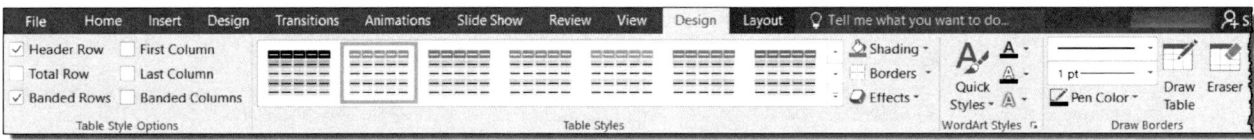

1. Select the table.

    When you select or click in a table, the Table Tools Design and Layout tabs become available, and the Design tab is displayed.

2. Display the full Tables Styles gallery, and observe the available gallery styles.

    Click the gallery's **More** button.

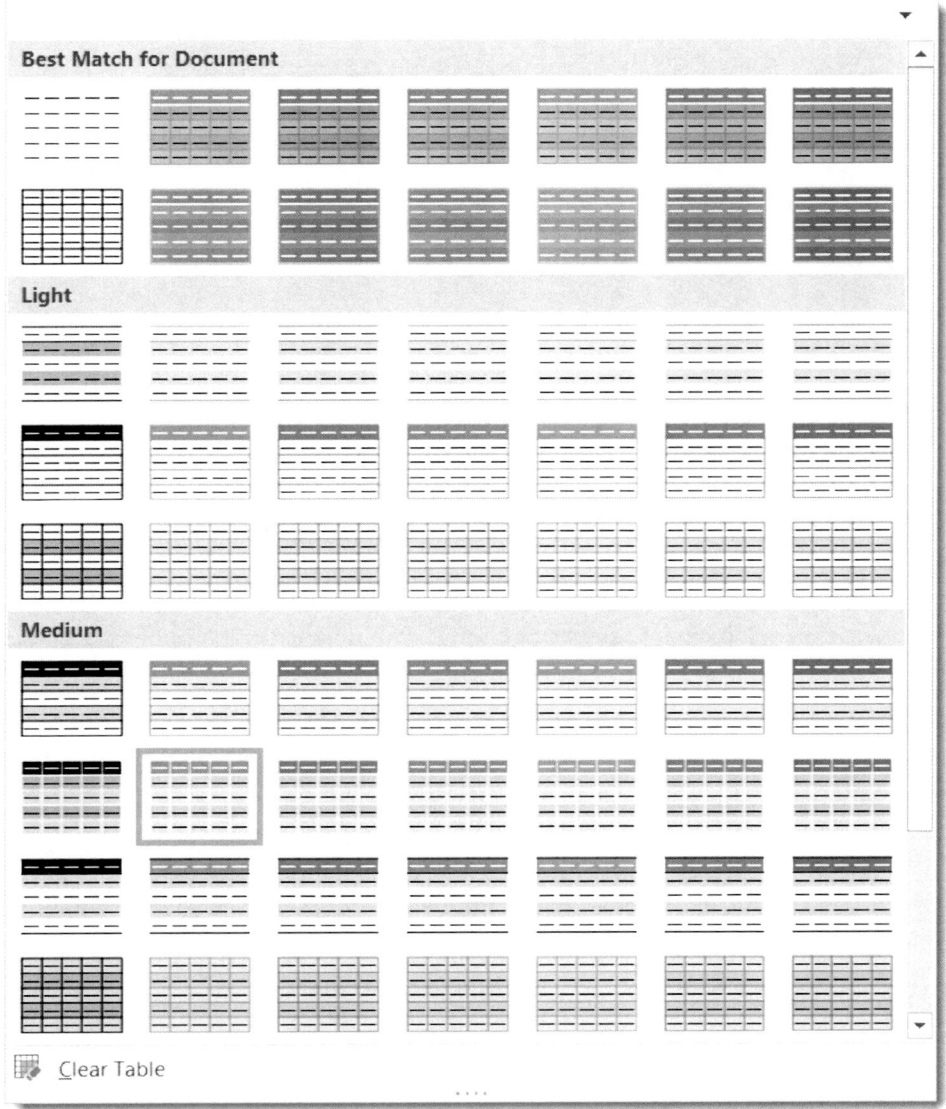

3. Hover over the different styles available, and notice the effect on your table.
4. Click a style from the gallery.
   To select it.

   The table is updated to the new style.
5. Apply any additional style or formatting elements you like.
   Use the tools in the Table Style Options group, the Draw Borders group, or any others.

The Table Style Options group

The Table Style Options Group, located on the Table Tools Design tab, contains important style options for working with tables. Check an option to turn it on; uncheck it to turn it off.

- *Header Row*: Applies a special format to the first row of a table, which normally contains column headings.
- *Total Row*: Applies a special format to the last row of a table, which often contains column totals.
- *Banded Rows*: Applies shading effects to alternating rows, making larger tables easier to scan.
- *First Column*: Applies a special format to the first column, which normally contains row headings.
- *Last Column*: Applies a special format to the last column, which sometimes contains row totals or subtotals.
- *Banded Columns*: Applies shading effects to alternating columns, making larger tables easier to scan.

Importing tables

You can import tables from other applications to use in your PowerPoint presentations. It's important to know that a table, a chart, a PDF document, or any such product of an external application is referred to as an *object* in PowerPoint. As always, when adding an object to a presentation, it's always good to start with a new slide, or at least one with an empty Content placeholder.

Once you've imported your table object, you can apply additional styles and formatting options using the tools on the Drawing Tools Format tab.

 MOS PowerPoint Exam Objective(s): 3.1.4

1. Select the destination slide for the table.
2. Click **Object**.
    In the Insert tab's Text group.

    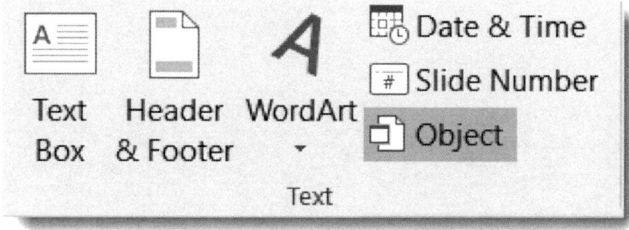

    The Insert Object window opens.
3. Select **Create from file**.
    The object that you create using this option embeds the external object in PowerPoint and links it to its source application.

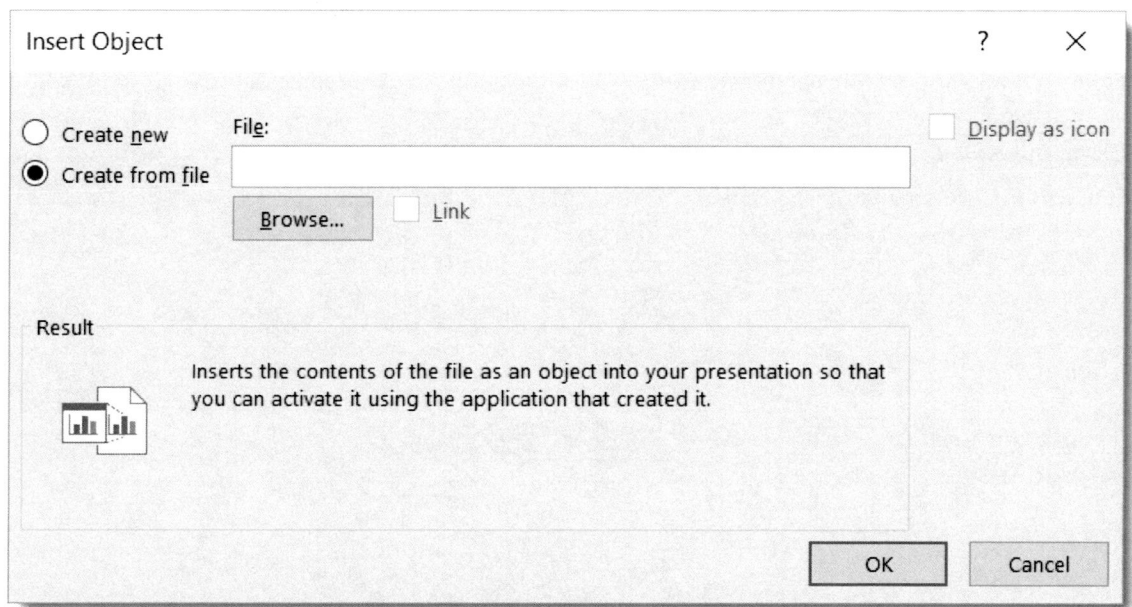

4. Click **Browse**, navigate to the source file, and click **Insert**.

   Checking the **Link** option allows you to maintain an active connection to the original Excel data: updating the original updates its linked slide object. However, because using this option results in only a picture of the data being pasted onto the slide, you can't apply many of PowerPoint's formatting and effects options to it. Also, you can only link to files saved in Excel 2013 or later.

   The imported table object is inserted onto the slide.

   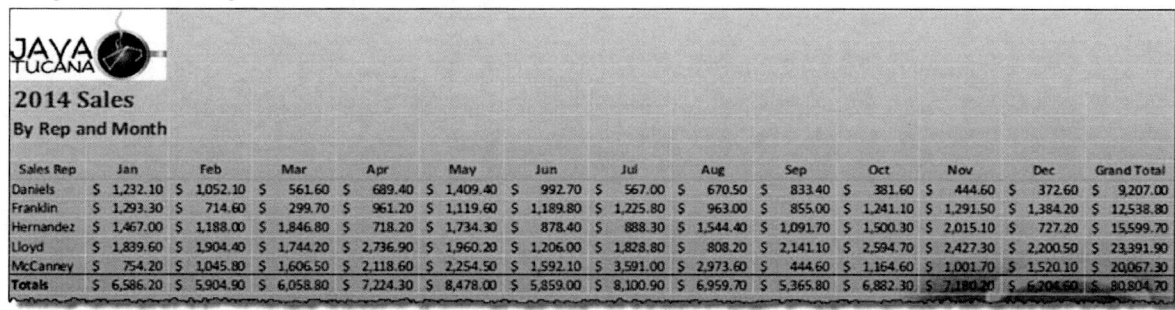

5. Double-click the imported object.

   The object opens in its source application for further editing, and so on.

6. When you're done editing the object in its source application, save your changes.

   The object is automatically updated in PowerPoint.

Exercise: Working with tables

You'll create a table, apply styles and formatting, and import an Excel spreadsheet as a table object.

Do This	How & Why
1. Open **JT Tables.pptx**, and save it as `My JT Tables.pptx`.	From the `Working with charts and tables` data folder.
2. Insert a table on slide 2.	This slide is blank.
a) Select slide 2.	
b) On the new slide, click the **Insert Table** icon.	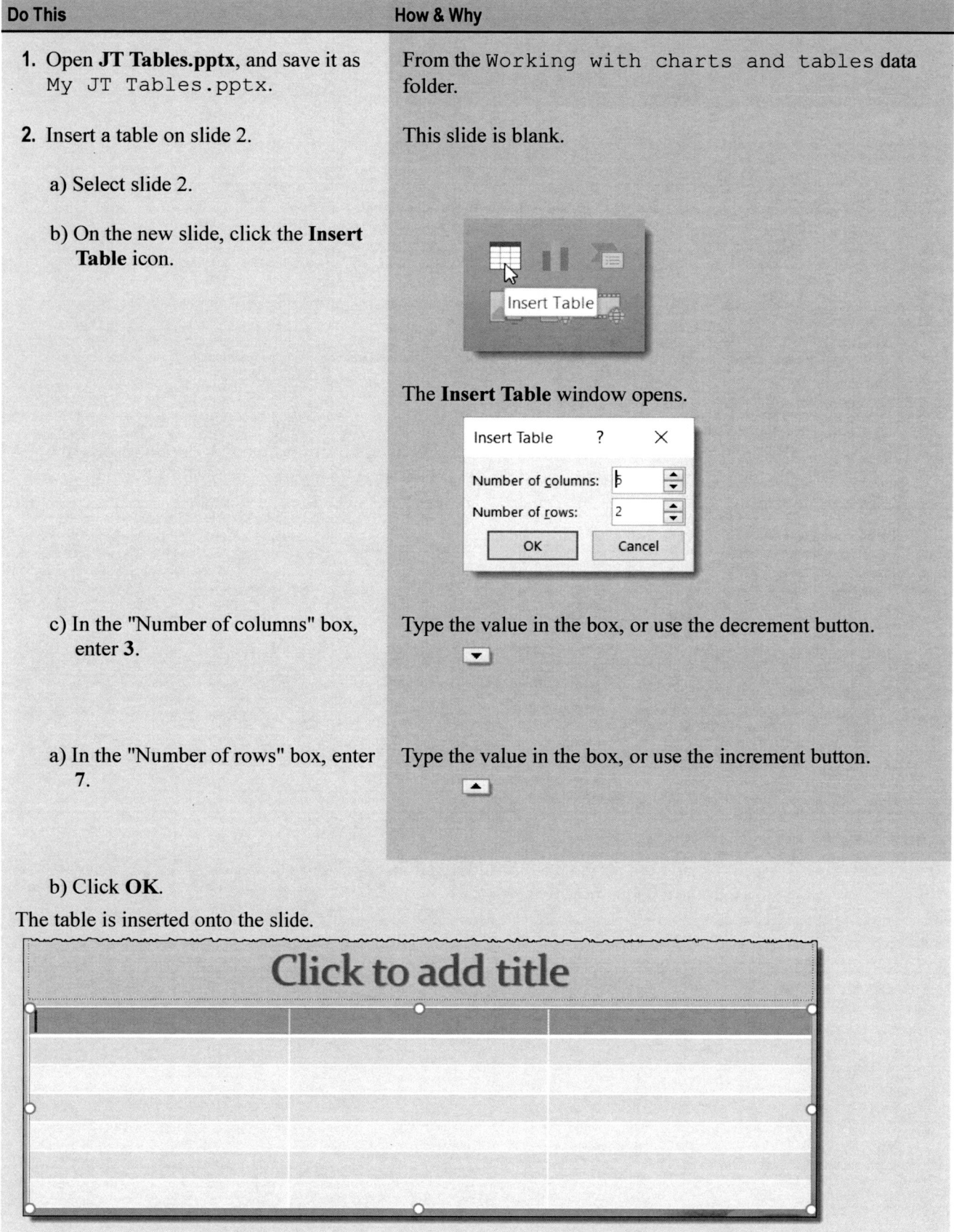 The **Insert Table** window opens.
c) In the "Number of columns" box, enter **3**.	Type the value in the box, or use the decrement button.
a) In the "Number of rows" box, enter **7**.	Type the value in the box, or use the increment button.

b) Click **OK**.

The table is inserted onto the slide.

Do This	How & Why

3. Enter the table data shown in the figure below.

Click in each cell and type the data. You can also use the **Tab** key to move to the next cell, and **Shift+Tab** to move to the previous cell.

Rank	Country	Millions of tons
1	Brazil	3.0
2	Vietnam	1.5
3	Indonesia	0.7
4	Colombia	0.7
5	India	0.3
	World	8.9

4. Open the Table Styles gallery, and hover over the various presets until you arrive at one you like. Then select it to apply the style.

On the Table Tools Design tab. Use the gallery's More button to view the entire gallery.

5. Make sure the **Header Row**, **Total Row**, **Banded Rows**, and **First Column** options are checked.

In the Table Style Options group.

6. Apply any additional style elements or formatting that you wish.

You can use tools from the Table Tools Design and Layout tabs, as well as the Home tab.

7. Resize the columns to best fit the data by dragging the column borders, then resize that table to nicely fit the slide.

8. In the slide's Title placeholder, type `The Top Five Green Coffee Producers`.

Do This	How & Why

9. Deselect the table, and observe your results.

10. Insert a new slide 3.

11. Insert the Excel table object **Sales - Rep and product.xlsx**.

   a) Click **Object**.

On the Insert tab.

The Insert Object window opens.

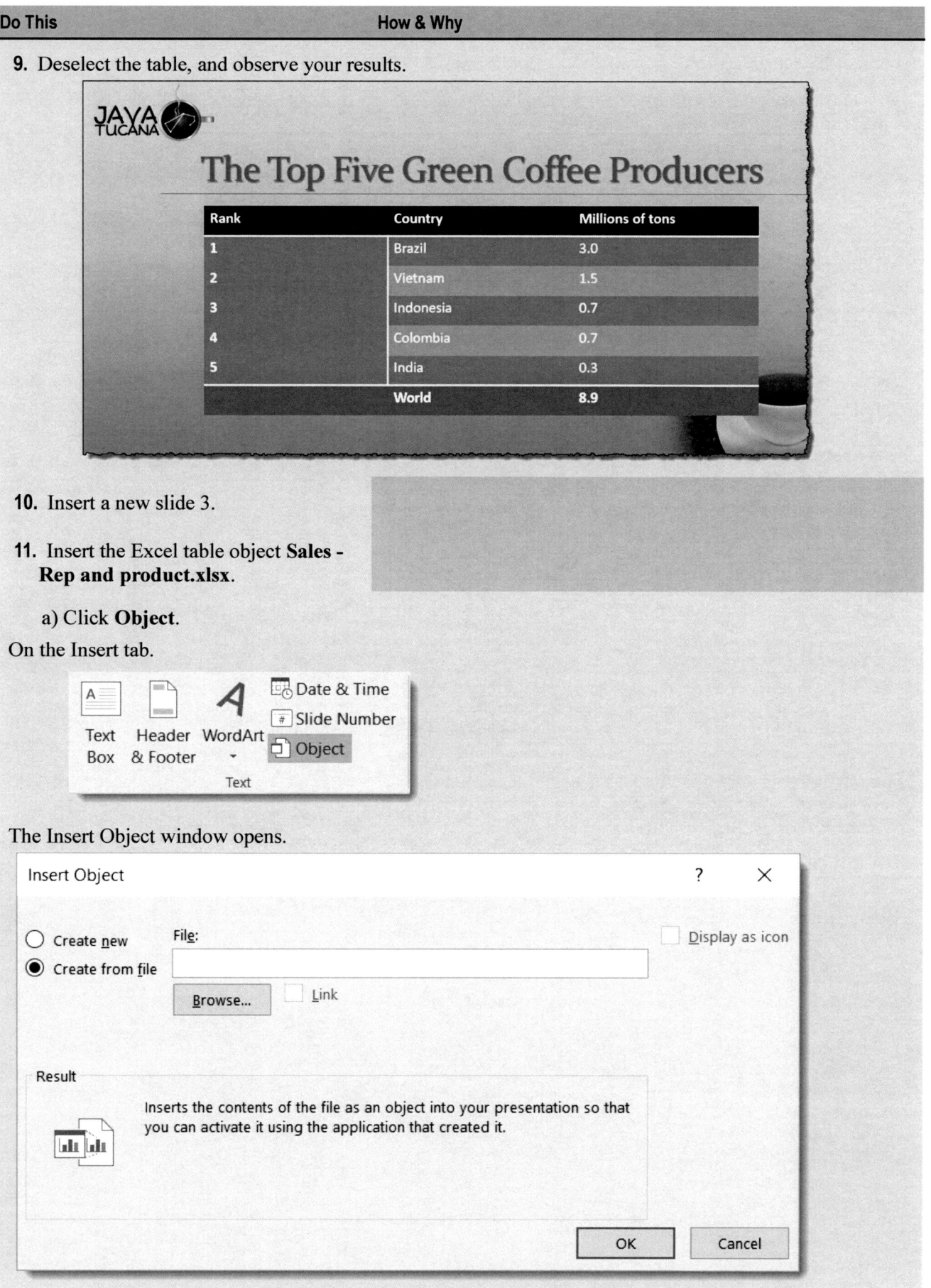

Do This	How & Why
b) Click Browse, navigate to the data folder, and select **Sales - Rep and product.xlsx**.	
c) Click **OK**.	

The Excel table object is inserted onto the slide.

12. Resize the table to fit the slide. Apply any formatting and style elements that you'd like.

13. Save and close the presentation.

Assessment: Working with tables

1. Which of these answers describes an easy way to create a table in PowerPoint?

    - Use the Table placeholder in the Content field.
    - Use the Table Creation tool on the Layout tab.
    - Use the Insert Table icon in the Content placeholder.
    - Use the Table tool in the Object group.

2. True or false? When formatting a table, it's a good idea to do all the minor formatting first, then select a style preset to apply, then enter the data last.

    - True
    - False

3. Which of these statements about importing Excel tables into PowerPoint is true?

    - Once imported, any additional formatting that you apply to a table must be done in Excel.
    - Once imported, if you need to edit table data, that must be done in Excel.
    - Once imported, the table is actually controlled by PowerPoint.
    - Once imported, the table becomes a Picture and is no longer an independent object.

Summary: Working with charts and tables

You should now know how to:

- Add a chart to a presentation; change its type, size, elements, and layout; apply a style to it; insert an Excel chart; and edit chart data
- Design and insert a table appropriate to the data it will contain, enter table data, apply a style and formatting, and import an Excel table

Synthesis: Working with charts and tables

In this synthesis, you'll add a chart to a presentation, modify its structure, apply styles and formatting, and edit the underlying data. Then you'll create a table using Excel data, resize it, and apply formatting.

1. Open **JT Charts-Tables Assessment.pptx**, and save it as `My JT Charts-Tables Assessment.pptx`.
    From this chapter's data folder.
2. On slide 2, use the Insert Chart icon to select an appropriate chart type, and insert the chart.
3. Open **Chart Data.xlsx**.
4. Select only the table data, including row and column headings, then copy the data.
5. Paste the data into the PowerPoint table on slide 2, using the default Paste option.
6. Close the spreadsheet to see only the chart.
7. Add the title `2015 Sales by Product and Region` to either the slide itself or the chart.
8. Change the chart type, add any chart elements you think should be displayed, and remove any that are unnecessary.
9. Apply a style to the chart, and add any additional formatting you wish.
10. Edit the chart data, and make sure the chart updates to reflect the changes.
11. On slide 3, import the Excel file **Excel Table - Assessment.xlsx** as a table object.
12. Resize the table, as necessary, and apply any formatting you wish, making sure the data are clearly visible on the slide.
13. Save and close the presentation.

Chapter 6: Customization

You will learn how to:

- Apply slide transitions
- Work with additional text features
- Work with printing options
- Create custom slide shows

Module A: Slide transitions

A slide show is by definition relatively static. At its most basic, there's no actual movement until you change slides. However, there are ways to make your presentations far more dynamic. One of these is by applying transitions to the slides in your presentations.

You will learn how to:

- Apply transition effects to all the slides in your presentation
- Apply transition effects to one or more selected slides

About slide transitions

 MOS PowerPoint Exam Objective(s): 4.1.2

PowerPoint provides many options for governing *how* your presentation flows from slide to slide, or *slide transitions*. The default way for a slide show to progress is to manually click through the presentation, switching abruptly to the next slide with each click. However, transitions allow you to set the presentation to move through the slides automatically. Perhaps more importantly, you can set the transition effect for individual slides, which is a powerful way to customize your presentation.

The Transitions tab on the ribbon provides the tools you need to create and modify the presentation of your slide show. It's divided into three main groups.

- *Transition to This Slide*: Here, you can select an effect type to transition to the current slide. You can then use Effect Options to modify the effect further.
- *Timing*: Controls the timing of the slide transition effect, as well as how the effect is triggered. Here, you can also select a sound effect to accompany the transition.
- *Preview*: Allows you to preview the effect you've selected for the transition to the current slide.

Applying the same transition to all slides

To apply a transition to all slides in a presentation, it's easiest to do so in Normal view or Slide Sorter view.

 MOS PowerPoint Exam Objective(s): 4.1.1, 4.1.2

1. Select a slide.
   You can select any number of slides, but there's no need to do so.
2. On the Transitions tab, select a transition.

   From the Transition to This Slide gallery. To display the entire gallery, click its More button ( ).

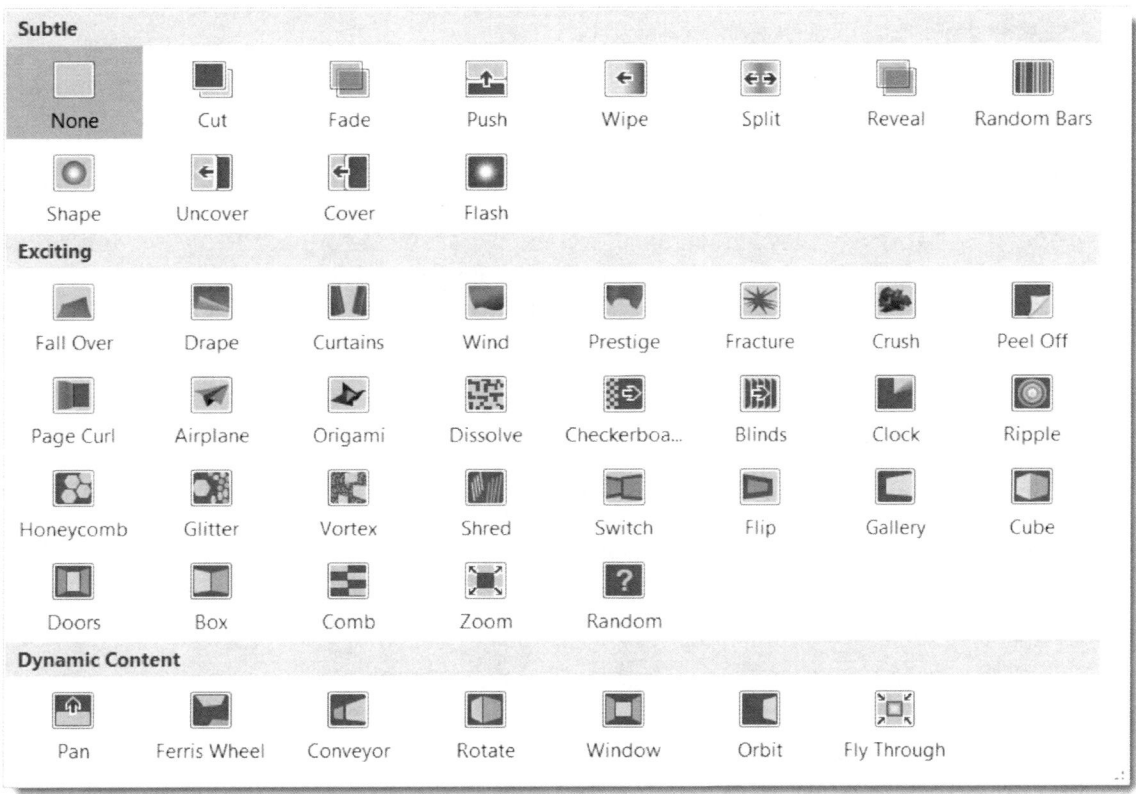

3. Select a transition preset, and observe the selected slide(s).

   The transition is applied, and the effect is previewed on the slide(s). To replay the effect, click the **Play Animations** icon in the Slide pane (or in Slide Sorter view). This icon appears next to a slide to which a transition (and/or animation) is applied, thus allowing you to replay the effect at any time.

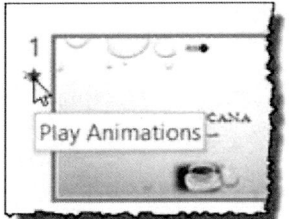

4. Apply an effect option.

   a) Click **Effect Options**.

   The effect options are displayed. They serve as a subset of the transition preset selected. Thus, the number and types of options vary with each transition preset selected.

   b) Select an effect option.

   Each time you select a new transition feature, the effect is previewed on the selected slide(s).

5. Set any timing options.

   In the Timing group.

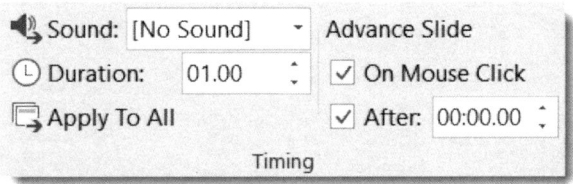

- *Sound*: Select a sound to play at the transition. The list of sounds provided is quite long, but should you wish to use your own custom sound, choose Other Sound, which lets you navigate to and load the sound file of your choice to apply to the transition.
- *Duration*: Set the length of time in seconds that the transition effect takes to complete.
- *Apply To All*: Applies all current transition effects to all slides in the presentation. For this reason, it's best to use this option after you've fine-tuned the transition.
- The Advance Slide area contains two options: *On Mouse Click* advances to the next slide only when you click. Set a value in the *After* box to have the slide automatically advance after that time elapses. Clicking both options creates a "whichever-comes-first" situation, so that you can still advance by clicking, but if you haven't clicked by the time the After value has elapsed, the transition will occur.

6. Click **Apply To All**.

   The transition effects are applied to all slides in the presentation.

    Note: It's important to remember that after you've applied transition effects to slides, if you decide to add or remove any options and you wish to apply those changes to all (or multiple) slides, click **Apply To All** (or select multiple slides before making the changes).

Applying transitions to individual slides

Apply transition effects to selected slides in Normal view or Slide Sorter view. If you're selecting many slides, however, Slide Sorter view is probably the better choice.

 MOS PowerPoint Exam Objective(s): 4.1.2

1. Open Slide Sorter view.

   On the taskbar, click 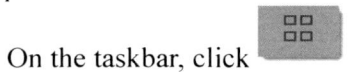 .

2. Select a transition preset from the gallery.

   On the Transitions tab, in the Transition to This Slide group.

3. Apply any additional transition effects.

4. Click the **Preview** tool.

   This is another way to preview the transition. If you've applied the transition to multiple slides, it previews all of them.

Exercise: Setting slide transitions

You'll apply slide transitions in a presentation.

Do This	How & Why
1. Open **JT Transitions.pptx**, and save it as `My JT Transitions.pptx`.	From the `Customization` data folder.
2. Navigate the presentation.	It consists of a few sections of information about Java Tucana.
3. Apply transition effects to slides 1–3, 6, and 18, all of which begin sections of the presentation.	
a) Switch to Slide Sorter view.	Click [icon].
b) Select slides 1, 2, 3, 6, and 18.	Press and hold **Ctrl** to make multiple selections.
c) On the Transitions tab, display all the Transition to This Slide gallery presets.	Click [icon]. The gallery opens.
d) Try clicking various presets from each category, and observe their effects as they're applied sequentially through the selected slides.	To replay the effect for a single slide, click its **Play Animation** icon. To replay it for all slides in sequence, click **Preview**.
e) With the slides still selected, use the **Effects Options** tool to fine-tune the transition.	Select an effect option from the list displayed for your transition preset.

PowerPoint 2016 Level 1

Do This	How & Why
4. Set any Timing group options you'd like to use.	*Except* for Apply to All. You'll use this option shortly.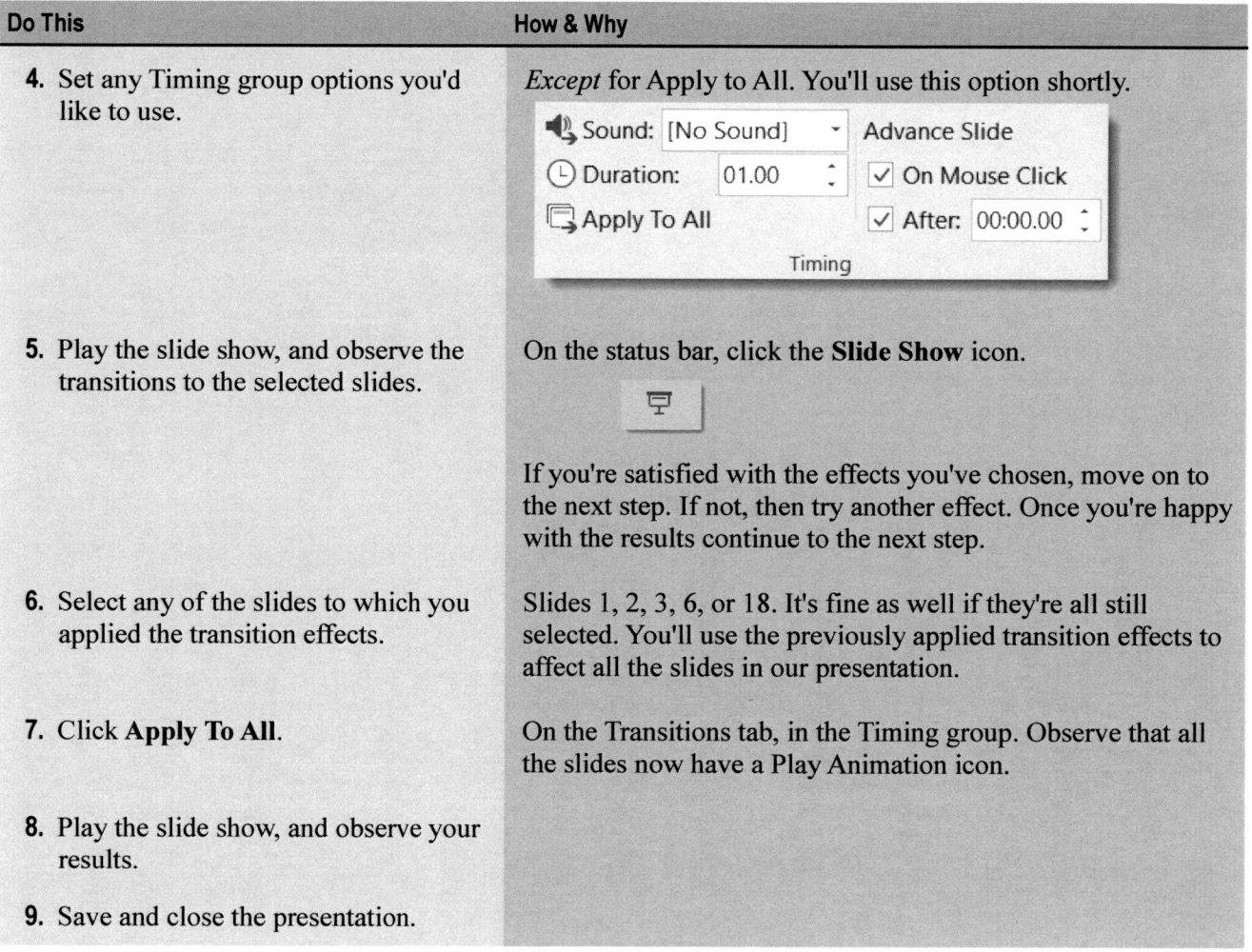
5. Play the slide show, and observe the transitions to the selected slides.	On the status bar, click the **Slide Show** icon. If you're satisfied with the effects you've chosen, move on to the next step. If not, then try another effect. Once you're happy with the results continue to the next step.
6. Select any of the slides to which you applied the transition effects.	Slides 1, 2, 3, 6, or 18. It's fine as well if they're all still selected. You'll use the previously applied transition effects to affect all the slides in our presentation.
7. Click **Apply To All**.	On the Transitions tab, in the Timing group. Observe that all the slides now have a Play Animation icon.
8. Play the slide show, and observe your results.	
9. Save and close the presentation.	

Assessment: Applying transitions between slides

1. True or false? To apply transition effects to all slides in a presentation, there's no need to select all the slides before doing so.

    - True
    - False

2. Which statement about transition effects is *not* true?

    - Transition effects can be previewed by clicking Preview or Play Animation.
    - The Duration option controls the length of time the affected slide is displayed.
    - Available Effect Options are context-sensitive.
    - You can use sounds from your own audio files to signal slide transitions.

3. True or false? In the Timing group, under Advance Slide, you can either check On Mouse Click, or check After and specify a time, but not both.

    - True
    - False

Module B: Additional text options

You can use text from other kinds of documents, created in many different kinds of applications. And there are different ways to add this text to your PowerPoint presentation, depending on the source, the type of file, the contents, and so on.

You will know how to:

- Import and outline from a Word document
- Import a PDF file
- Create WordArt from text

Text from other sources

You can incorporate text from many different kinds of sources into your PowerPoint presentations. Of course, you can always create the text within PowerPoint itself; however, its strength is as a presentation tool, not as a word processor. For this reason alone, a great benefit of using text from other sources is that quite often the source text is already formatted. And why "reinvent the wheel" when you can use the text as is?

A great many types of text documents are supported in PowerPoint. These can range from simple text (.txt) files created in programs such as Notepad or WordPad, to rich-text files (.rtf) or Microsoft Word (.doc, .docx) files. Of course, for small amounts of text from other sources, you often have the option of simply copying source text and pasting it onto a slide. However, certain applications don't allow you to do this very easily or very well. For larger amounts of text, importing the file—or in some case, text from it—can produce much more effective results.

Besides being able to preserve original source text formats, you do, of course, have the option of further customizing the look of text in PowerPoint. And you can do so whether you import the text or create it in PowerPoint. One such way of manipulating text to create more visual interest is to format it as WordArt.

A slide presentation lends itself to bits of information that are easily digested. Thus, when slides contain text, it's best to use elements such as titles, subtitles, bulleted or numbered lists, and so on, allowing them to be scanned fairly quickly. Put another way, slide text is best presented in something resembling outline form. For this reason, one very helpful feature is being able to import text documents (for example, Word documents or text files) in outline form, which can save you the trouble of having to create an outline from scratch in a presentation.

Importing a Word document outline

MOS PowerPoint Exam Objective(s): 1.1.3

You can import most text documents into PowerPoint. Particularly if the text has been formatted in the source application, resulting in titles, subtitles, and other kinds of headings, PowerPoint can retrieve this text in the form of an outline. When you import it, the outline items are placed on slides, saving you the time of having to create these slides from scratch.

The types of text formats that can be imported are many, and Word documents are, of course, among them. You can import these outlines into a new or existing presentation. The outline slides are added after the slide that was displayed before the import.

1. Click **New Slide > Slides from Outline**.
    Use the lower part of the New Slide tool.

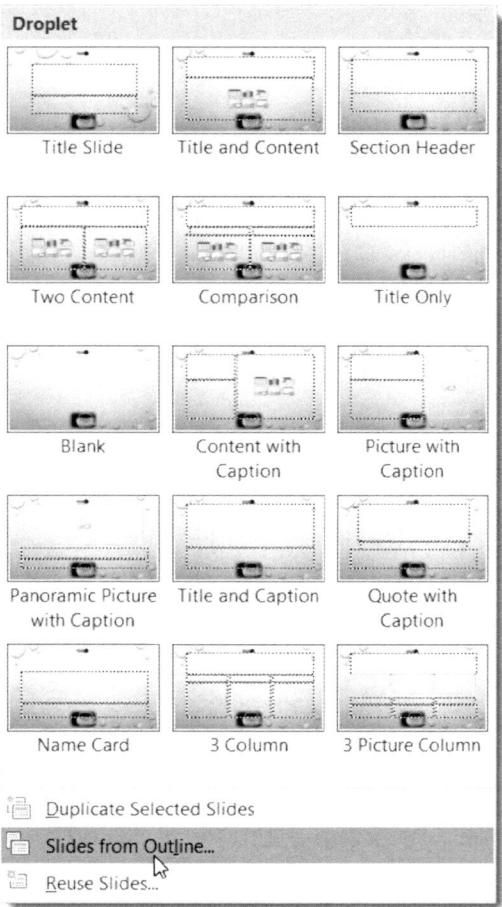

The Insert Outline window opens.

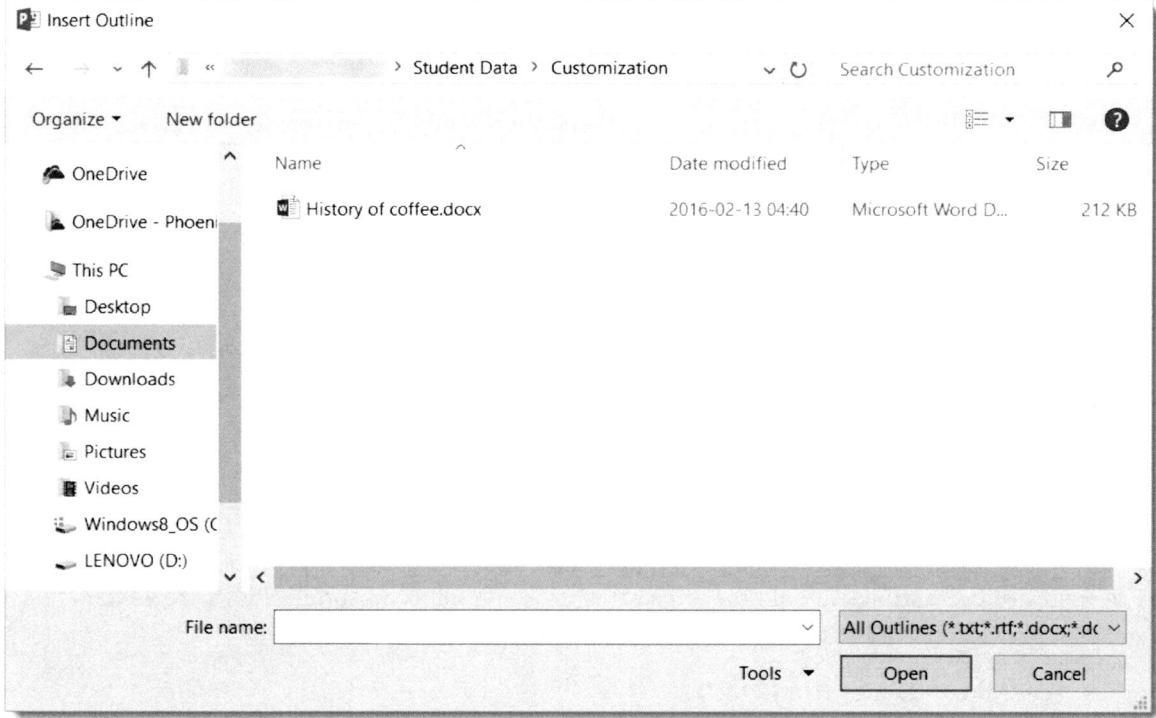

2. Navigate to the desired file, and click **Open**.

An outline of the file's text appears on new slides in the presentation.

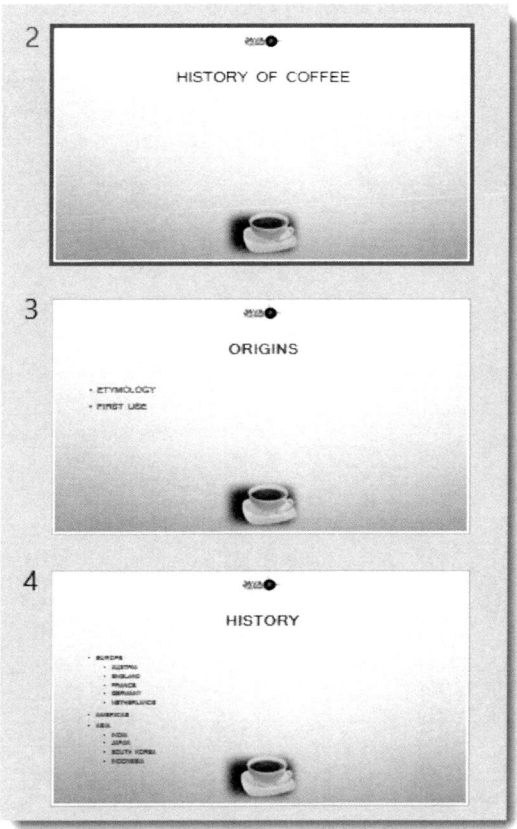

Importing a PDF file

You can import a PDF (portable document format) file into your PowerPoint presentation. Once you have imported a PDF file as an object, you can assign an *action* to it.

1. Import the PDF as an object.

   a) Select the destination slide, and click **Object**.

   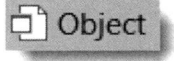

   b) In the Insert Object window, click **Create from file**, and click **Browse**.

   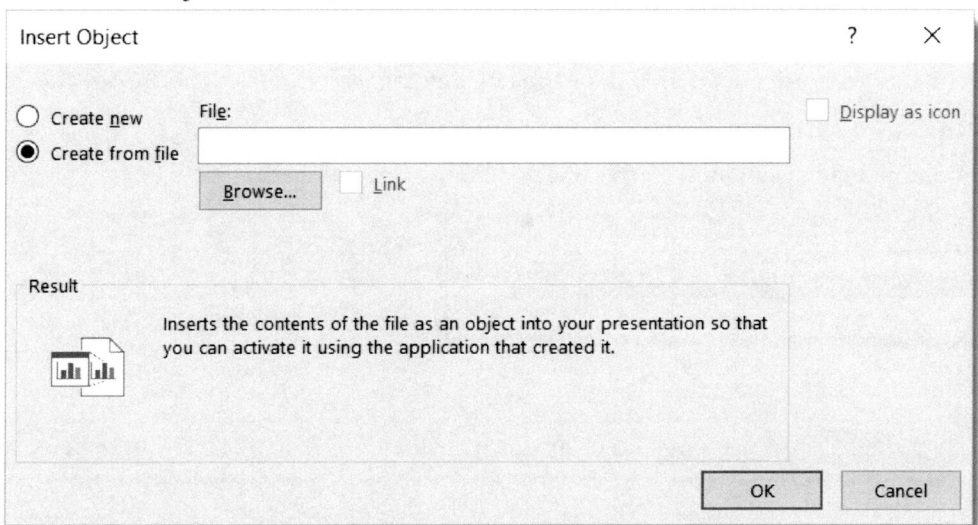

c) Navigate to and select the file, and click **Open**.

d) To display the file as a PDF icon on the slide, click **Display as icon**.
Otherwise, the PDF is displayed as a standard object in a frame with handles, with its opening text visible.

2. Select the object or icon, and click **Action**.
To attach an action to the PDF file object or icon. On the Insert tab, in the Links group.

The Action Settings window opens.

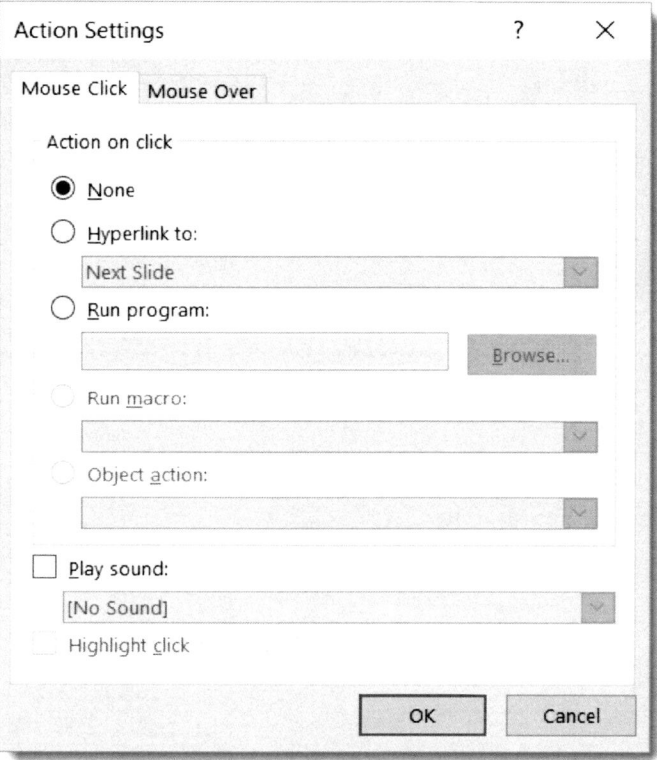

3. Select the desired tab.
   - To cause the action on a mouse click, click the **Mouse Click** tab.
   - To cause the action on mouse over, click the **Mouse Over** tab.

4. Select **Object action**, and make sure that **Activate Contents** is selected in the list.

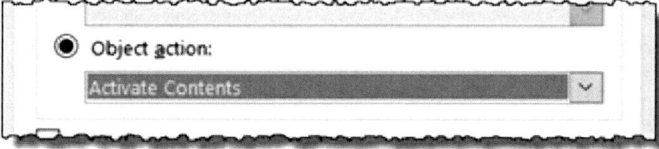

5. Click **OK**.
Now, during a slide show, when you click on or mouse over the PDF icon, the PDF file opens.

Creating WordArt from text

You can create WordArt from text and use it in your presentations. *WordArt* is a feature that was once available only in Microsoft Word (hence the name), but it's now available in other Office applications, including PowerPoint.

 MOS PowerPoint Exam Objective(s): 2.1.3

1. Select the text to be formatted.
2. Display the WordArt Styles group.
    On the Drawing Tools Format tab. This group contains a gallery of WordArt style presets, as well as other formatting options and effects.

3. Select a WordArt style preset from the gallery.
4. Apply any additional formatting and effects from the Text Fill, Text Outline, and/or Text Effects options.

Exercise: Using text from other sources

In this exercise, you'll import a document outline and a PDF file, and then you'll format text as WordArt.

Do This	How & Why
1. Create a new presentation.	Click **File > New > Blank Presentation**.
2. Display the New Slide options.	Click the lower part of the New Slide tool.

3. Click **Slides from Outline**.
The Insert Outline window opens.

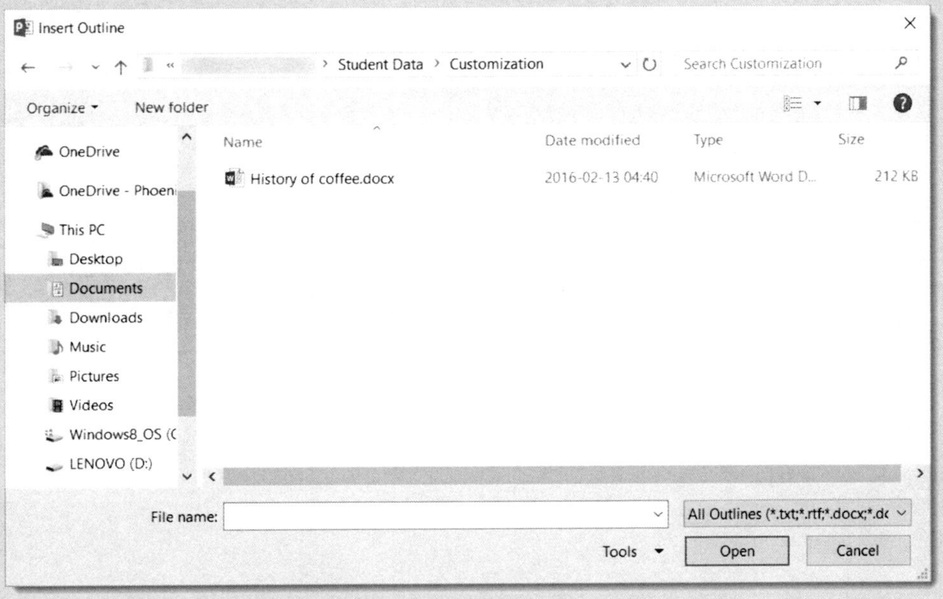

Do This	How & Why
4. Navigate to and open **History of coffee.docx**, and observe the results.	From the data folder. Select the file, and click **Open**. 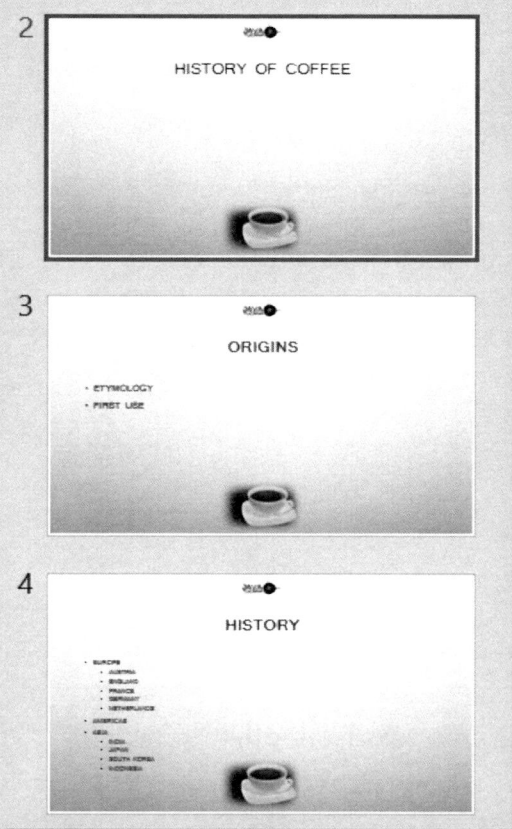
5. Add a new slide to the end of the presentation.	
a) Click just below the last slide in the Slide pane.	A horizontal I-beam insertion point appears there. 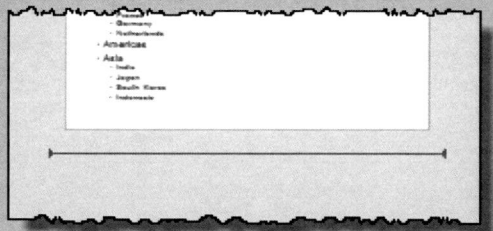
b) Click **New Slide**.	This is an alternative to first selecting a slide, and it's especially useful when you want to add a new slide 1 to the presentation. You can also use this technique in Slide Sorter view. The new slide appears at the end of the presentation.

Do This	How & Why
6. Onto the new slide, import the **History of coffee.pdf** file as an object.	The PDF icon appears on the slide. 
a) Click **Object**.	
b) In the Insert Object window, click **Create from file**, and click **Browse**.	
c) Navigate to and select the file, and click **Open**.	
d) Click **Display as icon**.	In the Insert Object window.
7. With the PDF icon still selected, click **Action**.	On the Insert tab, in the Links group. To assign an action to the PDF icon. The Action Settings window opens. 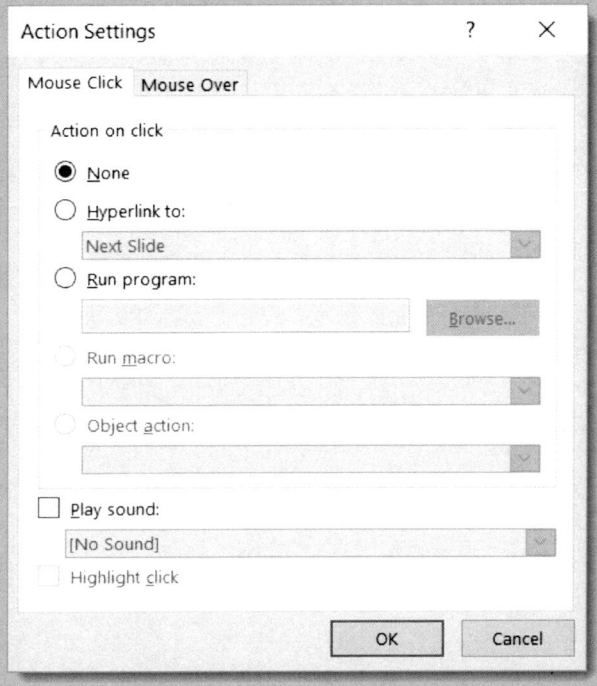
8. On the Mouse Over tab, click **Object action**, and ensure that **Activate Contents** is selected.	
9. Click **OK**.	Nothing appears to change, but this mouse-over setting only applies during a slide show. You'll get to test this shortly.

Do This	How & Why
10. On slide 2, select the "History of coffee" heading.	
11. Display the full WordArt Styles gallery.	On the Drawing Tools Format tab. 
12. Select a preset from the gallery.	
13. Apply any additional formatting and effects from the WordArt Styles group options.	
14. Save the file.	
15. Run the slide show, and be sure to hover the mouse over the PDF icon on the last slide.	
16. After running the slide show, make any additional change you wish, then save and close the presentation.	

Assessment: Using text from other sources

1. Which of these statements is true about importing a document in outline form?
   - It must be a Word file.
   - The source document can't be a normal text document; it must be written as an outline.
   - When imported, the source document is displayed one document page per slide.
   - Click Slides from Outline in the New Slide options to do so.

2. True or false? When importing a PDF file, you use the "Create from file" option in the Insert Object window.
   - True
   - False

3. Which statement about WordArt styles is true?
   - WordArt styles are complementary effects combined as individual presets.
   - To view the effects of WordArt styles, you must view the embedded object in Word.
   - You must set the Text Fill, Text Outline, and Text Effects options before applying a WordArt style preset.
   - To apply WordArt formatting in PowerPoint, Word must also be running.

Module C: Printing

Normally, the ultimate endpoint of the PowerPoint presentation trajectory is a slide show. However, at any time, and for different reasons, you might need to print any part of—or even all of—your presentations. To do so, you might also need to adjust PowerPoint Print Options.

You will learn how to:

- Preview your presentation before printing
- Work with Print Options
- Adjust Print settings to print handouts, notes, and individual slides
- Add the Quick Print tool to the ribbon
- Add the Quick Print tool to the Quick Access toolbar
- Print your presentation

Printing in PowerPoint

In order to print, you need a couple of things.

- Access to a printer, either by a local connection to your computer or through a network
- A printer driver for the printer you want to use

Generally, these things are set up for you at your workplace. After they are set up, printing in PowerPoint can be relatively straightforward. But you might find that a default printout doesn't give you what you want. There are also many available ways to specify your print job and many options for doing so.

The good news is that you can customize PowerPoint to better suit the way you work and your printing requirements. For this reason, you should preview your worksheets before you print them.

- *Print Preview*: In Backstage view. Whenever you intend to print, it's a good idea to preview your printout. In doing so, you might find some things to tweak in your presentation before taking the time (and using the paper) to print. You can preview all or any part of your presentation.
- *Print Options*: Also in Backstage view, this is where you set default options to control how PowerPoint prints in general.
- *Print settings*: On the Print Preview screen, you have access to settings for controlling each print job, including exactly what presentation components you wish to print. These include one or more slides, notes, handouts, or the entire presentation.
- *Quick Print*: As its name implies, this is the quickest way to print. Unfortunately, it's not available by default, but you can customize both the Quick Access toolbar and the ribbon to accommodate it.

Previewing your printout

In Backstage view, you can see a preview of how your worksheet will look when printed.

1. Click **File**, then click **Print**.

    To display the Print screen in Backstage view. Here, you can change print settings and see how they'll affect the printout.

    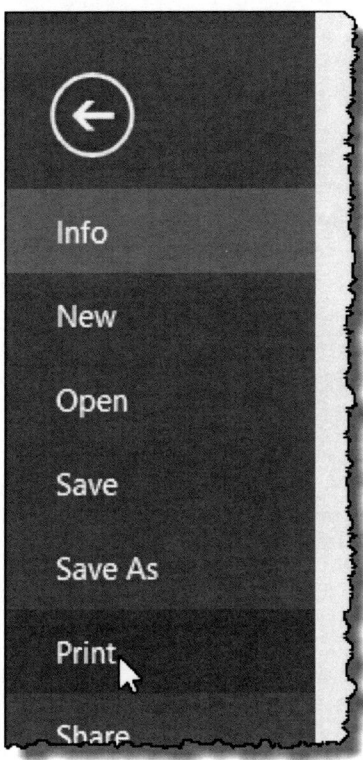

2. Click the preview, and then use the Page Down and Page Up keys to move through the preview.

    You can also use the page navigation functions below the preview. From here, you can print, adjust printer settings, or return to the presentation to make any additional adjustments.

    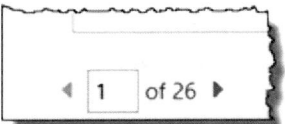

Setting Print Options

Use the Print Options settings in Backstage view to adjust general default printing options in PowerPoint.

MOS PowerPoint Exam Objective(s): 1.6.4

1. In Backstage view, click Options.
   Click **File > Options**.

   The PowerPoint Options window opens.

2. Click **Advanced**.
   In the left pane.

3. Scroll to display the Print options.
   These settings control printer-handling features such as print quality, resolution, color, and scaling.

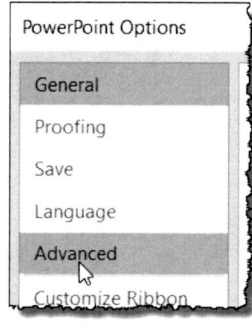
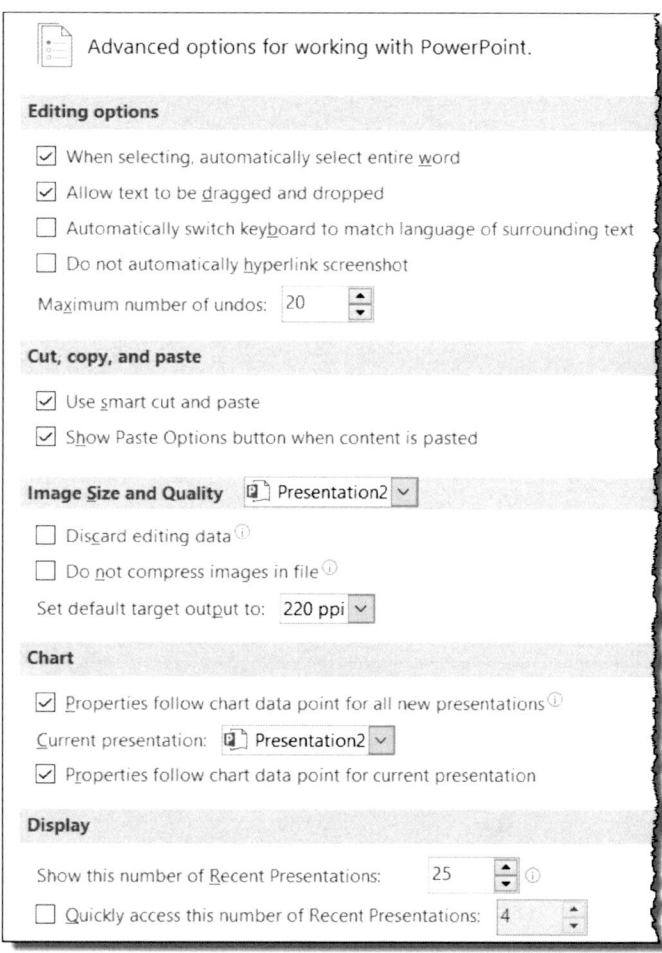

4. Once you've finished adjusting settings, click **OK** to implement your changes, or click **Cancel**.
   Either way, you're returned to the presentation.

Adjusting printer and print settings

You adjust printer and print settings from the Print screen in Backstage view—the same one you use for Print Preview.

 MOS PowerPoint Exam Objective(s): 1.6.1, 1.6.2, 1.6.3, 1.6.4

1. In Backstage view, click **Print**.
2. Make any changes to settings.
    Under Print, to the left of the preview pane.

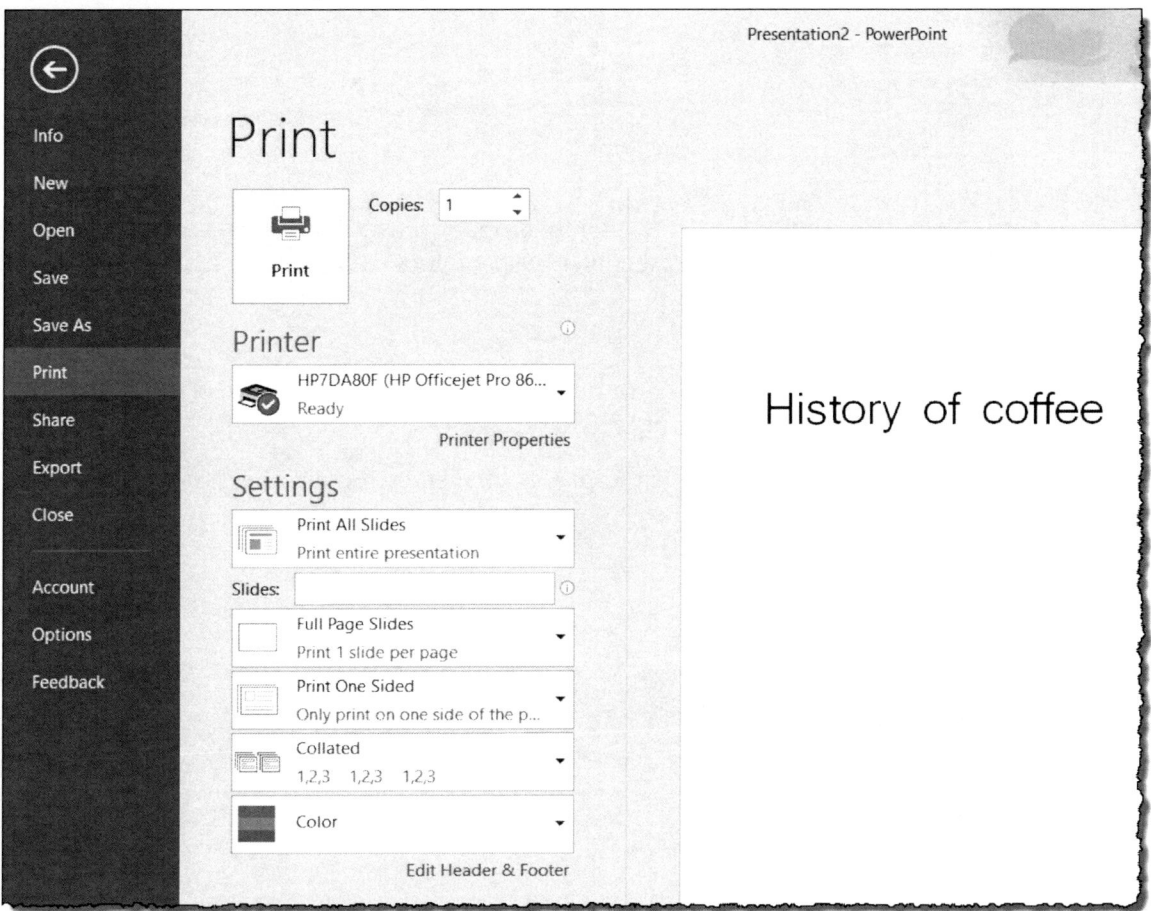

- Under Printer, you can select a different printer from the dropdown list, and click Printer Properties to adjust settings specific to the selected printer.
- In the Copies box, you can specify the number of copies you wish to print.
- Under Settings:
    - The Print All Slides dropdown list contains options for specifying exactly what slides you want to print.

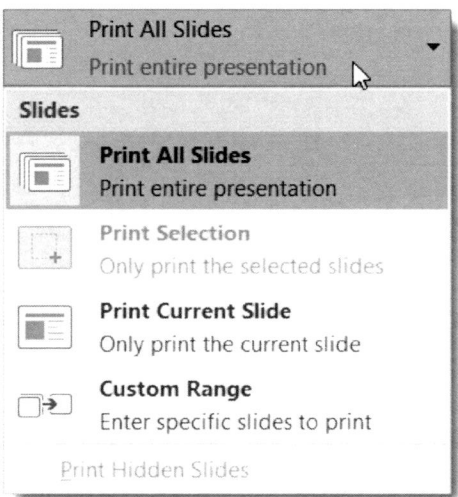

 Note: The options in the remaining dropdown lists depend, in part, on what option is selected here. In some case, other types of options become available, such as printout orientation.

- In the Slides box, you can specify the number(s) of the slide(s) you wish to print. For example, to print slides 6 through 10, you could type `6-10` or `6, 7, 8, 9, 10`.

- The Full Page Slides dropdown list displays options for printing slides, notes pages, and handouts, as well as others.

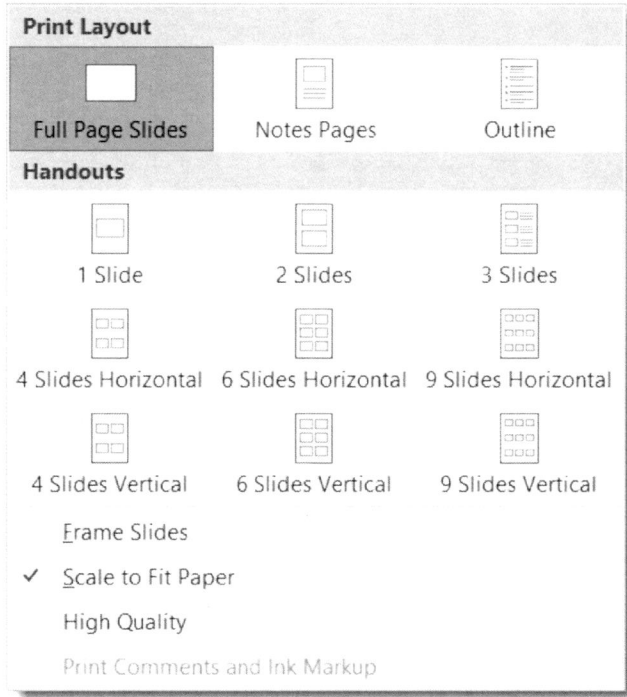

- The Print One Sided dropdown list

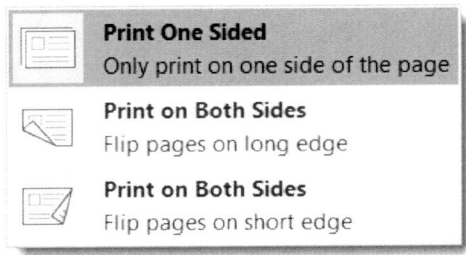

- The Collated dropdown list allows you to specify collated/uncollated printing.

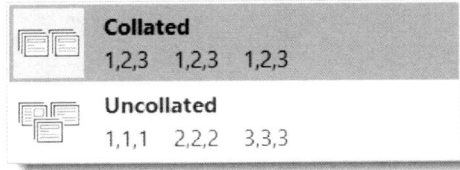

- The Color dropdown list allows you to choose whether you wish to print in color, black and white, or grayscale.

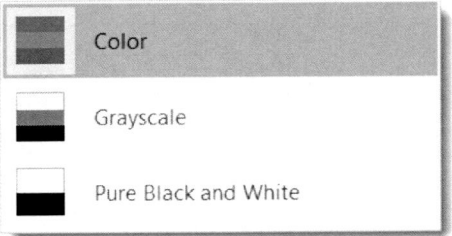

Printing
Once you've set your print option and settings and selected your printer, you need only print.

1. Open the Print screen in Backstage view, if necessary.
2. Click **Print**.

Adding Quick Print to the Quick Access toolbar
The fastest and simplest way to print in PowerPoint is to click the **Quick Print** tool. But this tool isn't available by default. One place you can add the Quick Print tool is on the Quick Access toolbar, which is handy because it's always available in the main PowerPoint window, regardless of what's showing (or hidden) in the ribbon.

1. Click the Quick Access toolbar down arrow.

    The Customize Quick Access Toolbar dropdown list opens.

2. Click **Quick Print**.

    To select it.

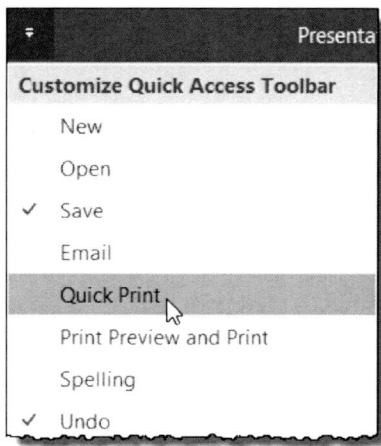

The Quick Print button appears in the toolbar.

Adding Quick Print to the ribbon

Another place to add the Quick Print tool is on the ribbon.

1. In Backstage view, click **Options**, and click **Customize Ribbon**.

    The Customize Ribbon screen is displayed.

2. Under "Choose commands from," in the list of tools, click **Quick Print**.
    You'll need to scroll down to see it.

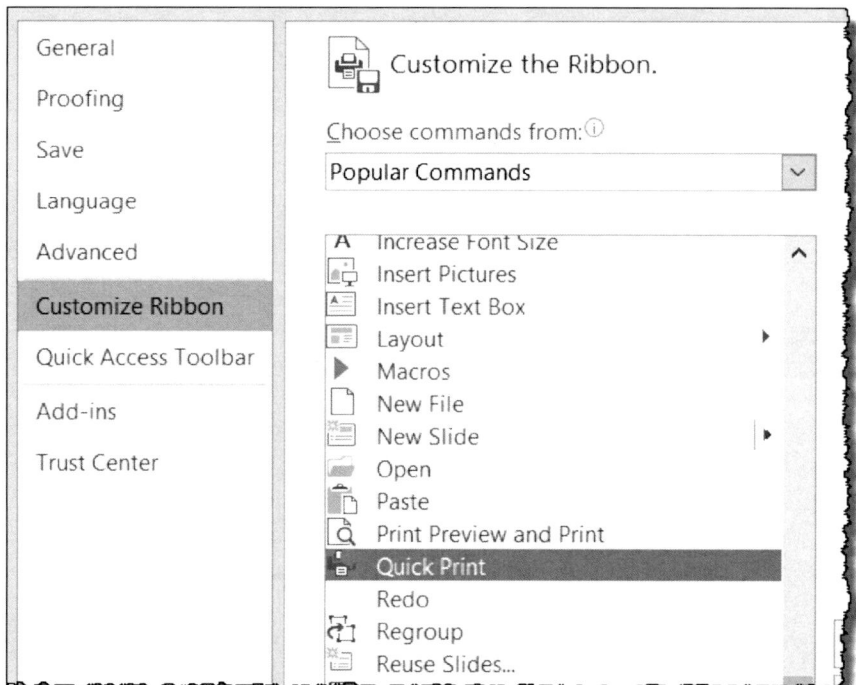

3. In the Customize the Ribbon tabs list, select a destination tab for the Quick Print tool, and click **New Group**.

    Quick Print is considered a "custom" tool in PowerPoint, so it has to be added to a special custom group. However, you can add that custom group to any ribbon tab.

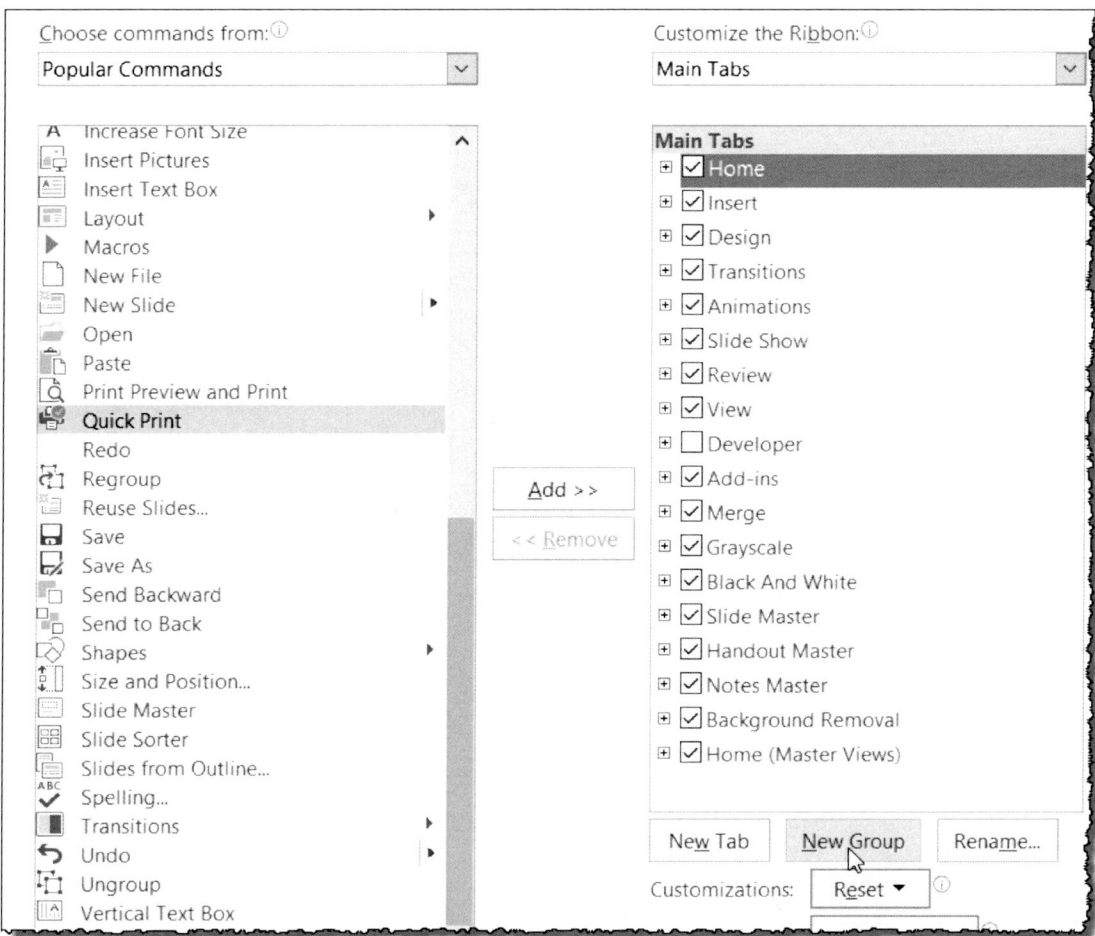

The custom group is added to the selected tab.

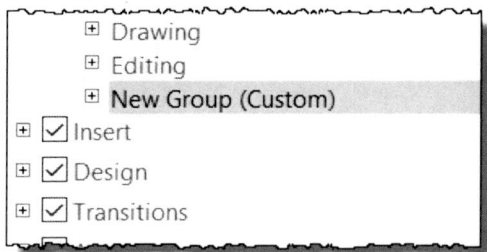

4. To change the position of the new group on its tab, click the up arrow or down arrow.
   To the right of the tabs list.

5. Click **Add**.
   Quick Print and New Group (Custom) should both still be selected.

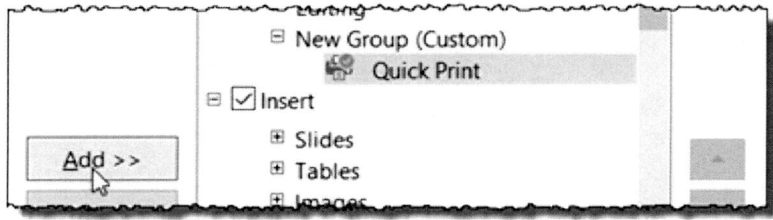

Note: To rename the new group, select **New Group (Custom)**, click **Rename**, and enter a new name.

6. Click **OK**.
   To save your changes.

7. Display the selected tab, and observe the Quick Tool in the new custom group.

Exercise: Exploring preview and print settings

Do This	How & Why
1. Open **JT Printing.pptx**.	In the Customization data folder.
2. Click **File**, and click **Print**.	The Print screen is displayed.
3. Navigate through the presentation in the Print Preview area.	Use the navigation area under the preview, or press **PgUp** and **PgDn**.
4. Observe the Print button.	If you click it, the current presentation will print on the current printer immediately, using all current settings. You're not going to do that now.
5. Click **Options**, and click **Advanced**.	In the PowerPoint Options window.
6. Observe the available Print Options.	You won't change any settings here.
7. Click **Cancel**.	
8. Return to the Print screen, and observe the available Print settings options.	Click **File > Print**.
9. Explore the available settings in each dropdown list.	
10. Open the Printer dropdown list.	Notice that besides being able to select printers, there are options such as printing to a PDF file and sending your presentation as a fax.
11. Return to the presentation.	You'll add the Quick Print tool to this toolbar.
12. Click the arrow at the right end of the Quick Access toolbar.	The Customize Quick Access Toolbar option are displayed.

Do This	How & Why
13. Click **Quick Print**.	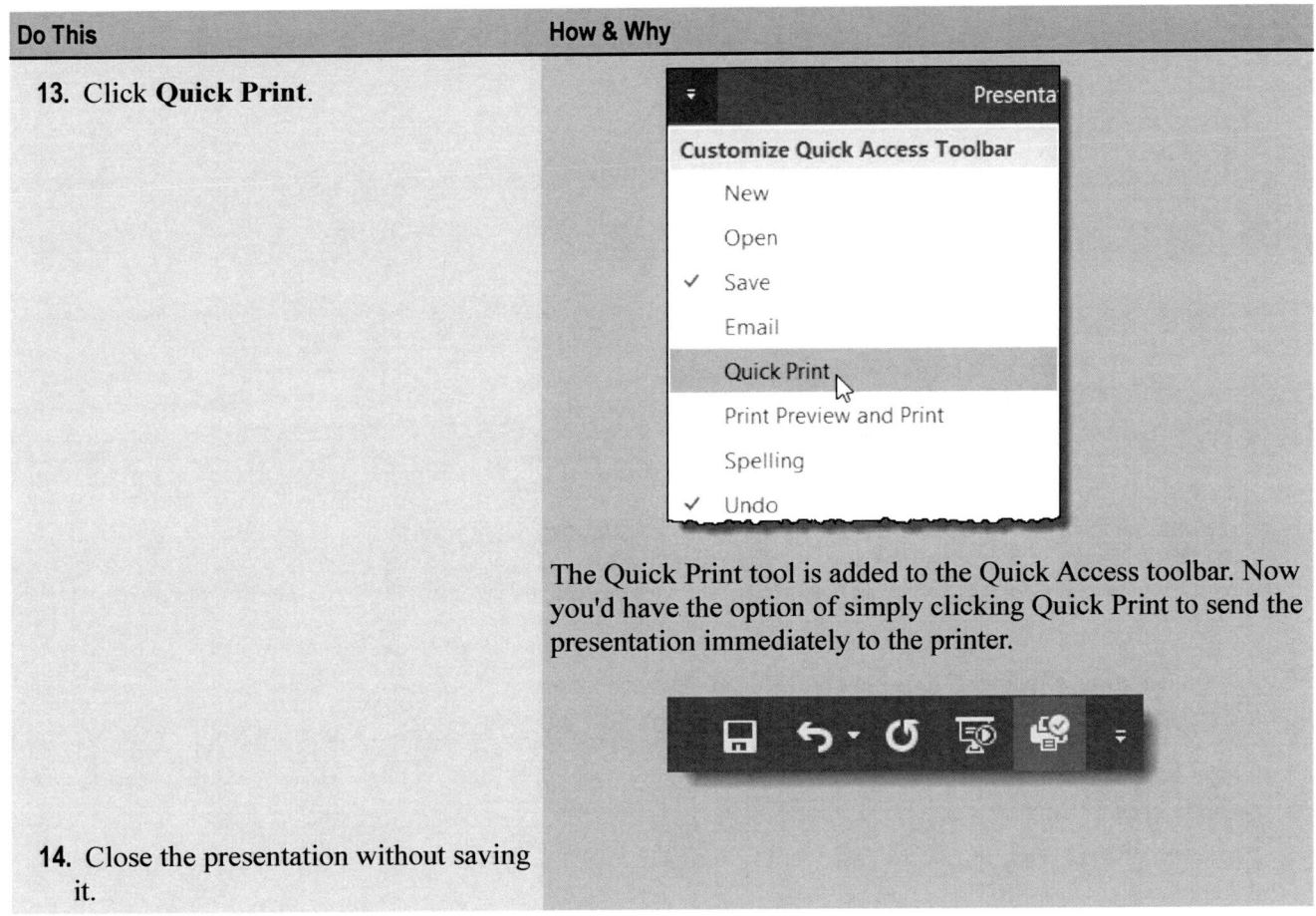 The Quick Print tool is added to the Quick Access toolbar. Now you'd have the option of simply clicking Quick Print to send the presentation immediately to the printer.
14. Close the presentation without saving it.	

Assessment: Previewing and printing

1. True or false? One way to preview your printouts is to use the Preview tool on the View tab.
   - True
   - False

2. Which of these options is *not* contained in the print settings?
   - Double-sided printing
   - Faxing
   - Collating
   - Color

3. True or false? The benefit of having the Quick Print tool in a custom group on the ribbon is that it's always visible.
   - True
   - False

Summary: Customization

You should now know how to:

- Apply transitions and transition effects to all or individual slides in a presentation
- Import text documents as an outline from applications such as Word, import a PDF file, and create WordArt from text
- Preview your printout, set print options, adjust printer and print settings, add the Quick Print tool to the Quick Access toolbar and to the ribbon, and print using either Print or Quick Print

Synthesis: Customization

In this synthesis, you'll apply transitions, import from Word and PDF files, create WordArt from text, preview your printout, set Print Options, adjust print settings, and print the presentation to a PDF file.

1. Open **JT Synthesis.pptx**, and save it as `My JT Synthesis.pptx`.
2. Apply transitions to a slide, and fine-tune the effects until they're exactly as you want them.
3. Apply the same transitions to all the slides in the presentation.
4. At the end of the presentation, import `History of coffee.docx` as a Word outline.
5. At the very end of the presentation, import `History of coffee.pdf` as an icon, setting it to activate content on mouse click.
6. Apply WordArt formatting to selected text in the presentation. Think about adding visual interest without drawing undue attention.
7. Preview the printout of the presentation, then return to the presentation and make any additional formatting changes you like.
8. In Print Options, check the **High quality** option.
9. Open the print settings, select **2 Slides**, **Collated**, **Portrait Orientation**, and **Color**.

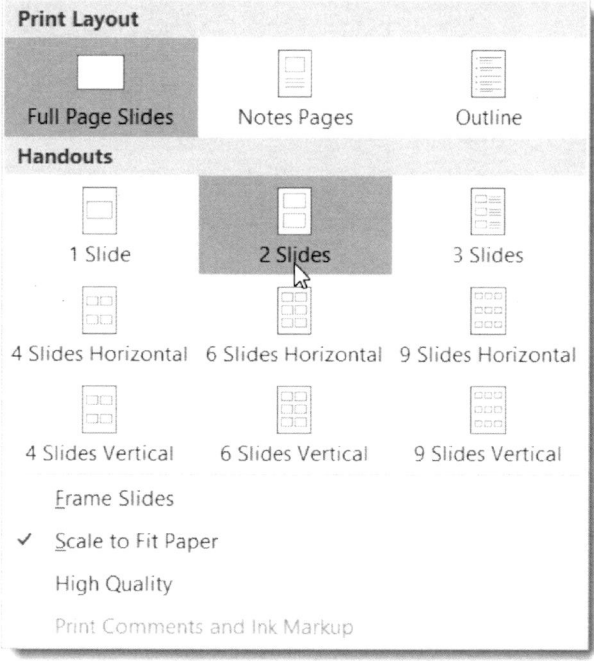

10. In the Printer options, select **Microsoft Print to PDF**.

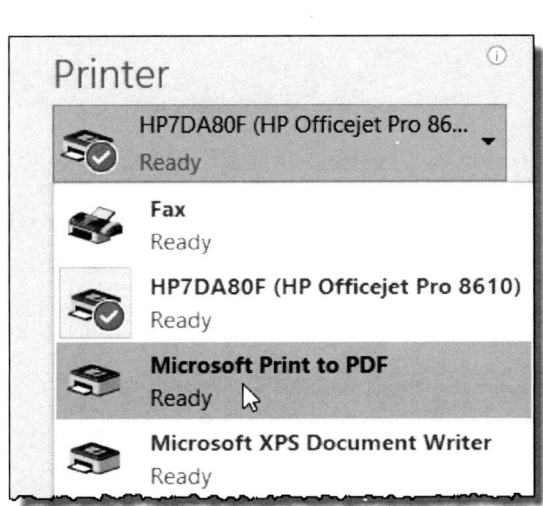
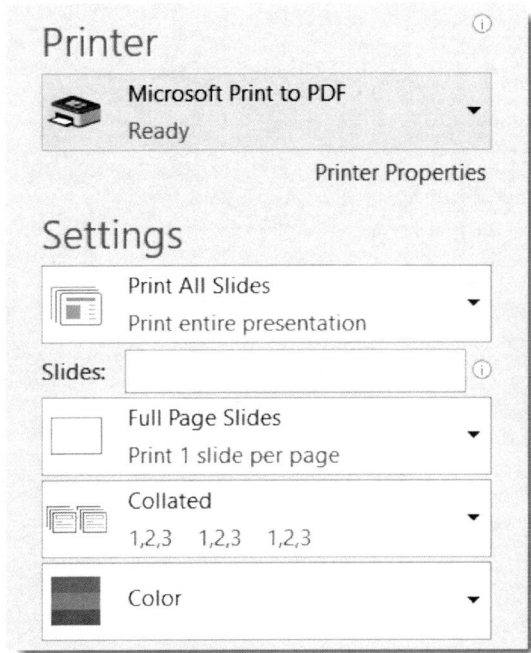

11. Return to the presentation.
12. Hover over the Quick Print tool.
    It's set to automatically print to a PDF file according to your print settings.
13. Click **Quick Print**.

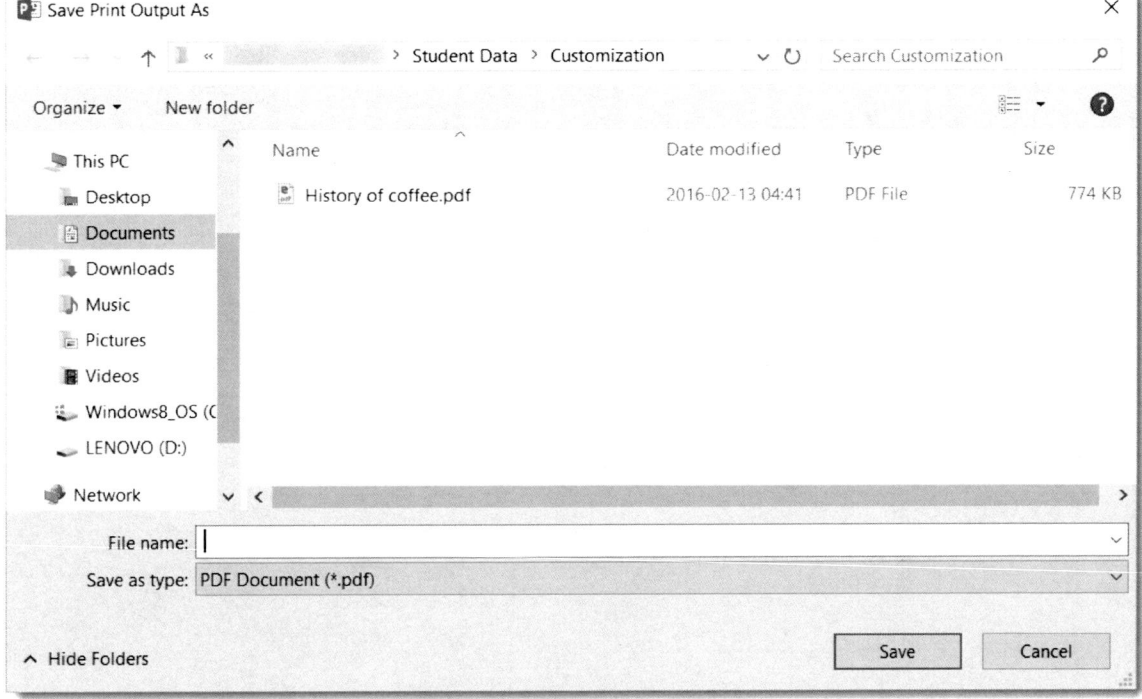

14. Name the file `My JT Printout`, and save it to the data folder.
15. Save and close the presentation.

Alphabetical Index

Aspect ratio..119
Backstage view..18, 179
    Info pane...18
    New pane..18
    Printing..179
Bulleted lists..75
    Creating...75
    Options..75
Bullets..75
Chart data..139
    Editing...139
Chart layout..136
    Changing..136
Chart style..138
    Applying...138
    Changing..138
Chart types..131, 135
    Bar...131
    Changing..135
    Column...131
    Line..131
    Pie..131
Charts...130, 131, 136
    About..130
    Adding..131
    Elements of..136
    Inserting...131
Context-sensitive..6
Cropping handles..120
Current slide..6
Curved shapes..100
    Placement and position of curves........100
Curves...96
Data...148
    Entering..148
Document outlines..165
    Importing..165
Entering data..148
Excel..148
    Enter box..148
Excel chart..138
    Inserting...138
File tab..18
Footer...56
    In masters..56
    On slides..56
Format Background pane.................................82
Formatting..73, 86
    Gridlines...86
    Text...73
Gettig help..11
    Tell Me box..11
Gridlines..86, 100
    Displaying..86
Groups...6
Guides...100
    Displaying..100
Handouts..59

Footers..59
Headers..59
Header..56
    In handouts and notes............................56
Headers and footers..56
    Date area..56
    Footer area...56
    Header area..56
    Number area..56
Help..11
    Getting..11
    Tell Me box..11
Hyperlinks..30
    Images..30
    Inserting...30
    Text...30
I-beam..24
Image files...34
    Inserting...34
Images.......................................34, 116, 117, 119, 120, 122
    Applying styles......................................122
    Background..117
    Bitmap..116
    Cropping..120
    Cropping options...................................120
    Inserting............................34, 116, 117
    Local...116
    Moving...119
    Online...117
    Picture files..34
    Pixels..116
    Sizing...119
    Types..34
    Vector...116
    Vector files...34
    Vector graphics..34
Importing...165, 167
    Outlines..165
    PDF file..167
    Text...165
    Text documents.....................................165
    Word documents...................................165
Layout..48, 65
    Modifying..48, 65
    Slide master...48
Layouts...65
    Applying...65
    Gallery..65
    Slide master...65
Line charts..130
    About..130
Lines..96, 98
    Drawing..98
New Slide..26, 65
    Layout gallery..65
Normal view..7
Notes...59
    Footers..59

Alphabetical Index

Headers 59
Notes view 7
Numbered lists 75
    Creating 75
    Options 75
Numbers 75
Object 167
    Action, assigning an 167
Objects 24, 150
    Hyperlinks 24
    Images 24
    Importing 150
    Non-text 24
    Shapes 24
    Text 24
Online images 36, 117
    Inserting 36
Online Pictures 36
Open shapes 96, 98
    Drawing 98
Outline view 7
PDF file 167
    Importing 167
Picture files 34
    Bitmap images 34
    Inserting 34
    Pixels 34
Pictures 116, 117
    Online 117
Pie charts 130
    About 130
Placeholders 24
    Graphics 24
    Text 24
Presentation 4, 18, 20, 29, 160
    Blank 18
    Create 18
    Creating 20
    Navigating slides 29
    New 18, 20
    Opening 4
    Slide transitions 160
    Templates 18
Print Options 174, 176
    Setting 176
Print Preview 174, 175
Print settings 177
Printing 174, 175, 176, 177, 179, 180
    Backstage view 179
    Previewing 175
    Print Options 176
    Quick Print 179, 180
    Requirements for 174
Printout 175
    Previewing 175
Quick Access toolbar 6, 179
    Customizing the 179
Quick Layout 136
Quick Print 179, 180

Adding to the ribbon 180
Reading view 7
Ribbon 6, 180
    Customizing the 180
Rulers 100
Shape layers 106
Shape styles 104
    Effects 104
    Fills 104
    Outlines 104
Shapes 32, 96, 98, 100, 103, 106
    Aligning 100, 106
    Creating 96
    Curved 100
    Drawing 96, 98
    Formatting 96
    Grouping 106
    Inserting 32
    Layering 106
    Resizing 103
Shapes gallery 32
Slide 57
    Date 57
    Footer 57
    Number 57
Slide backgrounds 82
    Applying 82
    Effects 82
    Fill 82
    Formatting 82
    Pictures 82
Slide master 48, 50, 65, 73
    Applying themes 50
    Format 48
    Layout 48
    Layouts 65
    Modifying 48
    Tab 48
    Text formatting 73
    Text style 73
    Tools 48
    Viewing 48
Slide Master view 48
    Layouts 48
Slide Sorter view 7
Slide transitions 160
Slides 24, 26, 29, 30, 65, 100, 160, 162
    Adding 24, 26
    Applying layouts 65
    Inserting 26
    Inserting hyperlinks 30
    Moving 24
    Navigating 29
    Objects 24
    Transitions 160, 162
    Zooming in/out 100
Slides pane 6
Starting PowerPoint 4
Status bar 6

Alphabetical Index

Styles..122, 148
    Applying..148
Table Style Options...................................150
Tables.....................................146, 147, 150
    Cells...146
    Columns..146
    Drawing...146
    Importing...150
    Inserting.......................................146, 147
    Rows..146
Tabs...6
Templates...20
    New pane..20
    Previewing..20
Text...24, 73, 165, 169
    Appearance..73
    Creating WordArt................................169
    Entering..24
    I-beam..24
    Importing...165
    Inserting...24
    Placeholder..24
    Sources..165
    Style..73

Text box...24
Text formatting..169
    WordArt..169
Text styles..74
    Formatting..74
    Individual slide.....................................74
Themes..50
    Applying...50
Tooltip...6
Transitions..160, 162
    All slides...160
    Applying.....................................160, 162
    Individual slides.................................162
    Slide..160
Undo..100
Vector graphics...34
    Inserting..34
Views...7
WordArt...169
    Creating..169
    From text..169
Zoom control..6
Zoom slider...100